The Best of
North American
Fisherman

A FISHING JOURNEY

The Best of *North American Fisherman*—A Fishing Journey

Printed in 2006.

Tom Carpenter
Creative Director

Michele Teigen
Senior Book Development Coordinator

Teresa Marrone
Book Production & Design

Laura Holle
Senior Book Development Assistant

Steve Pennaz
Kurt Beckstrom
Dan Johnson
Chris O'Brien
Terri Durgin
North American Fisherman Editorial Staff

Glenn Bamburg
Penny Berryman
Shawn Bjonfald
denverbryan.com
Larry Dahlberg
Merlyn Hilmoe
Bill Lindner Photography
Bob McNally
NAFC Archives
Steve Pennaz
Spence Petros
Tim Simos
Jon Storm
Mark Strand
Howard Tripp
Bill Vanderford
Don Wirth
Photography

The Green Agency
Cover Image

Chris Armstrong
Mark Atkinson
Wally Eberhart
Nancy Harrison
Jim Haynes
Duane Raver/USFWS
Janelle Sundberg
Cory Suski
Illustration

5 6 7 8 9 / 10 09 08 07 06
© 2002 North American Fishing Club
ISBN 1-58159-168-3

North American Fishing Club
12301 Whitewater Drive
Minnetonka, MN 55343
www.fishingclub.com

Contents

Come Along on
A Fishing Journey...

Fishing is full of journeys.

Of course, you take journeys just to go fishing. Maybe it's to a pond, lake, creek or river down the road: your home water, a place you love. Some journeys involve a little more adventure ... a trip north (or south or east or west, maybe even out of state) that takes you to a special place far from home.

Fishing also helps you make journeys that explore family and friendship. No matter who your fishing partners are—parents, siblings, offspring, coworkers, best friends, good buddies—being on the water with someone provides insights into the inner workings of any relationship.

Yes, the places we go and the people we fish with matter. But there's another type of fishing journey too: the continuing quest to get better and catch more fish, bigger fish, more often. There's nothing wrong with any of those goals!

This fishing journey is important too. Who doesn't like to catch fish? Sometimes it's easy. Sometimes it's not. Whatever the situation, you should always be challenging yourself, working to increase your knowledge and improve your skills. Learning fishing ins, outs, strategies, secrets, techniques and tips. Understanding fish biology so that you can unlock angling mysteries even when the going gets real tough. Not settling for the status quo but actively working to achieve success.

The book you're holding, *The Best of North American Fisherman—A Fishing Journey,* addresses all three kinds of journeys. Here are stories of special places, and of fishing partners that matter. And here is page after page of great angling instruction, the best you'll find anywhere, to help you on your journey to fishing success.

Members have asked for a book like this, and we're proud to be able to deliver it. Here, summarized in one convenient and handsome volume, are the best feature stories from *North American Fisherman* magazine in 2001.

Here is the year's best (and timeless) fishing information in one lasting package. Magazines get lost in the busy shuffle that is called life today. *The Best of North American Fisherman—A Fishing Journey* gives you a chance to reconnect with and preserve forever the year's fishing knowledge.

May you have good luck and great enjoyment on your own personal fishing journey, and may this book be of assistance in your quest.

Good fishing!

Bass

Bass can drive a guy (or gal) crazy.

One day they're whacking everything you throw. The next day you can't buy a hit at any price.

Of course, there is a rhyme and reason to all these bassing ups and downs. It just has to be figured out once and for all and for sure.

Until that happens, you've got this chapter … helping you figure out how to land more bass when the fishing is tough. Who needs help when the fish are coming easy?

Largemouths and smallmouths alike, bass are very special fish. Catching them can be hard work. But these pages will take away some of the mystery, and load you up with knowledge, ideas and insights so that the fish won't drive you quite as crazy.

And if they do make you completely crazy, there's no better way to go.

The key to catching cold-water bass is putting heavy metal lures squarely into the...

DROP ZONE

by Don Wirth

The hooks on my graph showed bass sitting smack on the bottom—the perfect scenario for a deep-diving crankbait, slow-moving spinnerbait or a big plastic worm, right?

Wrong. The fish were bottomed out at 62 feet—three times deeper than even the longest-lipped crank can dive. How about a spinnerbait? Naw, it would take forever to sink into the strike zone. A plastic worm? Great in warm water, but the temperature was a frigid 44 degrees.

Time to reach into the ol' tackle box and pull out some heavy metal. I'm talkin' tailspinners, spoons and blade baits … the lures that savvy fishermen reach for when largemouths, smallmouths and spotted bass are super-deep in super-cold water.

Metal bass lures have been around for decades, but overall they've kept a low profile. Major lure makers find them expensive to manufacture and tough to market to anglers who are more impressed by a flashy new crank or spinnerbait.

But the fact is when bass go deep in winter, heavy metal will outproduce other offerings 10-to-1.

By familiarizing yourself with the lures and presentations outlined here, you'll score consistently on big bass during the cold months.

Vibration Plus

Blade baits, such as the Silver Buddy, Bullet, Gay Blade, Sonar and Cicada, are razor-thin slices of metal, weighted at the bottom or head, that drop into the strike zone like a rock.

Pulling a blade on a tight line or reeling it quickly produces tremendous vibration, a super-tight series of pulses that provokes savage strikes. The ideal place to fish a blade bait is a deep, rocky highland reservoir or shield lake; one with little wood or weed cover.

Although they work in the shallows when retrieved quickly, their best application is in deep water. Indeed, blades cover the 35- to 60-foot zone faster and more thoroughly than any other type of lure. They can be jigged vertically like a slab spoon, but they really shine when fished horizontally, down stair-step ledges and cascading points.

They generally produce best in clear to slightly stained water, but are less effective than tailspinners or spoons in murky conditions.

The Precious Metals

The popularity of tailspinners, like (from left) the Craw George, Little George and Blitz Tailspin, is again on the upswing as more anglers are discovering how deadly they can be.

Jigging spoons are a perennial favorite among winter bass anglers. Among the top choices are (from top) the: Crippled Herring, Pirk Minnow, Glo Spoon, Hopkins Spoon, Mann-O-Lure, Kastmaster and CC Spoon.

Blade baits (clockwise from left) like the Sonar, Bullet Blade, Cicada, Gay Blade and Silver Buddy are the go-to lures when cold-weather bass cling close to the bottom.

Blade baits strongly mimic small pelagic baitfish, like gizzard shad, alewives and ciscoes that commonly inhabit deep, clear bass waters. When temperatures plummet in the winter, these menu items may die and sink slowly to bottom, where bass are waiting to snarf 'em up like popcorn. A fluttering blade bait triggers this seasonal feeding response like few other lures can.

Blades come in many sizes and colors, so when targeting deep bass, choose one that's heavy enough to sink into the strike zone quickly, yet matches the size of the prevailing forage. During winter, most anglers favor blades weighing ½ to ¾ ounce (about 2½ to 3 inches long).

Color is dictated by conditions. On a sunny day in clear water, a silver or gold blade emits tremendous flash that calls fish in from long distances. Under overcast skies, though, an unpainted blade simply mirrors the gray sky. Instead, use white, orange, chartreuse or another vibrant color that will catch a bass' eye.

A 6½-foot, medium-action baitcasting rod is the perfect tool for working a blade. Its relatively soft tip has enough give to allow a fish to inhale the lure deeply, ensuring a good hookset. In somewhat tangle-free water, 10- to 14-pound mono provides sufficient muscle to handle big bass.

The Depth Connection

Throughout most lakes and reservoirs in the southern and central U.S., shad are the principal forage of bass. In these waters, huge numbers of bass are caught on lures that look or act like shad. Thin-bodied, tight-wobbling baits like Rat-L-Traps, Spots and X-Shads have a shape and swimming motion like shad. Many topwater baits are designed to mimic, by sight or sound, a shad feeding at the surface. Add blade baits, tailspinners and jigging spoons to the list.

But during the cold months, shad, both gizzard and threadfin, occupy deep water, putting them and the bass that eat them out of reach of most lures. According to Jeff Boxrucker, fisheries research biologist with the Oklahoma Department of Wildlife Conservation, threadfin shad appear to congregate in deep coves with deeper water nearby, while gizzard shad orient more to the open water of Lake Texoma. As the water drops into the mid-40s, the temperature-sensitive baitfish start to die off. The stressed shad slowly sink to bottom, sometimes swimming erratically on their sides.

This phenomenon is akin to a lumber camp cook clanging the triangle at dinnertime. And a fluttering and flashing blade bait, spoon or tailspinner does a really good "dying shad" routine.

A likely key to metal bait success is the time of year, or more specifically, the water temperature. Again, the die-off begins when water temps drop into the 40s. But most anglers think bass quit feeding at 50 degrees. Not true. Although they feed less, and are less aggressive in cold water, recent studies show largemouths (even Florida-strain bass) continue to feed into the low 40s. Smallmouths and spots also feed when the temperature drops below 50 degrees.

How Deep Is Deep?

For years I have read bass-catching technique articles and tried to apply them to the lakes I fish. One thing that always perplexed me: how deep is deep? The answer depends on where you are fishing, but I can offer a general relationship about light intensity

Fluorescent lines are a plus, especially on those cold, gloomy winter days, because they're easier to see against the dark water. Another important tip is to use a small wire snap or snap-swivel on the line's terminal end. More than one blade bait has been sent into orbit on the cast by an angler who unwittingly knotted his line directly through the sharp-edged hole in the lure's back.

When should you tie on a blade? There are a number of situations that definitely stand out. First, if bass are holding on or within a few feet of the bottom, rather than suspending higher in the water column.

Also when they're parked on, or suspending just above, stair-step ledges on 45-degree rock banks, as well as the deep points at the end of these same banks. And when marks on your sonar screen indicate bass are holding near boulders or rock piles.

Notice that these situations all feature fast-breaking depth changes and a predominance of rocky cover. In winter, bass in highland reservoirs and deep shield lakes prowl ledges, drop-offs and other steep breaklines.

These chart recorder images perfectly show classic winter bass situations—largemouths hugging the steep side of a main-lake point (left), and bass suspended in open water (top). In the latter, you can see the jigging spoon. Note that the angler made about 30 jig strokes over the school, a testament to how lethargic winter bass can be.

Blade Presentations

Blades can be fished horizontally or vertically. Vertical jigging will catch suspended bass, sure enough, but a blade bait, with its two-hook design, tangles in the line more frequently than a spoon. Very frustrating!

For more consistent results, and fewer tangles, fish a blade bait horizontally by first making a long cast past your target. Keep the rodtip at 10 o'clock while the lure sinks on a tight line. When it hits bottom, lower the rodtip to 9 o'clock, reel up slack and snap the tip sharply back to 11 o'clock. This will cause the lure to pop off the bottom.

Lower the rodtip back to 9 o'clock as the lure drops. When it hits bottom, snap the tip back to 11 o'clock again.

Most anglers get hung up on the third step. After popping the lure off bottom, the idea is to drop the rodtip slowly, with just the slightest amount of bow in the line. If it's too tight, the lure won't look natural as it falls. Too much slack, and it may tumble and tangle in the line. Or, a fish may inhale the lure, and spit it, before you know it's there.

---

in water that you can connect with a metal-bait pattern.

The amount of light penetration decreases logarithmically as water depth increases. But we'll skip the mathematics and go with some general rules of thumb.

Humans can see down to a light intensity that's about 1 percent of full daylight. Drop a white lure, like a spinnerbait or blade bait, into the water, and mark the depth at which it disappears. At approximately double that depth is where light intensity is 1 percent of the intensity at the surface. Incidentally, this is also the depth down to which aquatic plants can typically grow.

Shad seek deep water during the cold months and bass follow. Extremely deep bass may not be able to feed by sight, instead they use their lateral lines to locate food.

Bass can see at about 0.1 percent of surface light. To estimate the depth where light intensity drops to that level, simply multiply the depth at which the white lure disappears by four. You now have an approximation of the depth down to which bass can find your lure by sight.

Do bass live at lower levels of light? Probably. Do they feed in the dark? Possibly. But if you are trying to trigger a cold bass, don't waste your time on fish that can't see your lure.

—*Dr. Hal Schramm*

Metal Working

Jigging spoons, tailspinners and blade baits are excellent lures for cold-weather bassin',' but like other artificials, they can benefit from minor tweaking. Here are three ideas that will improve your catch rate:

Fine Points

Many blade baits come with split trebles. When they are damaged by snags or repeated sharpening, simply replace them by adding a split ring and a standard treble. Some blades have a split double-hook on the belly. Replacing it with a treble will guarantee more hook-ups, as well, but it also increases the chances of a tangle.

Big And Slow

Replacing the blade on a tailspinner with a larger one offers a couple advantages. First, the increased vibration and flash will make the lure easier to detect in murky water. The larger blade also adds lift, causing the lure to helicopter more slowly on the drop.

Straighten the tail wire just enough to remove the clevis, swap out the blade, and replace.

More Action

Use a bench vise and a heavy-duty pair of pliers to put a slight bend in a thick, heavy jigging spoon. Even a slight curve in the lure's body will make it flutter more erratically as it falls. This enticing action mimics the throes of a dying shad—something that even the most reluctant cold-water bass will find nearly impossible to ignore.

Winter bassers on Dale Hollow Lake, Tennessee, use an alternate blade retrieve for big smallmouths. After casting the lure, they keep the rodtip rock-steady at 10 o'clock throughout the retrieve. Instead of twitching the rodtip, they make rapid turns of the reel handle to move the bait. The blade scoots frantically near the bottom like a crawfish, and can elicit arm-wrenching strikes from big bronzebacks.

Blade baits may require tuning. Either make sure the blade is straight, or go the opposite direction and curl the tail section with pliers. This makes the lure wobble more erratically, and sometimes more enticingly.

Compact, Yet Deadly

Legendary lure maker Tom Mann hit a home run when he designed the Little George tailspinner nearly 40 years ago. This tiny slab of metal with a single spinner blade at the rear has racked up countless numbers of giant bass over the years.

Today, Mann's Bait Company cranks out zillions of Little Georges; it's said to be the best-selling metal bass lure of all time.

There's been a recent resurgence of interest in tailspinners among tournament anglers, prompting the introduction of a number of new models including the Stanley Shad and Gama Shad. Tailspinners are the most compact of the metal baits, making them a good choice in cold water, when a bass' digestive process slows dramatically and small forage is preferred. Like other metal baits, they mimic small baitfish.

In most situations, choose a ½- to 1-ounce lure in a shad or chartreuse pattern, depending on water clarity and cloud cover. Tailspinners also work great in muddy water. To make it "thump" even more, bend the spinner blade slightly with your thumb to give it more cup.

In rocky waters, work a tailspinner where you'd fish a blade bait; it's equally effective in the super-deep zone. And if your winter bassin' takes you to a murky lowland reservoir, a tailspinner is the better of the two choices. The lure's design makes it perfect for dredging offshore structure—humps, channel drops—and its single-hook lets it rip through thin brushy cover with a minimum of hang-ups.

My favorite tailspinner rod is a 6½- to 7-foot, medium-heavy action baitcasting or spinning rod. Tom Mann prefers an 8-foot saltwater spinning stick to fish a Little George. Most bassers will find this war club too heavy for all-day use, though.

Because tailspinners are especially productive around deep wood cover, you'll want heavy, 17- to 20-pound abrasion-resistant line. No snap or swivel needed, however. Just tie directly to the line attachment.

Cousin to the traditional tailspinner is the marabou version, typified by the legendary Pedigo Spinrite, which is no longer produced. The Marabou Spin, with its long wire line-tie and marabou dressing on the rear treble, is a good clone, though.

Marabou tailspinners have a cult following among smallmouth chasers; Tennessee bronzeback guru Billy Westmorland caught a 10 pounder on a Spinrite. These baits are specifically designed for clear water; fish 'em on a stiff 6½-foot spinning or baitcasting rod with a slow-retrieve reel spooled with 6- to 10-pound mono.

Two Retrieves

Traditional tailspinners are meant to be fished in yo-yo fashion close to the bottom, much like a blade bait. In fact, if you follow the same steps outlined for fishing a blade you'll be right on the money with your tailspinner.

Marabou tailspinners, on the other hand, should be retrieved horizontally on the outer edges of gravel flats, in the headwaters of deep tributaries, across submerged roadbeds, and on gravel points with scattered stumps.

As always, cast past the target and keep the rodtip at 10 o'clock while the lure drops. Immediately after it touches down, point the rodtip just above the surface, and pop the rodtip slightly to get the tiny blade turning.

Reel slowly and steadily, swimming the lure just off bottom all the way to the boat. If you feel it drag bottom, speed up your retrieve. If you lose contact with the bottom for several seconds, slow down.

There's something about a marabou tailspinner than elicits powerhouse strikes in cold water. Smallmouths, especially, will hit these lures like a freight train, so keep a firm grip on the rod handle!

Solution For Suspenders

Bass often hang at mid-depths during the winter, but are suspended in deep, cold water; a jigging spoon is usually your best choice. In fact, short of fishing live bait, it may be your only choice.

In most cases, you can just about predict where bass will suspend in the winter. Among the most predictable are the ends of deep, rocky or stump-strewn points; close to, or out from, steep rock bluffs; in the middle of hollows (deep V-shaped tributary arms); above major offshore structures such as channel drops, ledges, humps and rock piles; and in open water, especially where baitfish are present.

It's possible to spoon-feed big bass in incredibly deep water. Anglers on Georgia's Lake Lanier routinely catch chunky spotted bass that are suspended 100 feet below the surface! Thirty to 50 feet is more common for largemouths and smallies on most bodies of water.

Virtually every major lure manufacturer offers a jigging spoon; time-tested favorites include the C.C. Spoon, Hopkins, Crippled Herring, Lazer Eye and Strata Spoon. Use a ½- to 1-ounce spoon for most winter applications. A 6- to 6½-foot medium-heavy baitcasting rod is ideal.

Low-stretch superlines of 10-

Fridgid weather or fair, when water temps drop in the fall, it's time to break out the metal.

to 20-pound test are ideal in this situation because they allow you to detect the lightest strike in deep water. And be sure to use a snap-swivel as jigging spoons can cause monumental line twist.

Color and finish are topics of considerable debate among winter bass anglers. Many prefer a chrome spoon with a hammered finish to mimic a dying shad. Painted spoons, however, are usually more productive on overcast days and in stained water.

Jigging Technique

A bow-mounted sonar unit is indispensable when jigging vertically. You want to be able to see the fish as well as the spoon.

Of all the metal lures, jigging spoons require the most straightforward technique. Simply position your boat directly above the suspended bass or ball of bait-fish visible on your sonar. With the rod at 9 o'clock, drop the spoon to the bass' level. Count it down, strip known lengths of line from the reel, or watch your sonar screen.

Lower the rodtip to 8 o'clock, then snap it up to 10. Pause for a split-second, then snap it again, to 12 o'clock. The hand movements should be sharp and deliberate, like cracking a whip.

Lower the rodtip back to 8, just fast enough so you can "feel" the spoon fall. Don't lower the rod too quickly or you'll throw too much slack in the line. Lower it too slowly, and you'll kill the spoon's enticing flutter.

As always, bass usually hit as the lure falls. If you "lose contact" with the lure as it drops, it's likely that a bass has scooped it up.

Remember that bass suspending in cold water are usually lethargic. Don't just jig the spoon a few times and move on—keep working the fish slowly and methodically. And here's a cool tip: keep a waterproof marker in your pocket. When you hang a bass, quickly mark the line at the rodtip before reeling in. This will allow you to quickly hit the same depth over and over again. ⌁

Contacts

Heddon (501) 782-8971 lurenet.com	**Mann's** (800) 841-8435 mannsbait.com	**Cotton Cordell** (501) 782-8971 lurenet.com	**Silver Buddy** (888) TO-BUDDY silverbuddy.com	**Hopkins** (757) 622-0977
Luhr-Jensen (800) 535-1711 luhr-jensen.com	**Elmer Taylor** Little Sparky (931) 243-6133	**Horizon** (800) 818-3026 horizonlures.com	**Northland** (800) SUN-FISH northlandtackle.com	**Strata & Lazer Eye spoons** (800) BASS-PRO basspro.com
Bullet Blade (423) 477-2033	**Sampson** (205) 582-2974	**Reef Runner** (419) 798-9125	**Marabou Spinn** (606) 298-5106	

Fix the Six

AVOID BASS FISHING'S SIX MOST COMMON MISTAKES.

by NAFC Bass Advisory Council Member Penny Berryman

I have a great job. I'm one of those lucky folks whose vocation and avocation are the same. I truly love fishing, whether it's for fun and games, or for big bucks on the tournament scene.

With the time I've spent on the water, I've experienced it all—the good and the bad. As human beings, we all have days when we just can't quite get it together—days when we make the mistakes and mental errors that keep us from being the best anglers we can possibly be.

From preparation to concentration to reading nature's signs, there is always something we "could have done better." I've come to learn that if I control some of my mental mistakes, I am a better, more successful angler. Here are the mistakes I strive to avoid:

Mistake 1: Lack Of Preparation

Whether you're a tournament fisherman, an avid angler, or someone who enjoys the occasional weekend on the water, time is of the essence. Some degree of preparation is always necessary, but stepping up your overall preparation and eliminating unproductive water will go a long way toward locating bass.

One solution is map study. I eliminate a great deal of water by first studying a map and determining where the fish will NOT be. Factors like time of year, water levels, water temperature and power generation are excellent clues. Sources for information abound, and one of the most powerful is the Internet. Before your trip, post a few queries on billboards, or view up-to-date reports on state fish and wildlife agency sites.

It's also important to make sure your equipment is functioning properly, which maximizes your on-the-water efficiency. Be sure your boat (batteries charged?), trailer and all your tackle are in prime shape before ever leaving home. And always get a good night's sleep before fishing. When fully rested, you'll handle problems like backlashes, broken rods and bad weather with much more patience.

Mistake 2: Concentration Lapses

The most successful bass anglers are always concentrating, especially during their initial search. Many NAFC Members are 100 percent mentally prepared for that first strike, and when they get it, it leads them straight to bite number two because they instantly analyze every strike to determine exactly what caused the fish to bite.

For example, say you get a strike while reaching for a bottle of Coke. That should tell you the strike came when you stopped reeling and reached for the drink. Sometimes a strike will come when you turn your head to answer a question from your fishing partner. Any time you change the rhythm of your retrieve and you get a strike, it's most likely the change in rhythm that caused the strike, so adjust accordingly.

Be observant. Water levels on this Mississippi oxbow fell overnight and the bass moved from shallow flooded brush to cypress knees, tossing out the previous day's pattern in the process.

A more serious problem is the steady erosion of concentration over a day of fishing. Really, it's very hard to concentrate intently on one activity for a long period of time, so eventually casts become sloppy, you work the lure with less attitude—everything dwindles and strikes become few and far between.

I think the things we carry around in our mind are probably our own worst enemies. When you've got a very hectic schedule or important event in your home life, for instance, part of your mind is over there and the rest is here, on the water. But it's critical you clear your mind and focus on the task at hand. Not only will you relax—an important healing aspect of the fishing experience—but you'll also catch more fish.

Mistake 3: Not Observing

This is a mistake I see a lot of anglers make, including myself. I know I've been guilty of it in the past and it's one thing I've really tried to work on. Most of us don't take the time to notice the subtle changes that occur in the environment from one day to the next. In our efforts to hurry and catch a fish, too often we rely on what worked yesterday.

Instead, we really need to tune into what the aquatic environment is telling us about today's conditions. Living on Arkansas' Lake Dardanelle, with its ever-changing conditions, has really forced me to be observant.

Avoiding the mistakes we're discussing can help you catch smallmouths too.

I eventually got it through my head that all I need to do, when I launch my boat, is to look at the water level on the weedline. A 2-inch drop in water is an instant sign that I need to fish stumps and rocks, instead of the grassbeds I fished yesterday. The river environment taught me to see each day with a new set of eyes.

It's the most natural thing in the world to hit the water and try to duplicate yesterday's successful pattern. Pick up that same spinnerbait, or that same crankbait, and go back to fishing the same pattern. But if you're really paying attention to little changes in the environment, you receive clues that allow you to adjust your patterns every day.

Be alert to the forage base, too, and nervous water. A scared minnow, for instance, is the number-one sign there's a predator lurking below. When I'm fishing, I'm hoping that predator is a bass. This fleeing minnow tells me that I need to switch to a Pop-R, or I need to throw a little crankbait to catch the predator that just revealed its location.

Mother Nature is full of signs; it's up to you to observe and interpret them.

Mistake 4: Not Capitalizing

Here's one blunder that we've all been guilty of from time to time—not fishing an area thoroughly enough to learn its subtleties and fish-holding potential. Too many anglers give up on an area too quickly, failing to exploit all the different spots that hold fish.

Although many of us may, more often than not, whisk through an area looking for active bass, I feel there are many times that we simply outwit ourselves, and in the process, fail to catch fish. If anglers slow down just a little, and take the time to explore all that's available, their overall success will skyrocket.

I have learned from my own mistakes that bass are not always actively feeding. Whereas a quick pass through an area may produce two bites, I realize that, if the area's capable of holding two fish that hit quickly, it has the right ingredients to hold many more fish that may be in a negative mood.

Before I leave an area that has good potential, I spend as much time as it takes to find out what those inactive fish might be relating to.

I'll use my trolling motor to cruise the area and study my sonar screen trying to find the subtle

> "Learning to fish deep structure and cover isn't nearly as difficult or mysterious as we are led to believe."

Preparation is a key to success, and maps are a big part of it. Using them, along with clues like water temperature, water levels and time of year, will help you eliminate vast tracts of unproductive water.

changes in the bottom contour, bottom content, or possibly some secondary cover, that is not obvious to other anglers.

Personally, with almost every tournament I was fortunate enough to win, I picked one or two main areas that produced well for me during practice rounds, then invested enough time in practice to learn all the subtleties of each spot. When an active bite slows down, being a little bit stubborn and forcing myself to fish every piece of cover at several depths and with several presentations has really paid off.

Mistake 5: Dependence On Shallow Water

I think it's safe to say that 90 percent of America's bass fishermen spend 90 percent of their time in shallow water. I'm guilty of this too. But I was lucky enough to learn, early in my fishing career, how to take advantage of the various types of offshore structure.

The first step in finding deep bass is to invest in a high-quality depthfinder, with plenty of vertical pixels for good resolution and target separation. I first learned the value of extra pixels in a summer tournament on Lake Tenkiller in Oklahoma, where I knew shade was going to be an important key in finding largemouths seeking refuge from the sun.

I had just received a new Humminbird Wide Panorama, and with it I was able to determine which brush piles were old and which ones had just been put out. Most of my better fish came from the newer,

Crankbaits are great search tools, but after you locate a productive area, always work it very thoroughly with a variety of baits.

"fluffier" brush piles that offered more shade. Just one example of the role electronics can play in finding deep bass.

And really, it's pretty easy fishing. Once you make contact with deep cover, maintain contact with it by fishing lures like a Carolina-rigged lizard, crankbait, spinnerbait, jig or Texas-rigged worm. I always stay tuned to what I feel on my line and after contacting some type of cover, I try to imagine what the bait has bumped into, then let it sit motionless for a few seconds.

Learning to fish deep structure and cover isn't nearly as difficult or mysterious as we are led to believe, so don't be afraid to stop pounding the shoreline.

Mistake 6: Failure To Learn

Even if you have reached the level of some of the most consistent anglers around, you owe it to yourself to keep an open mind. Be open-minded enough to learn new things from anyone you meet. Even today, I still learn from my amateur partners. I may be a professional angler, but I certainly don't know it all. I never will. I can't emphasize enough the importance of continuing to learn each and every single time out.

If you avoid the pitfalls I mentioned above, and continue to learn every day, you will come considerably closer to fulfilling your potential as a fisherman—and isn't that the goal of every bass angler?

Will Dropshotting Revolutionize Bass Fishing?

THE WEST'S HOTTEST TECHNIQUE HEADS EAST AND TURNS BASS FISHING UPSIDE DOWN.

by Jon Storm

Not so long ago, in a country far, far away, there grew a rig that may forever change the face of bass fishing. As it crept across the Pacific Ocean, as it slowly fed its way into the boats and minds of Western bass pros, it promised to turn everything we knew about bass fishing, literally, upside down.

In Japan, it's called the lucky rig and it's been a mainstream technique for nearly a decade. In North America, we call it "dropshotting," and *North American Fisherman* first reported on the rig in the December/January 1998-99 cover story "Polishing The Rocks."

Although the dropshot rig still garners a few laughs and taunts from the bass crowd—with such endearing monikers as "crappie rig" and "sissy bait"—it's still an exciting, versatile rigging option that works when nothing else will.

The best part is, dropshotting still dwells in relative obscurity. Any fish east of the Continental Divide has likely never seen it, and anglers looking for an edge up on the competition need look no further than this arrangement of hook, line and sinker.

No matter where you live—north, south, east or west—dropshotting can help you catch more largemouths, smallmouths and spots (plus other species). One must consider water clarity, however, for it's the one factor that overwhelmingly governs dropshot success. In clear water, the rig excels. Stained or muddy water? The jury's still out. So too, it's not the best rig to use when bass are active and feeding. However,

under difficult or pressured conditions, the dropshot rig is perhaps the best tool we now have to catch neutral or negative fish.

Tag End, You're It

Simply put, a dropshot rig is nothing more than a hook, tied with a palomar knot, and a weight secured to the tag end. Think of it as an upside-down Carolina rig and the advantages become obvious. With the weight resting on bottom and the bait tied directly to the line, rodtip movement is transferred directly to the bait. Just as important, the dropshot suspends the bait a fixed distance off bottom. And you can work it in place, unlike a Texas or Carolina rig, which requires an angler to move the entire rig to activate the bait. With a dropshot, the bait hovers in the same spot and dances with just a few twitches of the rodtip.

To rig a basic dropshot setup for clear water and no cover, start with a spinning reel, medium-action 6½-foot rod and light line, say 8-pound mono or fluorocarbon, or 6/20 superline. Hook choice is important, and the best hooks for dropshotting are small, live bait style hooks with an upturned eye. Good examples include Daiichi No. 2 Salmon Egg hooks, Gamakatsu No. 2 Split Shot hooks or Owner's new Down Shot hooks. Seldom will you need to make the rig weedless. If so, opt for small offset hooks and bury the hook point.

Tie the hook to the line using a palomar knot, leaving at least 1 to 2 feet of tag end, which you rethread through the hook eye. To the tag end, attach the appropriate size weight. Almost any style of weight works—split shots, mojo weights, bullet sinkers or Lindy's No-Snagg are excellent options. If using a split shot in snag-free waters, wrap the line around the shot once before crimping. Fish the heaviest weight you can get away with. I generally use ⅛- to ¼-ounce weights, but step up when fishing extra deep, in heavy wood or in heavy wind.

Another option is the new tungsten weights, imported from Japan (call J&T Tackle, (888) 96UFISH, to order). Tungsten is much denser than lead, so it sinks faster. Plus, tungsten is a highly responsive metal that makes it easy to judge bottom types like mud, rocks, pebbles or shale. Trouble is, tungsten costs about $2.00 per weight.

Perhaps the biggest problem with the dropshot rig is line twist. Using a spinning reel and fishing the rig down deep plays havoc with monofilament and fluorocarbon. One partial solution to line twist is a new brand of weight, called the Bakudan, imported directly from Japan. Designed specifically for dropshotting, the Bakudan incorporates a microswivel and unique line tie that makes it easy to adjust the weight up and down

> ## "The beauty of the rig is its versatility. It can be used to fish virtually any type of structure and cover ... "

the line. Make no mistake, Bakudans are expensive and a bag of six costs about $4.50 (call (909) 798-1732 to order), but for snag-free waters, they're hard to beat.

One other solution, or partial solution, to line twist is to use a superline. Barry Day, former field services manager at Berkley, spent the past year fishing dropshot rigs around the country. So has bass pro Gary Klein, a Berkley pro staff member. Both agree that FireLine is one solution to line twist.

Monofilament and FireLine twist at the same rate, but unlike

monofilament, FireLine stores little to no energy and even when twisted, won't coil and jump off the reel. Anglers may shy from superline's high visibility, but after conducting numerous field tests and catch comparisons, Day recorded little, if any effect on bites. He even fishes the bright green FireLine. When experimenting with FireLine, or other superline, just be sure to use small diameters (6/20 is a good start); or use a mono or fluoro leader.

Design Differences

The last step in assembling the rig is to choose a good bait. Here, the options seem limitless, and whether it's the custom-pour plastics from out West or mass-market baits like Berkley's new Drop Shot Powerbaits or the red-hot Lunker City Slug-Go (3- or 4½-inch sizes), they all share similar characteristics.

First, they all work. Second, good dropshot baits have either a straight, paddle or forked tail. The reason is simple. Curlytails need forward movement to activate, while plain tails are more active when worked in a vertical fashion. The third characteristic is a flat underside, which helps the bait catch water and sway on the drop. Finally, most of today's dropshot baits are small, running from 3 to 5 inches. Anglers are successfully experimenting with larger baits, however.

Along with their smaller-than-average size, dropshot baits tend to be translucent, with subtle colors or glitter (used sparingly). The translucent colors are a better choice in clear water and often mimic local forage— emerald shiner, for instance.

Beyond Bass

One reason for the dropshot's growing popularity is there's no easier rig to fish. Even in the hands of a beginner, dropshotting provides steady, multi-species action all day long. But experts can use it to target a number of species, as well, especially when fish are deep. Bluegills, crappies, bullheads, white bass, walleyes, you name it—if it swims, it'll bite a dropshot.

One reason it works so well is the smaller baits. I regularly fish a jig and plastic grub for crappies, but direct-tying the plastic is a great way to target crappies relating to deep points. Plus, you can dropshot smaller micro tubes and curlytails without compromising lure control. Where legal, I like rigging two, even three baits up the line, using a jig as my weight. Also, you can fish the rig alongside brush piles, drop it vertically into timber or work suspended fish over deep basins. Bluegills along deep weed edges are easy to target with the dropshot. I've even caught perch with it.

I do recommend you put the rig into the hands of beginners. If you're tossing spinnerbaits, for example, or burning cranks, let the youngsters fish a dropshot and they'll have plenty to keep them busy.

One problem with the dropshot is pike and pickerel. Although you do get the occasional lip hook with these toothy critters, most often they cut your line. I've learned to live with it, but in waters with tons of hammer handles, retying can get frustrating.

How To Fish The Dropshot

Fishing the dropshot rig is incredibly simple. First, pitch the rig four to five feet from the boat and let it sink to bottom (A). With some slack in the line, lift the rodtip and jiggle it. Next, drop the rodtip and let the bait fall back toward bottom (B). This is when most strikes occur. If you feel a fish, set the hook immediately (C).

Whenever possible, nose hook the plastic, much as you'd do with live bait. Fishing an exposed hook not only increases your hookup rate, it leaves almost the entire length of plastic free to jiggle and shake.

Simplicity, Not Science

Fishing the dropshot takes a little getting used to, but the cardinal rule is always: Keep it simple. Subtle shakes and lifts, rather than violent gyrations or large vertical lift/drops will generate more bites. Here's how to do it.

With your dropshot rig in hand, position the boat near or over the particular area you'd like to fish. Pitch the bait four to five feet away from the boat and let it sink to bottom on a slack line. Then, with a bow in the line and the weight riding on bottom, raise the rodtip slightly, twitch it three or four times, then drop the rodtip. This causes the bait to fall, and that's when

most strikes occur. It's critical that, when shaking the rodtip, you keep some slack in the line, which gives the bait more freedom to move.

Although it's primarily a vertical presentation, casting the dropshot works well, too. I often position along the outside weedline and make parallel casts to work a larger area. The beauty of the rig is its versatility. It can be used to fish virtually any type of structure and cover, from boat docks and rock piles to outside weed edges, submerged weedbeds, brush piles and even hydrilla mats.

Killer Apps

Through the rig's gradual evolution out West, certain bull's-eye applications have arisen. In short, we know the dropshot works great over deep-water rock piles, along deep, tapering points or at the base of bluffs and canyon walls. But what about other situations? East of the Continental Divide, bass habitat changes significantly. From matted weeds to prairie lakes, from strip pits to big rivers to the Great Lakes, and everything in between, there exist unexploited bass primed for the dropshot rig.

My first experiment involved the legendary smallmouth fishery on Lake Erie. In the dead of last year's hot summer, I took the rig to the Eastern Basin in Buffalo, New York. The water was dead calm; the sun bright and brutal.

It was a classic situation that posed a major problem— gin-clear water coupled with bright sun meant fish would be deep and likely off the feed. Immediately, I went to the drop-

Tying The Dropshot

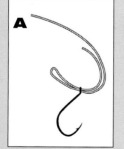

To tie the dropshot rig, hold the hook so the point faces up (A), run the doubled line through the eye, then tie a palomar knot (B), leaving 1 to 2 feet of tag end. After seating the knot, run the tag end back through the hook eye (C), and adjust the knot so the hook rides perpendicular to the line. Attach a weight anywhere on tag end (D).

Dropshot Options

Versatility defines this revolutionary rig, from the style of plastics you choose, to the type of sinker (or bait) that anchors it. Try tying the dropshot rig in one of these three ways:

SIMPLE SETUP	or...	TANDEM RIG	or...	JIG DROPPER

shot while a buddy rigged a tube. We were fishing the channel edge just outside Buffalo Harbor, and found a group of bass resting just atop the edge, relating to a large buoy chain.

A tube wasn't the answer. Activating the bait meant dragging it away from the "spot on the spot." The dropshot bait, on the other hand, stayed in a stationary position right at the base of the chain. Result: three 4-pound smallies on the dropshot, zero for the tube.

I should note that the wind eventually did pick up, and once we started drifting the breaks and humps, the tube went fish-for-fish with the dropshot.

The situation is telling; a perfect example of how a "Western technique" fits into Eastern conditions. Deep bass, clear water, definable features— dropshot territory at is finest. But it doesn't stop there. Lakes like Bull Shoals, Table Rock, Lake Lanier and Lake of the Ozarks are all primed and ready for dropshotting. And spotted bass, especially, are top targets for the rig.

"I've got a bunch of my friends who are fishing the rig," says pro Gary Klein. "Tom Mann on Georgia's Lake Lanier is a good example. He'll fish the lake with the conventional jig and shakin' worm they've been using down there for years. He'll fish an area hard and catch two or three spotted bass. Then, he'll pick up the dropshot and catch 10 fish straight. The dropshot will make them bite."

Klein, quick to use hindsight in planning his tournament strategies this year, looks back on his career wins. "One win was on Bull Shoals in late October, and I was the only angler in the field to catch a limit all three days. I was fishing a shakin' worm in 55 feet of water and had the fish to myself. If I'd had the dropshot rig, I'd have massacred 'em. Same thing on Lanier. I won that in December, but it was another situation tailor-made for the dropshot."

Other clear-water potentials include strip pits across the country, especially phosphate and spring-

"Dropshotting is also a great way to avoid that nasty soupy moss that collects on lake bottoms."

fed limestone pits, plus any water infested with zebra mussels. In fact, the dropshot is an outstanding tactic for elevating the bait above razor-sharp mussel beds. Lose a sinker? No big deal. Lose your bait? Well, you've lost the fish.

Why Not Weeds?

Fishing the rig on Erie piqued my curiosity. Sure, the smallmouths we were fishing are known to commit suicide, and sometimes it seems like a shoelace would catch 'em, but the real test came as I plied the rig on tougher waters—the natural lakes near my home in Minnesota. Here, the experiment involved the deep weed edge.

Aim High For Bass In The Grass

Aquatic vegetation is good for bass, and for bass anglers. It provides cover, oxygen, shade and attracts a variety of forage items. Most bass anglers quickly learn to fish weedbeds—inside edges, outside edges, notches and holes are all productive patterns at one time or another. But what about really thick weeds at the surface, like water hyacinth, alligator weed or surface-matted ("topped-out") hydrilla or milfoil? Do bass live there?

The answer, of course, is yes. But many anglers fail to understand the where and why. It's a somewhat well-kept secret that bass in matted vegetation are near the top of the weeds, not the bottom. The reasons are many. Water hyacinth roots, for example, provide high-density housing for aquatic insects, small crustaceans, grass shrimp, crawfish and small fish. Topped-out submergent vegetation is especially attractive to grass shrimp and small fish. I've collected dozens of large grass shrimp from a square yard of surface-matted hydrilla.

Naturally, feeding bass head for the food, which is often a foot or two below the surface. But it's also likely that less active bass may be hanging right under the mats, too, since decaying plant material often makes the bottom inhospitable. Matted weeds also block out sunlight and most oxygen production takes place near the surface.

Knowing this, I concentrate on targeting bass near the surface of the weeds. I fish hyacinths or topped-out hydrilla, for example, by flipping a plastic worm, craw or tube through the mat and letting it sink to bottom. Hits often come on the fall. If the bait reaches bottom, I immediately bring it back up and fish a foot or less beneath the mat. Another tip: When fishing floating plants, look for fresh, healthy ones—they have the best root systems. When fishing topped-out submersed vegetation, look for old vegetation with patches of filamentous algae, which appears as slick, shiny, smooth, bright green patches from several inches to several feet in diameter. Grass shrimp love the algae, and bass love the shrimp.

—Dr. Hal Schramm

When fishing floating plants or topped-out vegetation (left), bass are often nearer the surface than we think. Dropshotting is a great way to target these fish.

You'd be hard-pressed to find a fish that doesn't, at some point, utilize the deep weed edge. Bass like to cruise the edges, and I've always approached the situation with classic presentations—Carolina or Texas rigs, jigs, cranks and spinnerbaits. But the dropshot works, too. Works so well, in fact, that it's often difficult to target just bass because the rig attracts crappies, walleyes, 'gills, pike, even drum.

Dropshotting is also a great way to avoid that nasty, soupy moss that collects on lake bottoms. Any bait that hits the moss is instantly worthless until the next cast, but with the dropshot, the bait never touches it. Submerged weedbeds, too, offer their own particular set of challenges. Here, when bass are cruising above the weed tops, spinnerbaits and cranks can be fantastic, if you can dial in the right depth, but the dropshot is a viable option, too.

Western big-bass specialist and NAFC member Bill Siemantel encourages Eastern anglers to accept what he's learned. "One of my 12 pounders last fall came from a submerged grass mat, where the weeds were four feet tall. The fish were just above the grass and any other rig, even a Carolina rig, gets pulled down into the grass where the fish can't see it. I used the dropshot with four feet of tag end, which suspended the bait two inches above the weed tops. The bass never see this type of presentation."

Going back to thinking of the dropshot as a reverse Carolina rig, it's easy to understand its mechanics. No matter the change in bottom contour, a dropshot bait is always a fixed distance off bottom, so anywhere a suspended plastic is to your advantage, the dropshot should be tried. Siemantel also argues the merits of the rig in topped-out weeds. So does Western bass guru Rich Tauber, who's been one of dropshotting's biggest proponents and is responsible for bringing the Bakudan weight over from Japan.

> **"It's truly been a long time since anglers have had the opportunity to challenge themselves with a brand-new, revolutionary, go-to technique."**

"Right now we're almost finished with designs for a flippin'-style Bakudan and it should be available shortly," says Tauber. "Too often, anglers fish below matted weeds like hyacinth and hydrilla, right on the bottom. What the pros know, is that bass often tuck up close to the bottom of the weed mat, feeding on crawdads and other critters that live in the suspended root systems. To reach these fish, it's important to suspend the bait off bottom." (See sidebar, "Aim High For Bass In The Grass.")

The most common option is the jig or Texas-rigged worm, pulled up and twitched below the weed tops, but the dropshot offers an interesting alternative, since the bait remains in the same spot, yet is much more active. Plus, weights as heavy as 1 or 2 ounces can be used to punch through the mats with little to no effect on bait movement. However, dangling weights can hang up during a fight. Siemantel, when fishing the heavy stuff, ties the weight with two overhand knots so the sinker breaks off if it hangs during battle.

Fishing The Forest

In Texas, power plant lakes such as Richland Chambers and Squaw Creek are littered with standing timber. In places where water clarity allows, the dropshot is an excellent choice of presentations.

In our conversations, Gary Klein turned me onto a technique being used on Richland Chambers. Here, many savvy anglers work a Carolina rig through the tree limbs. When it bumps a limb, they keep the rig in place and bang the weight against it, which leaves the bait suspended in the trees.

Problem is, most action gets absorbed by the weight. Substitute a dropshot and the bait comes alive. Just be sure to use heavier line or you'll quickly lose a hooked bass in the tangles of timber.

Other times, the base of timber produces, and again, the dropshot can be worked vertically like a jig, or cast to the base of the tree and wiggled in place. Brush piles, too, can be fished effectively with a dropshot, as can fallen timber on natural lakes.

Pint-Size Power

Today's dropshot baits run small. From left to right: Roboworm Straight Tail; Gary Yamamoto Small Lizard; Dezyner Baits 4-inch Doodle; Dezyner Baits 3-inch Grub; Berkley Bass Minnow; Lunker City 4-inch Slug-Go; Competitive Edge Hawkeye; Angler's Choice Chubby Worm. Clipper shows relative size.

Again, the key is water clarity and mood of the fish. Muddy water or aggressive fish? A dropshot is probably not the best option. If the water's relatively clear and fish are neutral or negative, try it.

Fish This Rig Now

It's an exciting time to be a bass angler. So often, trends seem nothing more than a simple change in marketing strategies or tackle refinements—fat cranks versus thin, 7-foot rods versus 6, hot new fluorescent colors or sharper hooks.

It's truly been a long time since anglers have had the opportunity to challenge themselves with a brand-new, revolutionary, go-to technique.

Yet, so many questions still remain.

How will it perform in stained or muddy water, for example? Can we dropshot 8-inch lizards? What's the ultimate solution to line twist? And more.

I don't have the answers, but I'm excited to be starting on the journey toward understanding. You can be, too.

Think about the waters you fish and the particular challenges they present, then make room for the dropshot in your list of go-to techniques. The feast of success is but an experiment away.

ON SOLID GROUND

A THREE-SEASON GAME PLAN FOR CATCHING BASS FROM SHORE.

by Field Editor Spence Petros

I paused for a moment and scanned the lake. A high-powered boat had been flying by every couple minutes, but this time, the wait seemed longer than normal. Finally I heard a roar in the distance and hoped it would come close enough. Yes! A streaking boat buzzed within 75 yards of shore. Perfect.

Within seconds the waves began to slap the riprap bank. My 7-foot spinning rod helped me make a long, tight cast parallel to the rocky bank. I worked the shallow-running minnow plug with a pull-pause, pull-pause retrieve. Suddenly, a smashing strike! Just like the other dozen or so I'd gotten over the last hour. A chunky bass pushing 3 pounds cleared the water; I landed it without getting my feet wet.

When the feeding spree ended, I walked down the bank to a sandy flat where my boat was parked, cranked up the motor and headed out onto the open water to finish the day's fishing. I had parked the

boat to fish a wind-pummeled riprap bank with a weed edge that started a few feet out. A tough situation to fish quietly and effectively from a boat.

But not from shore.

If you think shore fishing is only for anglers who don't have a boat, or for those too young, too old or too inexperienced to operate one, think again. I would rather be a knowledgeable shore-bound angler than one in control of "200 horses" who doesn't understand bass and how they react to various weather, water and seasonal conditions.

The major reasons that get me walking the bank are: It's spring and my boat's not ready; I only have limited time to fish; or the biggest reason of all—a particular spot or area is more effectively fished from shore! I guess a little ego enters the picture, too, when you can catch more bass afoot than others flying around in $30,000 boats.

Shore Stuff

While shore fishing is an advantage in many instances, you have to use the right tackle. I prefer to use jig-style lures, especially in the spring. A

bottom-hopping bait combined with line watching becomes my "underwater eyes." I mentally keep track of the time it takes the lure to fall back down to bottom, which helps me locate slight changes in bottom contour.

With a no-stretch superline, it's easier to feel out particular pieces of cover. Plus, it's easier to achieve riveting hooksets, even on long casts. I generally use 10- to 14-pound Flame Green FireLine linked to a 3- to 4-foot leader of mono or fluorocarbon. Upgrade the pound test to cope with bigger-than-average bass and/or heavier cover.

I tend to use 7-foot rods for most of my shore fishing, as they allow longer casts (if needed), and provide better angles when casting parallel to the bank. Also, longer rods let me reach out past shoreline cover to cast, or to better control a fish after the hook-up.

Where It's Warm

The first warm trends of late winter/early spring signal the start of a shore-fishing bonanza. Many bass move into shallow, sun-drenched waters that heat up quickly. These areas, especially if wind-protected and exposed to a lot of direct sunlight, can easily be 10 degrees warmer than the main-lake waters. Look for these clues that help pinpoint areas of warmer water.

Feeder creeks spilling into lakes or reservoirs are always prime spots to check. Start at the creek mouth, paying close attention to any changes in water color—darker water usually contains more floating particles, which absorb and store heat. Darker water also attracts forage. Finding structure or cover at the creek mouth is a plus, too. Locating a lip, hole, small hump or scattered cover at the creek mouth may be the key to bigger bass. A good way to uncover these hidden jewels is with a jig, as I mentioned, along with high-visibility line.

Brush, willow or wood-lined banks are a common sight at many creek mouths. If the water is deep enough—18 to 24 inches is a good rule—you'll generally find bass holding there. This is the type of spot where it's common to contact several bass, then return a few hours later and do it again as migrating fish move in. Under higher water conditions, these areas really heat up.

Creek Mouths And Inflows

Creeks and streams flowing into lakes and reservoirs often hold active bass during early-spring warming trends. Casts should cover stained waters (A), and feel for any type of cover along the bottom (B) or any slight depth changes (C). Be sure to note wind direction, which pushes warm water along the shore. Also probe any shoreline cover at the creek mouth (D) that rests in at least 18 inches of water. Check up to the first pool, paying attention to any wood in the water (E) or fertile flat (F) that may support early weed growth.

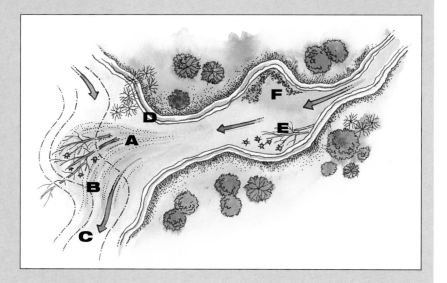

Cover-lined banks at the creek mouth, in the creek and around the first hole or pool in from the main body of water are all worth checking. I generally use the first widening, or hole, in determining whether to head farther upstream. If the first hole produces fish, I continue upstream to fish another pool. Slower-moving feeder creeks usually hold largemouths, while swifter creeks may draw early-season smallmouths. Any wood or rock cover is capable of holding bass, but also watch for protected flats on the north shores. These areas foster early weed growth and are always worth checking.

Other areas that warm quickly and draw bass like magnets are backwaters, shallower bays, man-made canals and channels, along with narrows that connect wider bodies of water. In all these instances, the faster a spot warms, the more likely it is to get the first wave of shallow-moving bass. A few more tips: dead-end or T-shaped canals usually warm faster, as do bays and backwaters with darker bottoms that are more sheltered from the main-lake water. Toss various types of cover into the mix and you have the potential for the lake's best spot.

When fishing visible cover in these areas, I've had great success with smaller spinnerbaits. A ¼- to ⅜-ounce bait with a single Colorado blade is a favorite, and I either slow-roll it or fish it with frequent drops. Spinnerbait strikes usually come on the fall, which is another reason to use a no-stretch, visible super-line. I generally don't use a trailer this early in the year, and if I start getting short strikes, I clip the skirt so it just comes to the end of the

Spence's two largest Illinois bass were caught from shore. This 23-inch, 7 pounder was pulled from an early-to-warm channel off a large lake.

The Inside Weed Edge

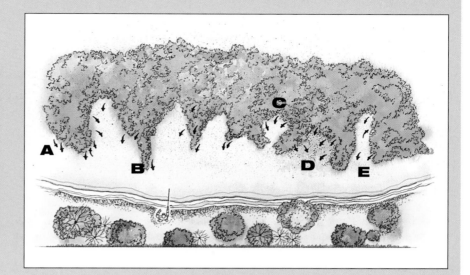

Inside weed edges are prime spots for a shore-bound angler. If you can easily see the weeds, cast to edges (A), points (B), holes (C), hard-bottom areas (D) and slots (E). Bigger bass usually hold tight to these features, but it takes precision casts to catch them. If the water is murky or weeds are too deep to see, feel them out with a lure. The shallower edges of weeds like cabbage, coontail and milfoil are great, but don't ignore the inside edge of reeds, or the shallow sections of a big pad field or "slop."

hook's bend. When not casting to visible cover, I cast parallel to the shore.

55 Degree Magic

Unless it's spring, I usually don't pay much attention to water temperature when bass fishing. But once the water temperature hits 55 degrees in the spawning areas, both small-mouths and large-mouths move in and become very active. This situation is very different from fishing the early-to-warm spots I mentioned above, as most of those areas were not good spawning grounds.

Fifty-five-degree water signals the pre-spawn period, when bass cruise the shallows and begin to search out spawning sites and potential mates. They begin to cross flats, cruise inside weed edges, migrate along channels and move into open bays related to the main body of water.

It's also the time when they'll knock the paint off a fast-moving lure, or quickly suck in a jig or live bait presentation. This aggressive bite lasts until the water temperature reaches the low 60s. Then, you've got to slow down to catch the bigger, non-chasing females.

During pre-spawn, the shallow "inside edge"

Soupy shoreline slop is a situation most boaters pass up. Catch the fish they miss while never leaving the bank.

of a major main-lake weedbed really starts to turn on. Many bass will spawn along this weedline, often around any type of cover between the weed edge and the shoreline. The most productive zones are the two- to six-foot depths where the edge occurs. If the inside weed edge is visible, it's easy to fish. If it's not easy to see, make sure to use a lure that allows you to feel it out, like a jig or spinner-bait. It's critical you hit that weed edge, since bigger bass often hold tight to the edge where they relate to small weed points, cuts, isolated hard bottoms, or where cover comes into play.

Furthermore, the inside edges of weedbeds are very important throughout the year. Not only are they hot during spring, but on many lakes and reservoirs, they can be better than the deeper, outside weed edge. Fishing pressure from boats along the deeper edge and over the weeds can be heavy during the warmer months, but fish along the inside edge often rest unmolested. Inside weedlines can also be very productive on lakes where larger predators such as muskies, pike or big walleyes "rule" the deep edge. They can also get hot under low-light conditions, at night or during fall

Do Northern Bass Need Spawning Sanctuaries?

Recruitment—the number of wild young fish that survive and grow to catchable size—is always a major factor in how many fish are in a lake. That said, does fishing during the bass spawn negatively affect recruitment? After all, black bass, like other Centrarchids, guard their eggs and fry, and the number of fry that survive is largely dependent on how well, and how long, the nest is guarded.

David Philipp, a Senior Scientist with the Illinois Natural History Survey, wanted to know more. Specifically, Philipp set out to discover the relationship between successful nests—those whose fry reached self-sufficient size—and year-class strength.

Over a 10-year period, Philipp and team studied a number of prime bass lakes in southeastern Ontario. Research teams swam the shorelines daily, locating, tagging and monitoring bass nests, then recording which ones were successful and the number of viable fry they produced. The number of successful nests and fry in a lake were then analyzed in relation to the subsequent year class.

Not surprisingly, Philipp found that nesting success directly influenced year-class strength in the waters he studied. It stands to reason, then, that any disruption of the spawning ritual —including the removal of the guarding males —will have a direct negative impact on the size of the fish population.

Philipp notes that, obviously, catch and harvest has the most negative impact. However, he also argues that catch-and-release

---

warming trends—all situations that tend to pull bass in shallower.

Another favorite shore situation that corresponds with 55-degree water temperature is fishing in bays or harbors. Moored boats can be especially productive, as bass mill around the attractive shelter. Be very careful not to hook the boat, or the rope or chain that anchors it. If in doubt, don't cast.

Working The Weeds

From the time they are tall enough to provide cover, until cold weather causes them to turn brown, weeds are a blessing to the shoreline angler. Since bass often follow them into shallow water for feeding, safety and spawning opportunities, you may think weeds related to deeper water are a big plus. This is not always the case, especially in this era of "intelligent" fishing pressure. So often, savvy anglers look for prime weeds adjacent to deeper water, and good spots get hit hard. Here, the shore-bound angler can target fish other anglers ignore.

So too, the shallower areas of thick, matted beds of vegetation such as "slop," reeds or pads can be nearly impossible to fish from a boat. Yet this heavy, shallow cover often harbors the largest bass a lake has to offer. The best shore-fishing opportunity is often the one that looks like it has the least potential to a boater. A wide, weed-choked flat yards from any depth change? Fish it!

It can be difficult to fish these thick weeds from the low angle of the shore, so I use lures made specifi-

cally for the heavy stuff. Top baits include Johnson Silver Minnows with a plastic or pork trailer, the Frogzilla and Weed Demon from Snag Proof, or the Uncle Josh Jumbo Pork Frog on a weedless hook. I tend to use baitcasting rods, rather than spinning, to accommodate heavier line.

When fishing standard weed conditions, such as a good-size bed of cabbage, coontail or milfoil, besides working the inside edge, another excellent condition is to have at least a foot or two of open water over the tops of the weeds. Weedbeds that haven't reached maturity, or those knocked down by fall weather or brisk winds, will have open water over the tops.

Unless the water is stained, the best fishing over the weed tops is usually under periods of lower light penetration, when bass tend to roam more. Low-light periods, cloudy weather, brisk wind or darkness are all conditions that trigger roaming bass. A willow-leaf spinnerbait is a great choice here.

A beach area surrounded by weeds can also be a night-fishing bonanza. After swimmers vacate the area, bass will often roam the edge of the weeds along the sand border. Other times, they cruise the clean sand flats where minnows probably move in at night. If you encounter this situation, think about swimmers using the area and be considerate of hooks.

Rocks Are Right

From acting as heat-absorbing bass magnets in cold weather, to harboring crawfish and baitfish in angling during the spawn negatively impacts a bass fishery. When the protecting male is hooked and removed from the nest, predators like sunfish, small perch and crawfish move in and begin feeding on the unprotected eggs or fry. Even if the male is immediately released, it may still abandon the nest if too many offspring have been lost. Catching males multiple times increases the odds of this happening.

Philipp and his team also tested the effectiveness of protecting prime nesting areas through the establishment of "spawning sanctuaries." These areas were identified through signage asking anglers to voluntarily refrain from fishing them. Interestingly, the signs had the opposite effect. Fishing pressure in the "conservation" zones was often greater than the rest of the lake, with some anglers actively (and illegally) targeting bedding bass, rather than legal pike, walleyes and panfish.

Spawning sanctuaries might find a place in fishing's future, as Phillips showed that bedding bass, at least in northern waters, need protection or anglers may threaten the very fisheries they treasure. But clearly, "volunteer sanctuary" status may not provide that needed protection.

—*Jon Storm*

warmer weather, rocks provide fantastic fishing opportunities. During the cold-water periods of spring and fall, rocks receiving direct sunlight draw bass like moths to a light. I've seen rock-lined banks on one side of a body of water attract bass in the mid-morning after soaking up direct sunlight, then go flat after the sun's rays shift. That's when the opposite shore turns on.

One of the first spots to check during the early season is where a rock-lined culvert connects two areas of water. If one is shallower, so much the better. Under sunny, warm conditions, schools of baitfish frequently hold at the mouth of the discharge pipe, and a bunch of bass usually aren't very far behind. The bass and minnows are easily spooked by a boat, but a shore-bound angler can have a field day here, often returning several times a day to catch additional fish. Use lures that splash down quietly.

During warmer weather and into fall, rocks that have "something else going on around them" can be consistent producers. Conditions that can make one area of rocky bank better than another are: where deeper water swings in a little tighter to the shore; when adjacent wood, weed cover or structure exists;

around points, turns or necked-down areas; when rocks are pummeled by wind; if current influences a particular spot; or where deeper, scattered rocks exist. Parallel cast with shallow-running minnow baits, bigger-lipped floating/diving crankbaits (they usually float out of snags when you stop cranking) and spinnerbaits.

A number of different situations draw bass very close to the rocks. Most often bass will be tight to the bank if the rocks break quickly into deep water, or if the water is cold but sun has been heating the rocks. Also, stained water or fishing pressure can draw bass tight to the bank. In all cases, shore anglers can really get to 'em with tight, parallel casts along the rocks.

A good "secret weapon" in summer and fall along riprap is to fish scattered rocks or rubble that rests slightly deeper than the deep edge of the rocks. Many anglers believe the base of riprap is a straight edge. Not so. Deeper rocks are often scattered along the edge as a result of erosion, a difference in bottom taper, or some rocks rolling further down into the water than others. Often, shore anglers can find and fish these areas effectively, especially with a Carolina rig.

Instead of using a barrel-shaped sinker, however, I opt for the banana-shaped No-Snagg sinker from Lindy-Little Joe. To further reduce the odds of hanging up, elevate your plastic offering off bottom by using a floating bait rigged with a thin-wire hook, and a small snell float like those used by walleye anglers.

There are a lot of situations when fishing for bass from shore can be more effective than fishing from a boat. Follow the bass through their seasonal cycles and focus on prime targets. You'll better understand the logic of fishing afoot, and in the end, score more bass from shore.

> ## "Savvy anglers look for prime weeds adjacent to deeper water, and good spots get hit hard. The shore-bound angler can target fish other anglers ignore."

Editor's Note: Whether you fish bass, crappies, walleyes or other species, Spence Petros' Chicagoland fishing classes will make you a better angler. For more information, call (815) 455-7770.

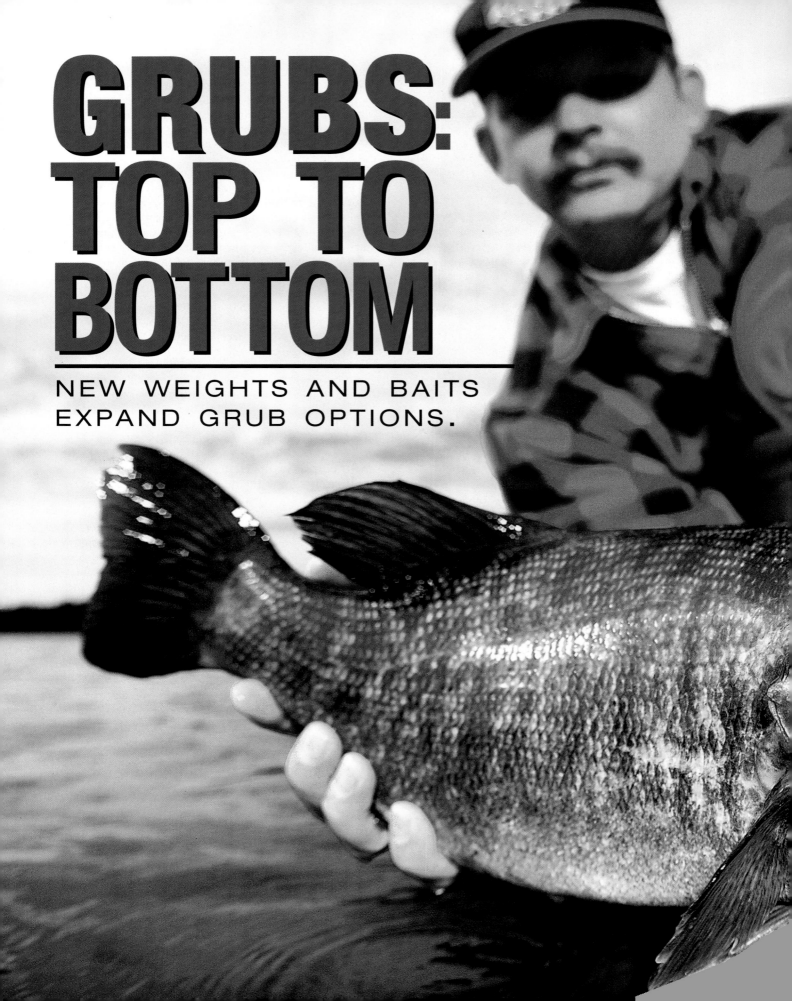

GRUBS: TOP TO BOTTOM

NEW WEIGHTS AND BAITS EXPAND GRUB OPTIONS.

by Jon Storm

Nice smallie, huh? The angler took it on a grub, a bait I consider the most versatile lure on the planet. Fish it deep, fish it shallow or use it to tempt those annoyingly neutral suspenders—the grub will not let you down.

As an editor of North America's largest multi-species fishing magazine and a bassaholic, I read everything I can about bass. I also chat with leading bass anglers, sometimes on a daily basis. And through the years, I've come to the conclusion that the grub, despite the fact that it's an extremely effective largemouth bait, will be forever pigeoned-holed as a smallmouth lure.

Hence the smallmouth photo. But the grub is a deadly largemouth bait. And the new grubs and rigging options now available make it even more so. As Penny Berryman told me the other day: "I can tell you all the top pros are quietly experimenting with the new baits and new rigs that are out there. The new grubs, with greater bulk and bigger profiles, aren't just for finesse situations any more."

Swimming A Grub

One of the most exciting grub developments in recent years is the idea of center-weighting. By moving the weight away from the head and distributing it along the body of the bait itself, grubs assume a more natural action. Rather than falling headfirst, they fall horizontally, or semi-horizontally, just like a wounded baitfish. The grub is easier to control on a steady retrieve and acts more like a crankbait than a jig. Just as important, the hook-point is often located closer to the tail, resulting in more hook-ups with short strikers.

Bait Rigs president Joe Puccio describes the genesis of the company's Slo-Poke Grubmaster, one of the newest center-weighted jigheads on the market. "As with so many things, the Grubmaster came as a result of wanting to solve a problem," says Puccio. "The idea came from Sturgeon Bay guides Gary Nault and Tim Dawidiuk. Smallmouths in this part of Lake Michigan have been relating more to weeds and heavy cover. Perhaps that's a function of the clearing water. Nault began sticking our original Slo-Poke walleye jigs inside grubs. This caused the bait to fall horizontally, and just as important, the hook stayed in an upright position, behind the line, so it was much easier to bring through weeds.

"As we upscaled the Slo-Poke to size 2/0 and 3/0 hooks, we transformed it into a bass jig, but at the same time made an exciting discovery. Smallmouths can be very discriminating when it comes to color. By inserting the colored Grubmasters into clear and translucent baits, we created new colors that no one else could replicate. A blue Grubmaster inside a smoke grub looks remarkably like an alewife. A pink head inside a gray body imitates a juvenile rainbow trout. The jigheads work just as well inside tubes, too."

The Grubmaster catches smallmouths in all situations—from skinny-water, pre-spawn patterns to deep summer and fall feeding zones. It can be crawled along rocky bottoms and through moderate weeds. It's also a fantastic swimming presentation. It's long been believed that the best way to swim a grub was with short pops of the rodtip, but there are times when a straight, crankbait-like retrieve works best. Most often it's in clear water with a pelagic forage base like shad, ciscoes and alewives that suspend at various depths. Smallmouths in these waters will often suspend near roaming schools of bait or adjacent to some type of structure.

Targeting these suspended smallmouths, once you find them, is straightforward. Cast the grub out, let it fall on semi-slack line, then burn

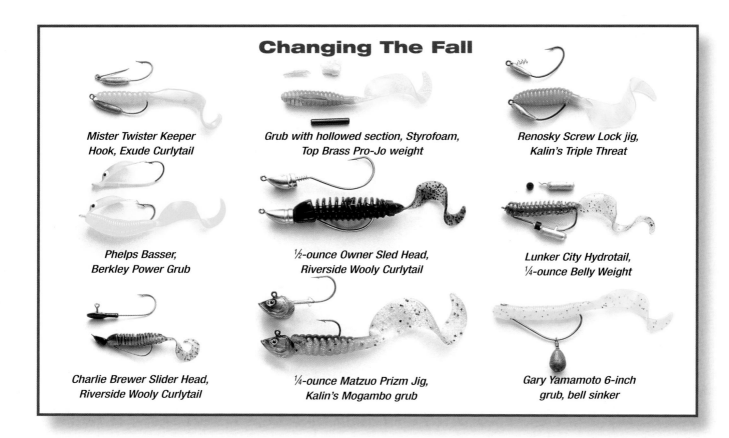

Changing The Fall

Mister Twister Keeper Hook, Exude Curlytail

Grub with hollowed section, Styrofoam, Top Brass Pro-Jo weight

Renosky Screw Lock jig, Kalin's Triple Threat

Phelps Basser, Berkley Power Grub

½-ounce Owner Sled Head, Riverside Wooly Curlytail

Lunker City Hydrotail, ¼-ounce Belly Weight

Charlie Brewer Slider Head, Riverside Wooly Curlytail

¼-ounce Matzuo Prizm Jig, Kalin's Mogambo grub

Gary Yamamoto 6-inch grub, bell sinker

it back to the boat. Experiment with different countdown times, and retrieve speeds, until you're reaching the depth the smallmouths are using—usually somewhere near the thermocline, but higher if the feed is on. It's also a great search technique that covers water quickly.

Largemouths, Too

Other ways to rig and swim a grub are with Kalin's Ultimate Grass Slasher or High Rider jigheads. Dave Burkhardt, a tackle industry consultant and seasoned veteran of Florida's vast largemouth bass fishery, turned me onto a summer largemouth pattern with grubs.

"I fish the Harris Chain, Butler Chain and St. Johns River in Florida," says Burkhardt. "During the peak of summer, the water gets extremely warm and, many times to catch largemouths, we need to down-size significantly—6-pound line and ⅛-ounce weights

are typical. One of the hottest patterns going is to use a Kalin's High Rider jighead and a natural-pattern grub like bluegill or black back/white belly. Working the grass, or right above weeds about to top out, swim the grub on a steady retrieve. If you come across holes in the grass, pause and let the grub flutter down. If you want to work deeper through the weeds, swim the grub with an Ultimate Grass Slasher head, which cuts through the greenery a little better."

The idea of swimming a jig is nothing new, but the new tools make it much easier and offer the fish a different look. To add a little flash to your grub, try one of Northland's new Thumper Spins; or if fishing in low-light periods, try a Northland glow stick on the jighead. To make the grub act more like a crankbait, attach an Eagle Claw Eaker Shaker in front.

Blakemore's Scoo-Tin is another great swimming head for grubs. The Scoo-Tin's tin alloy head glides through the water without undue drag, and it can be worked in a variety of ways. Try sharp jerks of the rodtip to rip the grub from side to side, or a steady retrieve with occasional pops for a more subdued swim. And when you stop the bait, it continues to glide forward and down. It's perfect for working a foot, or even less, below the surface.

How you rig a swimming grub is important. Rig

> **"The idea of swimming a jig is nothing new, but the new tools do make it much easier and offer the fish a different look."**

it tail up and precisely in the center and it will track straighter and appear more subdued and natural. Rigging it tail down makes it a better drop bait. It won't track as well when swimming, but then you're striving for a more erratic action anyway. As always, experiment.

The Fall Is All

Maybe it all started with Charlie Brewer's Slider heads. Back in the late '60s, Charlie Brewer, Sr. found it was getting tougher and tougher to catch fish in the reservoirs near his home. He developed the Slider head design while experimenting with smaller baits and lighter lines. The original head was nothing more than a dime soldered to a hook. In the decades that have followed, the original Slider design transformed into a varied lineup, including new models with larger, heavier Mustad Ultra Point hooks.

The Slider head not only swims grubs effectively, it creates a slow, wobbling fall that triggers fish when nothing else will. Another way to tweak the fall is with weighted hooks. Hooks like the Mister Twister Keeper Hook and Renosky weight-forward Screw Lock offer weighting options beyond simple leadheads.

Belly-weighting achieves a few things. First, as the grub swims, the weight acts as a keel to keep it from rolling. Second, the bait doesn't fall straight down, but more "down/forward." Of the weighting systems mentioned, though, Lunker City's Belly Weights are the most versatile, allowing acute adjustments to weight placement along any length of exposed hook.

There are times when you really want a bait to hang in the strike zone. Usually, the solution is to go to an unweighted grub. Gary Yamamoto grubs, which are 50 percent salt, are great for fishing weightless because they fall faster then regular soft plastics and you can fish them in up to 10 feet of water without losing patience.

The Phelps Weedless Basser is a little different, as it achieves near-neutral buoyancy. When

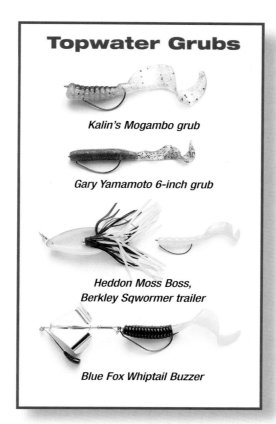

Topwater Grubs

Kalin's Mogambo grub

Gary Yamamoto 6-inch grub

Heddon Moss Boss, Berkley Sqwormer trailer

Blue Fox Whiptail Buzzer

rigged with a grub, it will still sink, but very slowly. The float rides up on the fall, so the hook point rides up, too. Plus, it's weedless and can be retrieved subsurface. A perfect situation for this grub presentation would be a quiet bay or pond, with weeds about to top out and various scattered cover.

Another rigging trick comes from NAFC member Bill Garbinsky from downstate New York. For over 25 years, Garbinsky has been fishing the East Coast bass circuits, and when the bite gets tough, he resorts to finesse grubbin'.

"Grubs themselves have a lot of action," says Garbinsky, "but there are times when you need to give them a little more. The problem is, it's tough to create action without fishing the bait faster. So you're faced with a paradox.

"What I do is slit open a grub with a razor blade and remove some of the material. I insert a small piece of commercial Styrofoam—the dense stuff, not puffy packing peanuts—then reseal the grub with a worm iron. I rig the floating grub on a split shot or mojo rig. The grub has so much action, you barely need to move it. It's a great rig for bedding bass, but I also use it to suspend the grub above new vegetation and shallow weeds, or to drag it along hard-bottom areas."

Another off-beat weighting tip comes from Russ Comeau, a former commercial striper fisherman, retired Wall Street financier and now the mind behind bassdozer.com.

"I've used center-weighted hooks, but a rig that I prefer incorporates a bell sinker. I take a

"The new grubs, with greater bulk and bigger profiles, aren't just for finesse situations any more."

–Penny Berryman

wide-gap hook, like the Gamakatsu EWG, and match the size to my bait, a 3- to 6-inch grub. For example, if I am using a Series 19 Yamamoto grub, which is a 6-inch grub, I take a 5/0 EWG hook. I rig the grub weightless, with the tail pointing down, but before I sink the hook back into the body, I slip a regular bell sinker on it. It's important you rig the grub with the eye of the hook about ½ inch back from the front of the bait. Just insert the hook point behind the head and Texas rig as you normally would a plastic worm.

"This is a shaking technique. I cast the grub out and shake it as it's falling. When it hits bottom, I'll keep shaking. The sinker stays put, but the bait rocks back and forth. The advantage over all the other center-weighting systems is you don't have to buy any special hook or head. You get a tremendous amount of movement out of the grub because the bell sinker is effectively on a swivel.

"It's a great technique for hard-composition bot-

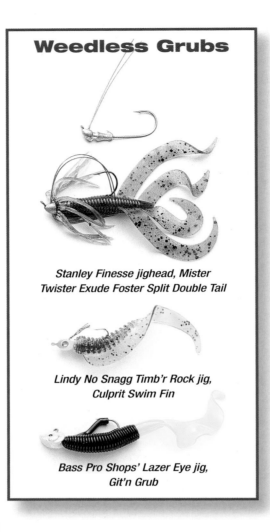

Weedless Grubs

Stanley Finesse jighead, Mister Twister Exude Foster Split Double Tail

Lindy No Snagg Timb'r Rock jig, Culprit Swim Fin

Bass Pro Shops' Lazer Eye jig, Git'n Grub

toms like sand, gravel, rocks and clay. It's also a good rig for clear water because the fish won't see the sinker. They'll be looking around for crawfish and they'll see the jiggling grub right there in front of them."

There are times when you want to front-weight a grub through Texas rigging, which is an effective presentation when bass are holding tight to cover or when you need a straight drop along visible cover elements. When Texas rigging, consider choosing one of the new fixed jigheads made especially for the purpose.

Owner's Sled Heads and Ultra Heads, or the Jobee Pro Hook, for example, are fixed-weight, high-performance hooks with extra-wide gaps that place the vector of pull directly in line with the hook point. Another option is the Gambler Florida-Rig screw-in weight, because it's a fixed weight that lets you fish any hook you'd like.

Matzuo's brand new Prizm jighead, built of acrylic, or Cabela's Livin' Eye resin jighead, are two more front-weighting options. These amazingly lifelike jig-

Good Scents: Do Attractants Affect Mortality?

Each year, new bodies of water are subject to special regulations. Some rules make sense. Others, like a somewhat recent law change in Canada, are baffling. In 1998, the Canadian Park Service prohibited anglers from using chemical or scented substances within national park boundaries. Simply put, anglers can't use, or even possess, fish attractants or scented soft plastic baits within national parks.

Researchers Steven Cooke of the University of Illinois and Karen Dunmall of the University of Waterloo (Canada) set out to discover whether fish attractants had any influence on hooking mortality. They took their study to one of the parks in question—Point Pelee National Park on the Canadian side of Lake Erie.

In a controlled experiment, anglers fishing from shore used five different types of baits on identical jigheads: dead emerald shiners, Berkley Power Grubs, salted Gary Yamamoto grubs, grubs scented with anise oil, and unscented plastic grubs. All baits were smoke color and roughly 4 inches long.

Over a four-day period, encompassing 16 hours of angling, the group caught 238 smallmouth bass. All fish were landed within 30 seconds. Notes were made on hook location, time it took to remove the hook, the depth of the hook in relation to the throat, and whether there was bleeding. The fish were placed in a 12-square-meter holding pen, monitored for 72 hours, then released.

Not a single bass died, nor was there any sign of disease that would lead to post-release mortality. Furthermore, after examining the data, there was no difference in hooking depth while using scented or unscented baits.

Biologically, it appears the Canadian Park Service regulations make no sense. Some feel the move was made to discourage angling in these protected areas.

Curiously, the research team also tracked the angling skill of each participant in the study. After cross-referencing data, it was discovered that skilled anglers tended to hook fish more deeply than unskilled anglers. We suspect that skilled anglers sense a bite more quickly than novices and set the hook while the bait is still deep in the fish's mouth.

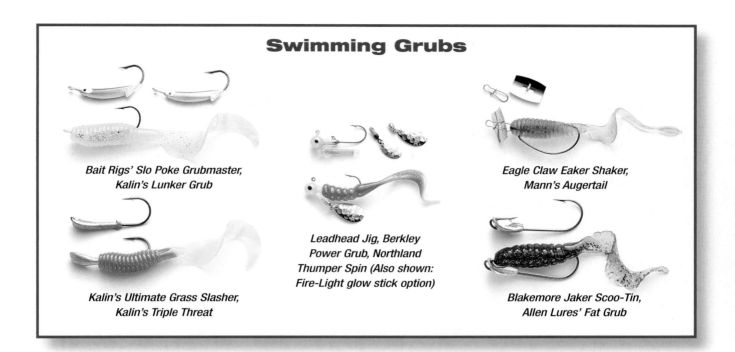

Swimming Grubs

Bait Rigs' Slo Poke Grubmaster,
Kalin's Lunker Grub

Kalin's Ultimate Grass Slasher,
Kalin's Triple Threat

Leadhead Jig, Berkley
Power Grub, Northland
Thumper Spin (Also shown:
Fire-Light glow stick option)

Eagle Claw Eaker Shaker,
Mann's Augertail

Blakemore Jaker Scoo-Tin,
Allen Lures' Fat Grub

heads are much lighter than leadheads, and their cupped chins create a unique action on both the swim and the drop.

New weedless options bear mention, too. If you need to cast or swim the grub through heavy weeds or wood cover, a few exciting new innovations include the Stanley Finesse jighead, the Lindy No-Snagg Timb'r Rock jig and the Git'n Grub from Bass Pro. The heads from Lindy and Stanley are unlike any other weedless system, and their applications branch from grubs into tubes and other soft plastics.

Grubs On Top

Whether you consider grubs shallow- or deep-water baits, and whether you fish them for smallmouths or largemouths, don't neglect topwater. Running a grub across the surface is deadly any time a topwater bite is happening, and they offer a particular advantage over traditional topwaters. When buzzin' weeds or boulders, for example, you can kill the retrieve at any point and the bait will fall slowly. This is something you can't do with a buzzbait or hardbait.

One of the best rigs, and one that's particularly hot right now, is a Kalin's Mogambo grub. Rig it on a wide-gap hook, like a 5/0 Mustad Mega Bite or Gamakatsu Oversize Worm Hook. Texas rig the bait weightless, with its tail down. The shank of the

hook acts as a keel and keeps the bait upright and buzzin' straight.

Key areas to hit include dollar pads, emerging vegetation and wood or rock cover. Kill the retrieve at any point and the Mogambo will descend slowly. Also try buzzing other large grubs like the Yamamoto Series 19 and Berkley's giant Power Grub.

A great topwater trick comes from guide and tournament angler Dave Lefebre from Pennsylvania. Like others, he buzzes Mogambo grubs, but he also fishes topwater spoons like the Heddon Moss Boss.

"It's common for bass to strike and miss topwater baits," says Lefebre. "An old tactic is to keep a rod rigged with a worm or other soft plastic, which you toss back to the bass that missed. Instead, when fishing a bait like the Heddon Moss Boss, I'll tie a 2-foot, 25-pound mono leader off the back of the Moss Boss' hook and rig the trailing grub Texas-style. If a bass misses the Moss Boss, I pause and let the grub flutter down. Nine times out of 10 the bass will nail it."

There are so many approaches, so many depths and strategies to fishing grubs, the subject is an entire book in itself. From topwater to deep water, and all the depths, structure and cover in between, grubs are the do-all, catch-all baits. Fish 'em hard for all species of bass and you'll understand much better how truly versatile the grub can be.

Weightless Wormin'

SOMETIMES A TEXAS OR CAROLINA RIG IS NOT THE WAY TO FISH A PLASTIC WORM.

by Don Wirth

The reservoir was high, and as I idled my boat toward the back of a tributary, hundreds of willow bushes inundated by rising water gave proof to the fact. I picked up a spinning rod rigged with a floating worm, a straight-tail plastic 'crawler impaled on an offset hook.

Talk about a plain-Jane rig—no sinker, no rattle; not even a wiggling twister tail to entice Mr. Big. But there was something off-the-wall about its color—shocking pink! The color of one of those gaudy Cadillacs driven by women who sell Mary Kay cosmetics for a living.

Any bass angler schooled in the art of finesse would no doubt have viewed the neon-colored worm with amusement. It looked like a cheap novelty that some prepubescent boy might drop down the back of his sister's blouse.

I cast the worm to a flooded bush and let the weight of the hook pull it slowly down. A twitch of the rodtip sent the worm darting, and the biggest bass I've ever seen shot out, opened its bucket-size mouth and sucked it in.

Even at casting distance, the take was easy to spot. One second I saw bright pink and the huge, dark shape of the fish. The next second, no pink, and the shape was on the move. I set the hook.

The bass boiled angrily beneath the surface, then bulldozed for the bush. Suddenly, the line cut upward as the fish tried to jump, but it was simply too big to clear the surface. When it shook its head, I saw pink at the corner of its mouth, the hook point buried solidly.

Two more bulldog runs followed, then I lipped the bass with both

Topwater Worm

There are many ways to catch bass using floating worms. A great presentation I stumbled on years ago was to turn a worm into an erratic surface lure. To get extra casting distance, crimp on a large split shot about 18 inches above the hook. Then, during the retrieve with a 7-foot spinning rod, wave the rodtip from side to side, holding the sinker above the surface. This certainly offers a different look, one the bass aren't conditioned to. Plus, it covers a lot of territory.

I use 10- to 14-pound superline tied to a small swivel, along with an 18-inch mono leader. Rig the worm with an exposed hook, or weedless, depending on the cover. When a bass strikes, drop the tip and delay the hook-set a second or two. A long spinning rod allows you to make longer casts, and lets you more easily swing the weight back and forth above the surface to create the side-to-side dart that triggers strikes.
—*Spence Petros*

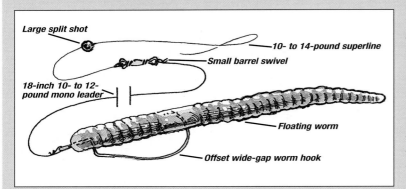

Large split shot
10- to 14-pound superline
Small barrel swivel
18-inch 10- to 12-pound mono leader
Floating worm
Offset wide-gap worm hook

hands. It weighed 9 pounds, 15 ounces on a digital scale.

I caught 14 more bass that day from 1 to 6 pounds on that goofy pink worm. And unlike bass caught on a crankbait or Carolina rig, every fish hit in plain sight. Bass fishing, my friends, just doesn't get more exciting than this.

Return Of Floaters

"Bass anglers have been fishing the so-called floating worm for 50 years, but lately the method has skyrocketed in popularity," says Wayne Kent of Creme Lures. "Ever since Nick Creme invented the plastic worm in 1949, bass anglers have learned to rig them in endless ways, including on a plain hook.

"Of course, bass fishing is a game of trends, many of which are driven by pro anglers on the national tournament circuits. For years, the Texas rig with a sliding sinker was the gold standard in wormin'. Then came the Carolina rig, with a heavy sinker, swivel and leader. Now the big buzz on the pro tour is the floating worm."

One reason the floating worm is enjoying a high-visibility status among the elite bass anglers is because major tournament circuits, including B.A.S.S. and FLW, have revamped their schedules. Fewer

"The biggest question is whether you should use a bright-colored worm, or one that is subdued and realistic."

events are held during the summer these days, more in the spring, and spring is when floating worms are especially effective because so many bass hold in shallow water at this time.

This spring-heavy schedule also tilts the playing field in favor of pros who are adept at targeting bedding bass. Keen-eyed competitors know the floating worm is one of the deadliest of all sight-fishing lures.

Although there are variations on the theme, the basic floating worm rig is a 6- to 8-inch straight-tail plastic worm rigged with only a hook to make it sink. Virtually every soft plastic manufacturer makes a worm specific to this technique. The best floaters, including Creme's Scoundrel, are made with high-grade plastics cooked at exactly the right temperature to achieve the desired buoyancy. Unrigged, they ride the surface. When rigged on a hook, they sink very slowly and respond with sinuous action to the slightest twitch of the rodtip.

Outrageous Vs. Natural

Color is always a hot topic among bass fishermen, including floating worm aficionados. And the biggest question is whether you should use a bright-colored worm, or one that's more subdued and realistic. Many anglers (myself included) prefer hot colors such as pink, school-bus yellow or white when fishing a floater. Not only do bass often react aggressively to these high-vis shades, they're easy for the fisherman to see. Alabama pro angler Randy Howell, one of the youngest stars on the tournament circuit, feels the ability to see the worm provides a tremendous advantage.

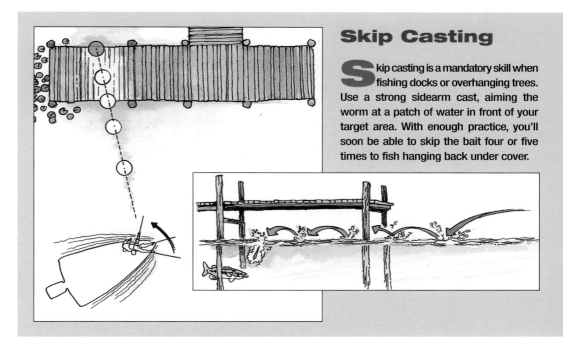

Skip Casting

Skip casting is a mandatory skill when fishing docks or overhanging trees. Use a strong sidearm cast, aiming the worm at a patch of water in front of your target area. With enough practice, you'll soon be able to skip the bait four or five times to fish hanging back under cover.

"Erratic movement is one of the most important factors in triggering a strike," he says. "If you're fishing a brightly colored worm near the top of the water column, you can easily see it a cast-length away. When you spot a bass moving in, you can 'kill' the worm (stop the retrieve so it sinks slowly), twitch it slightly, or swim it rapidly, all the while watching how the bass reacts.

"This is harder to do with a realistic looking worm that blends into its surroundings, and impossible to accomplish with a Texas or Carolina rig in deep water. I usually fish a white worm; it glows like a neon tube in the water."

Sometimes, he admits, bass will follow a bright-colored worm without striking, or fail to respond at all. In either case, it's time for a more natural hue. "Try to match the predominant forage," he says. "For example, when you're fishing around overhanging trees or bushes, green is good because it mimics a live caterpillar. Water snakes hatch in spring and are easy targets for bass along the margins of the lake; a black-and-yellow floating worm is a convincing imitation of a baby snake."

Pros Fish Floaters

There's more to fishing a floating worm than flipping it out and twitching it back. Randy Howell, along with Jay Yelas of Texas and Rickie Harp of Alabama, are three of the best when it comes to flinging floaters. Each of these competitors has earned thousands of dollars using these buoyant baits. And they all have specific ideas about the most productive ways to fish them.

Howell: Arrow Straight

"My biggest bass on a floating worm weighed 10 pounds even. I typically use a 6½-inch Hawg Caller rigged on a 4/0 hook with an offset shank. This gives

me enough weight to get the lure down to that 'twilight zone' where you can barely see it, and plenty of bite for hooking big bass.

"A 6½-foot, medium-action spinning outfit, strung with 10- to 12-pound mono, provides the flex to cast a light lure, and enough muscle to fight the fish.

"I'm a real stickler for a straight worm. It should hang dead straight when you hold it by its head. If it's got a kink, its action will be unnatural and will twist the line as it comes through the water.

"Often when you take a worm out of the package or your tackle tray, it's got a bend in it from sitting in storage for a long time. I lay several worms on the deck of my boat at the start of the fishing day so the sun will soften them and make the kinks disappear. Finally, the worm must be hooked absolutely straight, not off to one side even slightly, or it'll twist your line.

"A floating worm is most effective from pre-spawn to post-spawn, in water from 55 to 75 degrees. I fish it around laydown logs, isolated weed patches and other shallow cover. It's also a dynamite bait around boat docks, brush piles, weedlines, you name it.

"Anybody, even a kid who's just learning to cast, can catch a big bass on a floating worm, but for anglers who can skip cast, the chances of hanging a trophy escalate dramatically. When fishing the back of a cove or the banks of a creek arm, both classic situations for floating worms, an overhand cast will either get hung up or won't reach many of the fish. When bass are pressured, as they often are during a tournament, they tend to retreat back into flooded bushes and other shallow cover, and skipping is the way to reach them.

"Skipping a worm is like skipping a stone. You want the lure to hit the water with enough speed so it

skitters into the fish zone. The idea is to make a sharp, sidearm snap-cast so the lure hits the water in front of your target. If you make a whip-cracking stroke with the rod, you can skip the worm four or five times so it scoots under overhanging branches and into spots overhand casters only dream of reaching. Here's where the medium-action rod comes into play: you can't get the whip-crack effect with a rod that's too light or one that's too stiff.

"I fish a floating worm pretty fast, alternately turning the reel handle, twitching the rodtip and letting the bait sink a little, always keeping it high enough so I can see it when standing up. Many anglers fish this lure way too slow. Use it to trigger a reaction strike from bass, to shake 'em up a bit and elicit an immediate response."

Yelas: Ready Backup

"The floating worm is a great lure for clear to moderately stained water. I fish a 6-inch Berkley Power Floatworm, pink mostly, on a wide-gap 4/0 hook with a 6½-foot, medium-action spinning outfit and 10-pound mono.

"Skipping is definitely the key to catching quality bass on a floating worm. Any guy or gal who can skip a worm under overhanging trees and boat docks will outfish an overhand caster 10-to-1. Like riding a bicycle, the skipping technique is hard to describe in words, but with practice you'll get it right.

"I've caught some huge bass on floating worms in tournaments. It's even more fun than fishing topwaters, because you can see everything—the lure, the fish's approach, and the take. In fact, the floating worm is so exciting to fish, the greatest danger is that it'll entice you into staying with it too long.

"Bass will turn off this lure as quickly as they

turn on to it, so you must be prepared to leave it in favor of another lure when the bite subsides. Fortunately, it's easy to tell when the floating worm begins to lose its magic—just watch the way bass react to it. If they rushed out of cover to eat it an hour ago, and now only nip its tail or follow it half-heartedly, it's time to switch to a backup. Good choices include tubebaits, finesse worms, lizards and centipedes on a pegged worm sinker, or jighead, and fished on bottom.

"During bedding season, it's critical to view these backup lures as part-and-parcel of your floating worm program, not as separate lures and presentations. I seldom present the same lure to a bedding bass two casts in a row. Instead, I keep several rods rigged with all the baits mentioned and, to keep the fish agitated, I rotate among them.

"I fish each of the backup baits the same way, by holding the rod at 10 o'clock and gently shaking the tip. The idea is to keep the weighted head on the bottom while the lure pulsates."

Harp: Extreme Wormin'

"I won a berth at the 2000 Bassmasters Classic by winning a Federation tournament on Tennessee's Fort Loudon Lake on a yellow Creme Scoundrel floating worm. It was the only lure I used during three days of competition, and caught more than 27 pounds of bass. Once, when pre-fishing another tournament, I caught seven bass weighing 41 pounds on this worm. It's an awesome lure for big fish.

"I take the floating worm to extremes. I rely on it in clear or muddy water, shallow or deep, nearly year-round. I'll fish it from early spring through late fall, whenever the water temp is above 55 degrees.

"My favorite worm is an 8-inch Scoundrel on a

6/0 offset worm hook. The hook is much heavier than what most anglers use because my line is 6/30 Spiderwire, which has zero stretch, and my rod is a 6-foot, medium-action baitcaster. The super-tough line, heavy rod and big hook let me put maximum pressure on big fish in thick cover.

"I use an underhand cast, keeping the worm close to the surface, to get it as far back into cover as possible. A lot of strikes occur as soon as it hits the water. Super-line helps me stick fish that would probably come unbuttoned on stretchy mono.

"Let the bass tell you how to retrieve a floating worm. I vary retrieves from active to very slow, depending on the fish's mood. When bass are surface-feeding, fish the worm on top like you'd walk-the-dog with a stickbait. If that doesn't work, twitch it out from the cover quickly, then gradually slow it down as it moves toward the boat, letting it sink to around six feet.

"After bedding season, bass that were hanging around shallow wood and grass move out in front of the cover and suspend in deeper water. Slow-twitching the lure at their level can pay off big.

"Changing colors is critical with this lure. I'll often make a half-dozen loops around an area, using a different color worm on each pass. On sunny days, dark colors like purple and black seem to work best, while brighter colors produce better on overcast days.

"When a bass takes the worm, wait a second or two before setting the hook. I've watched big bass swim up and chomp down on the middle, carry it off a few feet, spit it out, then take it again from the head. If you set the hook immediately, you'll miss a lot of fish."

Fish It

The biggest mistake you can make with a floating worm? Not fishing it. This lure is a deadly tool, and it puts the fun back into bass fishing. And every serious angler could stand to have a little more fun.

Alternative Worm Rigs

Floating worms are as versatile as they are productive. You can rig them a number of ways to fit any specific need. Here are a few examples, but no doubt you'll discover others as you become more experienced with the lure:

Swivel rig—Rig the floating worm as you normally would, but add an 18-inch leader of abrasion-resistant mono and a small barrel swivel. The leader should be at least the same strength as your main line, heavier if you're fishing snaggy wood cover. This rigging method substantially reduces line twist.

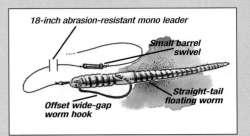

18-inch abrasion-resistant mono leader
Small barrel swivel
Straight-tail floating worm
Offset wide-gap worm hook

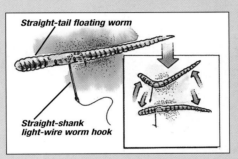

Straight-tail floating worm
Straight-shank light-wire worm hook

Wacky Worm—Pierce the middle of a straight-tail worm with a straight-shank, light-wire hook. Cast, and allow the worm to settle a bit, then twitch the rodtip. Both ends of the worm will alternately flare backward, then straighten out. The wacky worm is a great presentation when bass are holding in weedbeds topping out a foot or so below the surface.

Swimming Worm—Legendary big-bass angler Doug Hannon showed me this rigging method. "The Bass Professor" has caught largemouths up to 16 pounds on it. Run an offset worm hook through the head of a straight-tail worm as you normally would when Texas rigging, but before reinserting the point into the body, twist the body slightly with your fingers. Hannon fishes his swimming rig on a 12-inch leader of 30-pound mono

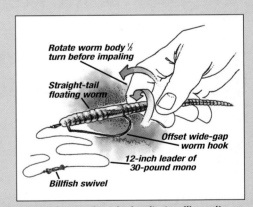

Rotate worm body ½ turn before impaling
Straight-tail floating worm
Offset wide-gap worm hook
12-inch leader of 30-pound mono
Billfish swivel

behind a billfish swivel, casting it to grassy points and retrieving it steadily so it swims across the surface like a water snake.

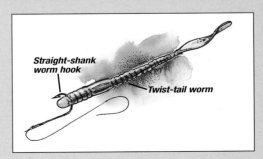

Straight-shank worm hook
Twist-tail worm

Open Hook—For maximum action, run a straight-shank hook above the thick ring of a twist-tail worm, letting the point protrude. Twitch the rodtip repeatedly so the body arches and tail wiggles. This is a great presentation when bass are holding around boat docks and weedlines.

Jig Hopping

Top pros Mark Menendez and Mickey Bruce urge anglers to adopt this little-known, but deadly, bass jigging technique.

by Jon Storm

Unless you fish the Tennessee River Valley or follow the professional bass tours closely, odds are you've never heard of "jig hopping." Known also as "stroking" and "jig-jerking," it's a relatively obscure technique practiced by top pros like Mark Menendez and Mickey Bruce that has never truly caught on in other parts of North America.

But, as these two gentlemen have proven time and again, jig hopping is at home anywhere bass inhabit clean to clear waters. And if you think spinner-baits, or other "moving" baits, are the only way to provoke reaction strikes, you're about to discover a brave new world of jig fishing.

Mickey Bruce used jig hopping to place third in the '93 BASS Masters Classic, and employs it frequently on the trail, from Lake Lanier to the Louisiana Delta. It's practiced most on Kentucky Lake, but works anywhere you're faced with deeper water and inactive fish. The whole jig-hopping philosophy is, as red-hot pro Mark Menendez describes it, "a system within a system that includes tackle, line, jig and trailer, in various combinations."

But the most amazing thing about the system is the actual technique itself. "I rip that jig so hard, you'd think I was setting the hook on a 10-pound fish," says Bruce. "Each and every rip is that violent."

Hopping: Where, Why

For most bass anglers, the jig is the perfect weapon for fish holding tight to cover—pitch and twitch, hook a fish. The jig excels along the bottom, too, and draggin' jigs has dredged up countless big bass. But when bass are relating to cover, but not covered up—when they're suspended above and around structure or cover—most anglers go to a spinnerbait, crank or other fast-moving lure to provoke reaction strikes. Sometimes it works, other times it doesn't, and then it's time to hop a jig.

This technique is really at its best in the post-spawn through early summer period, when water temperatures reach 70 to 72 degrees and fish move out of creek arms en route to summer residences. But it's good right now, too, as the bass follow shad migrations back into creek arms.

According to Menendez: "During October, you can get on any major creek channel and follow the shad. Somewhere along that creek channel, from the mouth to the back end of the creek arm, you will encounter a population of fish, and that's the place you want to hop a jig. The top of the drop may be only four feet, and the bottom of the channel may only be eight, but this is a deadly technique in that situation."

Deadly in other situations, too, like summertime when fish set up on deep ledges or rocky points, or when they relate to rock humps and sunken islands, but suspend far enough above or away that bottom-fishing won't provoke their ire. And it's a three-punch combo, effective on largemouths, smallmouths and spots.

Rip It Good

To prepare for jig hopping, mark the structure you plan to fish either mentally or with a marker buoy, and position the boat in deep water, perpendicular to the area you wish to fish.

Once you've marked a ledge, flat or other area, and can mentally picture what's below the water, cast the jig and let it settle to bottom. Next, align the rod with the jig and hold it at the 10 o'clock position. There should be some slack in the line. Now, get ready to rip.

"See how hard you can jerk that rod a minimum of three feet," is how Mickey Bruce describes it. Menendez adds: "When you stroke that rod up, and you do it right, your line should sound like a bow and arrow. If you hear a 'wheeoush' you'll know you're on the right track."

You really can't rip the jig too hard, but you can rip it too far. Be sure to end the stroke above your

How Hopping Works

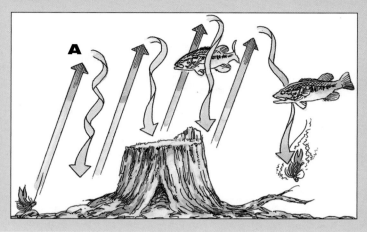

Violent ripping, combined with slack line, creates a rubber-band effect, lifting the jig vertically off bottom, even when done from a distance. When fish are loosely relating to cover, or suspended above it, the technique puts the jig squarely in the strike zone. Most hits come at the apex of the hop (A).

head, in about the 1 o'clock position, then pause and let the jig fall on a semi-slack line. By ripping the jig so violently, it shoots vertically off the bottom, then descends back down. It's a way of getting a jig straight up off the bottom, and right on the nose of a fish, even when the jig is far away from the boat.

Both pros agree 95 percent of the bites occur just as the jig reaches its apex and begins to sink back down. The other 5 percent of the time, a fish will pick the jig off bottom, and when you go to rip again, it will darn near break your wrist. Setting the hook, however, is not easy. With the rod behind you at 1 o'clock, if you feel a tick or thump, the best you can do is reel back down to about 11 o'clock and try to take up slack. It's a chance game, and you might get him, you might not.

Menendez discusses the payout. "You're going to lose more fish than you're going to catch with this technique, but the trade-off is you'll get more bites. So your ratios may be different, but your catching is going to be the same or better."

Tackle Balance

The combination of violent ripping and hit-or-miss hooksets directly affects which setups work best. Foremost, use a high-speed reel; a minimum of 6:1. This lets you take up line as quickly as possible and get a handle on a lightly hooked fish.

For rods, Menendez and Bruce differ in their approach. "I use a 6½ footer," says Menendez, "which is the best go-between for moving the bait vertically in the water column, and moving it horizontally toward the boat. Anything longer, and the stroke moves the bait out of the strike zone. It also needs to have a heavy to medium-heavy action, with a short handle—either straight or pistol grip. I'm working with Shakespeare right now and we're releasing a rod made specifically for jig hopping."

Mickey Bruce largely agrees, but his jig-hopping rods run a little longer. "I use a minimum of 7 feet, most often a 7½ footer, so when I rip the jig and the rodtip is at a high angle, I can follow that jig down

How To Hop

1 Cast the jig, then let it settle to bottom. Raise your rodtip to about 10 o'clock, making sure there's some slack in the line.

2 Rip the rod as hard as you can, stopping at about the 1 o'clock position.

3 Pause, and let the jig fall on semi-slack line. A strike will register as either a "tick" or solid thump. Most hits come as the jig reaches the high point of its hop.

4 If you feel a strike, reel down quickly and set the hook. Understand, you will lose some fish.

with a limp, but not totally slack, line and detect a strike. The length gets the slack out quicker."

When building your own system, try a 6½- to 7½-foot rod, coupled with a high-speed reel. But here's where things get tricky. Yes, the rod and reel are integral pieces, but the real key is balancing the jig, trailer and line to achieve the rate of fall that works on a particular day.

Basically, each component affects the manner in which the bait hops and falls. Changing one affects the entire system, so you must consider the whole package.

We'll start with line. Menendez prefers lighter monofilament. "I use 10-pound Triple Fish Camoescent for two reasons. First, its hard coating makes it very stiff and sensitive. Second, it's highly abrasion-resistant. When you stroke that jig, if you're hitting brush or rocks, you need a tough line. Also, the 10-pound diameter allows the jig to fall at the correct speed. You get bites on 12-pound, but not as many, and even fewer with 15-pound."

Bruce goes heavier. "I use 16-pound Momoi saltwater mono. When casting, it combines the smoothness of monofilament with the low stretch of superline, and it's the best go-between I've found."

Selecting the jig and trailer gets a little more complicated, and again, each pro differs somewhat, but agrees that experimentation is mandatory. They provide their systems as a starting point only.

"My most productive combination is 16-pound mono with a ⁹/₁₆-ounce Stanley jig and Zoom Big Chunk trailer," says Bruce. "I also keep rods rigged with ⁷/₁₆- and ¾-ounce Stanley Jigs, with smaller and bulkier trailers close at hand. If a jig doesn't come with rattles, I try to add as many as I can on the jig, trailer or both."

Menendez fishes Riverside jigs, and claims, "The key size is ½ ounce. I rarely use a ¾-ounce jig. Since this technique really started with a No. 11 pork frog, I use the Riverside Beavertail Chunk, which is of a similar size, but won't dry out when I set it down. If I want the bait to fall faster, I go to a craw worm, like the 3-inch Big Claw.

"Generally, in the spring you want a faster-falling jig. During the summer, I slow down and that's when I use the Beavertail Chunk. In colder water, I'll go even bigger, using a ¾-ounce jig paired with either a 5-inch Riverside Big Claw craw worm, or something else equivalent to a No. 11 pork frog. Plus, the fall turnover milks up the water and I want a bulkier jig with a bigger profile. Use a hook with a thin point and small barb to help get the hook started."

Of course, line diameter plays into each change in jig weight and trailer, but there's no universal rule. Having a few rods rigged with different combinations will start you down the path, and by adjusting to water temperature, clarity and mood of the fish, you'll eventually dial in a pattern that produces.

Color is the least important factor in jig and trailer selection. Bruce describes it perfectly. "Basically, I'm using a brand-new color they've just come out with, and it's kind of a secret on the pro tour. It's called black-and-blue." Good one, Mickey.

Black-and-blue typically scores best, but if the water is clear, try a translucent color like pumpkin with green glitter, or other crawdad imitator. Menendez adds a few Kentucky Lake combinations to the mix by suggesting black/blue/brown, which he starts using in July when the water starts to clear, plus black-and-brown for very clear water.

Branching Out

Once you have the system down, there are a few more refinements that deal largely with the structure or cover you're fishing. It's a great ledge technique, and works on flats, too, plus points and humps, as mentioned. But it's important to decipher where, exactly, the bite is occurring and fish that depth precisely.

For example, if fishing a ledge, Menendez starts with his boat perpendicular to the ledge, then casts from deep to shallow. However, if he discovers the fish are biting just as the ledge drops off, he'll reposition the boat at a 30- to 45-degree angle, which maximizes the time his jig hops along, rather than down, the drop-off.

"This technique targets three specific groups of fish," explains Menendez. "It's perfect for catching fish suspended above and around cover, as well as fish

Bill And The Boomerang Rig

Let's highlight a product from Renosky Lures called the "Boomerang Fishing Pro." The concept is simple: improve a dropshot rig by incorporating a length of elastic spectra fiber. It's similar to the theory behind hopping a bass jig, because it keeps a bait off bottom, and in the strike zone, for a longer period of time.

Since we first reported on the Boomerang, it's undergone significant modification, thanks in large part to NAFC Life Member and big-bass specialist Bill Siemantel.

"Joe Renosky sent me a prototype of the rig and asked for some feedback," recalls Siemantel. "Immediately, I knew the setup was ingenious, but it needed some simplification. I started tying the hook directly to the line with a palomar knot, as I would in normal dropshotting. I then attached the line to the 'boomerang' section of spectra elastic, and affixed a Bakudan-style weight below. But I later modified it by flattening the bottom, and angling it slightly, to resemble a walleye walking sinker.

During just his second day of testing the new Boomerang, Life Member Bill Siemantel stuck this 26-inch, 14-pound largemouth on California's Lake Castaic.

"The system still amazes me. I've already caught bass up to 14 pounds on it. Really, the sky is the limit because the action is so unbelievable. You can do things with the Boomerang that you simply can't do without it. For example, one of my favorite new ways to fish a crawdad uses a new glider jighead, instead of a standard hook, tied above the elastic Boomerang cord and weight. With this setup, I raise my rodtip to lift the crawdad (Riverside Craw Bug) off the bottom and stretch the Boomerang cord, then drop the rodtip quickly. As the line goes slack, the Boomerang snaps back, turning the craw backward and sending it scurrying back toward the weight. You have to see it in person to believe it. It's the most natural action for a crawdad I've ever seen.

"I use this rig below docks, near shore and especially along the deep weed edge. Bass have never seen a bait that sticks its nose out, then backs up and disappears into the weeds."

To order the new Boomerang Fishing Pro, contact Renosky Lures: (800) 207-6611.

Fishing a craw? The elastic Boomerang cord (left) gives it an action unlike anything else available. Lift rod to stretch cord, then drop rodtip to introduce slack line. The elastic cord will snap back, turning the craw tail-first and scurrying backward. No other presentation gives artificial crawfish such realism.

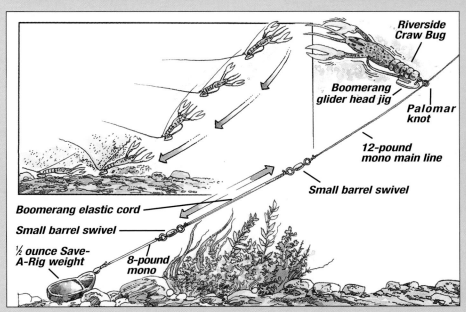

Riverside Craw Bug

Boomerang glider head jig

Palomar knot

12-pound mono main line

Small barrel swivel

Boomerang elastic cord

Small barrel swivel

½ ounce Save-A-Rig weight

8-pound mono

---

suspended just off a drop-off, or those using the drop-off itself for cover."

Bruce often targets specific cover elements atop a ledge, or attempts to understand exact fish positioning in relation to the ledge. "If there's a stump or brush pile atop the ledge, I'll usually cast beyond it and start ripping. If the fish are relating to the ledge itself, you need to envision exactly what's happening underwater. Sometimes you may only rip it three feet but it falls 10 feet, according to the steepness of the drop, yet ripping it up that three feet puts the bait right on the nose of the fish."

Menendez also expands the technique to other baits. "This whole technique, from my understanding, basically came from Toledo Bend. Larry Nixon was a guide there in his younger days, and he used the lift-and-drop technique to win the Classic in '83, but with a worm. There are many times when, if they won't bite a jig, I'll try hopping a Texas-rigged Big Claw craw worm or Riverside Ribbon Tail worm. "It also works on the Great Lakes, but with a tube bait. I've found that many times, when you get into high-pressure areas on Lake St. Clair, Erie or Ontario, most guys are dragging tubes. Now that's a very effective technique, but if I can find a flat with a little drop, even three or four feet, and I know there's fish there, I'll try hopping a tube. Most often, it's a ⅜- or ½-ounce insider weight on a 4-inch tube."

There's really no limit to what jig hopping can accomplish, given the right conditions. Whenever bumpin' cover fails to produce, whenever you mark fish relating to cover but not buried inside, prepare for a good workout and start hopping jigs. It's a "secret" technique that's a secret no more. ➤

by Don Wirth

Stripers can be notoriously hard to come by during the heat of summer. Such was the case on Nashville's Percy Priest Reservoir, where I'd been fishing since before dawn with guide Jim Duckworth. Although it was only 6:30 in the morning, it was already insufferably hot and muggy on the 14,000-acre lake. We'd drifted a smorgasbord of live threadfin shad, gizzard shad and bluegills over a submerged hump, but so far, the linesides had ignored our offerings.

"I'm not believin' this," Duckworth muttered. "That school of fish has been here all week!" On his graph, the barren hump looked exactly like a soup bowl turned upside down on the lake's pebbly

bottom. "Maybe they've moved off toward open water," he said as he veered the boat away from the hump with his trolling motor. We were over the very tip of the structure when all four of our rods began rattling in their holders.

"Must be stripers nearby," I said optimistically. "Our baits are panicking!"

Just then, every rod in the boat doubled over as an entire wolf pack of stripers attacked at once. What happened next on that hot August morning can best be described as a Chinese fire drill. Duckworth grabbed the stick nearest the bow and set the hook; I did the same with the rod at the stern. We then placed these rods back in their holders, picked up the two rods in the center of the boat and set their hooks, returned these rods to their holders, then began fighting the fish hooked on the first pair of rods.

SUMMER EEZE

In the mad rush, I kicked my open tackle box off the boat's rear deck; hooks, sinkers and striper lures flew everywhere. Duckworth landed the first fish, an 18 pounder, on the bow rod while I battled and landed a 25 pounder at the stern.

We quickly tossed the fish back into the lake and took up the fight with the two other stripers, which by some miracle hadn't tangled their respective lines. I power-cranked my next fish, a sleek 12 pounder, into the boat, but Duckworth's second striper wasn't about to give up.

Jim held the rod high, and the fish peeled off 20-pound mono as it raced for the snag-infested sanctuary of the river channel. "Start up the big motor and follow him," he instructed calmly. "And hurry—he's about to spool me."

I slipped Duck's outboard into gear, pointed the bow of his boat toward the fast-moving fish and gave the V6 a little gas. Only a few wraps of mono were left on the reel's spool; Jim turned the handle like a madman, gradually regaining precious line as I idled toward the fish.

"This one's a real hog," he exclaimed as the striper made another power dive. After a few minutes of steady pressure, the striper cut for the surface, where the battle continued until it finally lay on its side near the boat—a magnificent 40-pound fish. Duckworth hefted the beast into the boat, I snapped some photos, and we released it back into the reservoir, where it suspended motionless for an instant, flicked its great tail, and darted away.

That's the way it is with summer stripers. One minute you're wondering why you aren't at home, enjoying the air conditioning instead of bobbing around a steamy lake with a towel over your head. The next, you're battling an entire school of fish. *North American Fisherman* asked me to pass along a few strategies you can use to take these fighters right now on your home waters. If you thought you had to wait until fall to hang into a trophy striper, stay tuned—you're about to get your string stretched!

Summer Squeeze

"Besides baitfish availability, two factors—water temperature and dissolved oxygen levels—determine reservoir striper location in hot weather," explains Duckworth, a veteran striper guide.

"Stripers prefer water temps from around 62 to 68 degrees, and dissolved oxygen levels of around 4 to 7 parts per million. As the reservoir warms, this forces stripers to go deeper to find cooler water. But in summer, dissolved oxygen levels are often highest at the lake's surface, where wind, waves and boat traffic aerate the water.

"The deeper the stripers go, the less dissolved oxygen is available to them. This can put the fish in a precarious situation during the summer—a scenario we striper fishermen refer to as 'the squeeze'."

This so-called "squeeze" is one reason why some Southern states are cutting back on striper stocking programs in favor of the more heat-tolerant hybrid (wiper). It's also a reason many Southern striper fans lose interest in the summer months.

"Fishermen complain that when it gets hot, they can't catch stripers," Duckworth says. "True, once the water heats up and dissolved oxygen levels drop, the fish become almost dormant. Imagine how you feel when the air gets thin at extremely high altitudes, and you get the picture. But summer stripers are still catchable. You may have to present live bait right in their face to get 'em to cooperate, but they'll eventually bite."

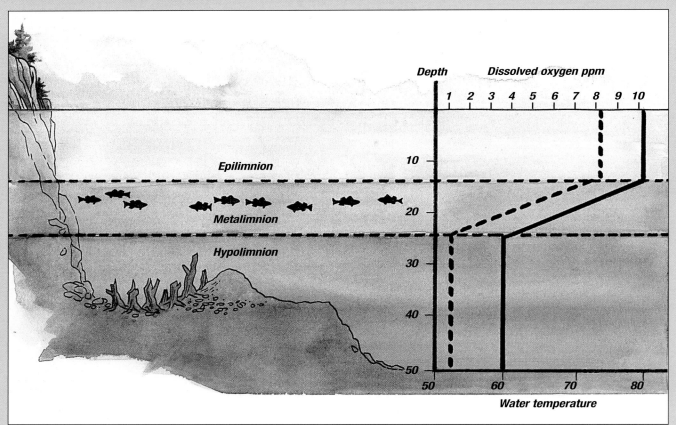

Squeeze Play: Stuck In The Middle

Yes this looks intimidating, but it's the best way to show exactly what's going on beneath the surface of your favorite stratified striper lake. Locating midsummer stripers is a matter of finding water that is not only within their preferred temperature range of 62 to 68 degrees, but that also contains enough dissolved oxygen (4 to 7 ppm). Use the chart to trace the oxygen level (dotted) from the top axis, and the water temperature (solid) from the bottom axis, to the cool, well-oxygenated middle layer of water called the metalimnion, and you'll see why stripers stack there. The water above is too warm; the water below doesn't have enough oxygen. Guides call this the "Summer Squeeze."

Which Method, When

Possible Situations	Presentation
Water temperature (at the striper's level): 62 to 70 degrees; dissolved oxygen: 5 ppm or higher; active fish.	Troll crankbaits or jigs
Water temperature: 70 to 74 degrees; dissolved oxygen: 4 to 5 ppm; neutral fish.	Vertical jig
Water temperature: 74 degrees plus; dissolved oxygen: 4 ppm or less; inactive fish	Down-line live bait

In the Tennessee impoundments where he guides, Duckworth consistently finds stripers in the thin midsection of cool, well-oxygenated water called the metalimnion. Most serious anglers give lip service to this area, often referring to it as the thermocline (which is located there), but Duckworth, a former commercial diver who's logged thousands of hours beneath the surface, has experienced it at the striper's level.

"As I descend from the surface of a reservoir to the bottom in summer, I first feel the water cool very gradually. Then, all of a sudden, I pass through a narrow zone where the temperature gets dramatically colder—the thermocline. To demonstrate how narrow this zone really is, when my hands first feel the cold water, my torso is still warm—that's a band of around two feet."

Of course, you don't have to jump in the lake and sink to the bottom to find the metalimnion. A thin layer of tiny, suspended particles often rests on the layer of dense, cold water below the metalimnion—an area called the hypolimnion. "Just put your graph in the manual mode and crank up the sensitivity until a slight band appears," Duckworth explains. "That's it."

Once Duckworth locates the metalimnion, he looks for water temps somewhere in the 60s, and

Guide Jim Duckworth nailed this 40-pound "Summer Squeeze" striper with a live shad. In still-water reservoirs, stressed stripers hug the thermocline to find water ranging from 62 to 68 degrees with oxygen levels between 4 and 7 ppm. This makes them easy to find. Both live bait and lures will take these fish.

dissolved oxygen levels of at least 4 ppm, just above the band of chilly water. "At Priest Lake, I typically find stripers suspending around 20 feet down in 68-degree water with 4 ppm dissolved oxygen in July," he indicates. "These fish will actively hit a trolled lure or slow-drifted live bait. But by late August, the dissolved oxygen levels may fall below 4 ppm in the stripers' preferred temperature zone, and the fish will become very lethargic as a result. I'll have to park over 'em with live bait or vertical-jig 'em to get a bite."

If finding this elusive comfort zone sounds like rocket science, fear not. An inexpensive electronic tool makes finding the thermocline and the striper's hot-weather hangout a snap. It's a combined temperature/oxygen meter, available from mail-order merchants like Bass Pro Shops and Cabela's for about $50. The compact unit, which runs on two AA batteries, has a 50-foot probe that also meters water visibility—good information to have when selecting lure colors for trolling.

Summer Structures

In the summer, the striper guides I fish with usually target the lower third of a slack-water reservoir. If the lake has a flowing creek arm, they'll fish this as well,

though such tributaries are more common in river-run reservoirs with well-defined current.

Summer stripers relate loosely to several open-water structures. Humps, or sunken islands, are Duckworth's top summer spots: "At Priest Lake, stripers commonly suspend 18 to 22 feet deep over humps," he says. "Unlike bass humps, which are often weedy or stumpy, striper humps can be as slick as a baby's backside."

Duckworth also likes rock bluffs, which he says are surprisingly overlooked by anglers. "Bluffs funnel baitfish migrations into specific areas feeding stripers can focus on, and often provide current as well," he explains.

Long points are good spots to fish, too. "Look for stripers suspending at the tip, close to deep water."

Other top areas include standing timber, around which summer stripers often gang up in huge numbers seeking baitfish; roadbeds, over which Duckworth often finds suspended fish; and channels, both creek and river.

"I call 'em striper highways," he explains. "Stripers often suspend at the thermocline over channels running 40 to 65 feet deep."

Trolling Time

Trolling big minnow-shaped crankbaits is a great way to butt heads with summer stripers, especially when dissolved oxygen levels are high enough that the fish aren't too lethargic. This approach is especially effective for covering large structures such as channel edges and rock bluffs.

In deep reservoirs with plenty of open water and not much standing timber (Norris Reservoir, Tennessee, and Lake Cumberland, Kentucky, come to mind), downriggers work great. Fish a shallow-diving plug with plenty of wobbling action, like a Cordell Red Fin, about 30 to 40 feet behind the release.

In mid-depth reservoirs with some standing timber (like Priest Lake, Tennessee), flatline trolling works better. Run a deep-diving lure like an Excalibur Fat Free Shad, Storm Big Mac or Rapala Magnum about two cast lengths behind the boat. Good colors include chrome, blue back/silver, white, red and firetiger. Tailor your trolling speed to the fish's activity level; somewhere in the 2 to 4 mph range is usually best.

Duckworth also trolls wire spreader rigs like Bass Pro Shop's Hyper Umbrella, which allow him to fish multiple lures (usually ½- to ¾-ounce leadhead jigs tipped with 3- to 5-inch, white curlytail grubs) at the same time. The rig simulates a school of baitfish, often with surprisingly deadly results.

"It's actually possible to hook up two or three stripers at once on the umbrella rig, so keep your reel's drag fairly loose," Duck advises. He trolls the umbrella rig 3 to 6 mph.

Vertical jigging with large blade baits, heavy spoons and big twister or shad-body jigs is another top summer technique. After locating suspending stripers on your graph, lower the ¾- to 2-ounce lure straight down to the fish's level, and start jigging.

> **"Since the stripers are extremely inactive, they aren't apt to hit a bait that's bouncing around a lot, even if the movement seems subtle to the person holding the rod."**

"Vary the cadence and intensity of your rod movements until you find what the stripers want," Duckworth suggests.

"Some days they want the bait barely moving through the water. I've even caught fish by simply lowering the jig, then putting the rod in a holder and waiting for a striper to strike."

Live Bait

When the water temperature is high, dissolved oxygen level low and stripers lethargic, live bait is usually your best bet, since it can be fished at a virtual standstill. Down-lining is often the best way to present it.

Born on the classic striper waters of the Southeast, it's a deadly way to tempt sulking stripers.

"A down-line is nothing more than a vertical Carolina rig," Duckworth explains.

"Slide a 1-ounce egg sinker onto your 20-pound main line, and tie a heavy-duty swivel to the tag end. Attach a 2-foot leader of 20-pound mono with a 6/0 bait hook at the business end. Bait up with a live shad, bluegill or trout (where legal), lower the rig to just above the thermocline, and place the rod in a holder. Don't try to hold it yourself."

The latter is a key point in down-lining. Since the stripers are extremely inactive, they aren't apt to hit a bait that's bouncing around a lot, even if the movements seem subtle, even nonexistent, to the person holding the rod.

"Never hold a down-line rod in your hand," says Duckworth. "The gentle bobbing of the boat imparts enough action to the bait; in fact, more movement

River Run Reservoirs In Summer

Reservoirs with ample current running through them are ideal striper spots in summer. Current moderates the water temperature and mixes oxygen from top to bottom, creating excellent striper (and bait-fish) habitat. Finding stripers in these long, snaky lakes, however, can be frustrating.

"In a slack-water lake, you pretty much know the fish will suspend right above the thermocline around open-water structure," says veteran guide Jim Duckworth. "But in a cool, well-oxygenated, river-run reservoir, the water may not stratify, allowing the stripers to scatter at different depths."

During midsummer, Duckworth targets the upper end of such reservoirs. "At daybreak, stripers will be shallow, herding bait onto gravel bars, shoals and points," he says. "Surfacing fish will hit big topwater plugs, but once the sun comes out, they drop back into deep, snaggy holes. That's when I'll switch to a catfish-type presentation, and fish cut shad or herring on a Carolina rig on the bottom, sometimes as deep as 50 feet."

often turns off the fish. Plus, even if you can keep the bait very still, if you're holding the rod when a striper bumps the bait, you may react too quickly and jerk it away from the fish. Don't take the rod out of its holder until the striper puts a bend in it."

Humps, channel drops, roadbeds and other similar fish-attracting spots are ideal for down-lining. To fish such areas effectively, Duckworth first idles over the structure, dropping a series of marker buoys to delineate the bottom contours and special features, then uses his bow-mount electric trolling motor to s-l-o-w-l-y maneuver his boat around the area as he fishes.

"Use sonar sparingly," he warns. "Once you're over fish, shut it off. The sonic pulses will spook suspending stripers. I recommend the 600-watt Lowrance X75 for stripers; never use a super-powerful deep-water graph."

At daybreak and sunset, times when stripers are most likely to be near the surface, freelines, planer boards and/or balloons become viable options.

"These techniques are great for picking up surfacing stripers, along with bonus bass or hybrids," says Duckworth.

"Freeline a big gizzard shad or skipjack herring about two cast lengths in back of the boat. Use a balloon or float rig with a shad, trout or bluegill, suspending the bait six to 10 feet below the surface. You can also use your electric to troll any of these baits 40 to 60 feet behind a planer board."

Summer striper fishing may not have the greatest reputation for fast action, and the conditions are surely not for the faint of heart. But then, faint heart never won fair maiden, or in this case, monster stripers. Follow Duckworth's tips and you're well on your way to hot fishing all summer long.

A combination oxygen/temperature meter like this Temperature Plus Oxygen unit from Environmental Concepts is extremely helpful for pinpointing the depth of summer stripers in stratified reservoirs. The meter is available from Bass Pro Shops, (800) BASS-PRO, and Cabela's, (800) 237-4444.

Note: To book a summer striper trip with Jim Duckworth, call (615) 444-2283; or visit his website: www.jimduckworth.com.

Walleye, Pike & Muskie

*I*t takes a different breed of angler to become a dedicated walleye, pike or muskie fanatic.

Walleyes present challenges all their own, with their picky, choosy, finicky and fickle ways. You need a lot of finesse to boat walleyes regularly … and an exceptional knowledge of the fish.

As for pike and muskies—who can't get excited about doing battle with these top-rung predators? Yet these fish too can be incredibly difficult to catch … unless you're armed with the right strategies.

So here are walleye, pike and muskie insights, tips and techniques that will help you catch more fish, along with a very special tale to remember.

If you fish for any or all of these predators, you understand the addiction. These stories will throw you further into their grip.

Welcome to the Jungle

CATCH THE WALLEYES YOU'VE BEEN MISSING.

by Field Editor Spence Petros

Show of hands—who likes fishing walleyes in the weeds? Anybody? That's what I thought. Despite the growing number of weed-oriented opportunities on lakes across the continent, the vast majority of otherwise cutting-edge walleye anglers still suffer from an extreme aversion to fishing in vegetation.

I say suffer because in many cases, walleye fishermen who refuse to fish weeds are literally taking themselves out of the game by failing to target the greenery. Like it or not, weed walleyes are neither fluke nor flash in the pan.

Far from it. Due to pollution and natural aging, many of America's lakes are becoming increasingly fertile and weedy, which means more walleyes relate to weeds more often. Plus, because of their popularity, walleyes have been stocked in thousands of shallow, weedy "bass lakes" across the country. The number-one holding area in these waters? You got it, those leafy greens sprouting from the bottom.

So don't write weeds off as a waste of time or too much hassle. Hate weeds? Get over it. Learn to fish 'em and you may come to love that green stuff. Walleyes are often associated with mature weeds, but patches of emerging vegetation only a foot or two high can be hotbeds as well. The best early weeds typically sprout in shallow, fertile, quick-to-warm spots like flat, dark-bottom bays on the north side of the lake. If an incoming creek pumps warm, nutrient-rich water into the bay, so much the better for weed growth.

Fish begin to frequent these areas in early spring, drawn by the warm water, schools of baitfish and insect hatches. The fishing can be a bit tricky, though, because walleyes in such situations are frequently on the move, and spook easily in the relatively barren, skinny water.

One of the best presentations is long-line trolling just over the weed tops. Use a lightly weighted spinner rig (comprised of a blade, beads and single hook on a 3- to 4-foot leader), baited with a nose-hooked 'crawler or lip-hooked minnow. I also like a thin-profile crankbait such as a Berkley Frenzy Minnow, Storm ThunderStick or Bomber Long A. Shad Raps are a good choice, too.

If the wind is right, try controlled drifts, making long casts with an ⅛- to ¼-ounce jig tipped with plastic. Or, let the wind carry a buoyant slip-float rig, baited with a minnow or leech, over small sections of weeds.

Tackle considerations are critical in the shallows. For sensitivity and solid hooksets at long range, I wouldn't troll with anything but low-stretch super-line, usually 10-pound test. In clear water, add a fluorocarbon or mono leader.

For jigging, use a 6½- to 7-foot, soft-tipped spinning rod and a reel spooled with mono you can see. Switch to a medium-action 7 footer, like South Bend's System Series P-255, when drifting slip floats and bait over emerging weeds.

Warm Weather Weeds

Fortunately, all weedbeds are not created equal. This helps us pick out the ones with the best features, and that, along with the knowledge of how walleyes relate to weeds as the seasons progress and weather conditions change, helps us zero in on the conditions where our chances are the best.

Cabbage—also called pike weed, redtop, pickerel weed and bass weed—is hard to beat. Walleyes tend to favor its broad leaves over narrow-leafed varieties, and it's easier to fish a lure or bait through the crisp stalks than through clingy vegetation like coontail.

Cabbage generally grows on a firm bottom with a clay base. One exception is the wider, brown-leafed tobacco cabbage, which thrives on softer, more fertile substrates. While tobacco cabbage can be productive from late spring into early summer, it usually dies off during the heat of summer, and is generally of little value later in the season.

Bushy-leafed plants such as coontail, milfoil and a number of other clingy, deep-growing weeds also hold walleyes. Many of these varieties are found in more fertile, darker waters than cabbage, but some lakes may have both.

It's good to know the different types of weeds, but keep in mind you're looking for the best weed

Spence with a dandy walleye plucked from the deep weedline.

growth a lake has to offer. Depending on the lake and time of year, that may be something as simple as a reed or cane bed in four to six feet of water.

In general, the bigger the expanse of weeds, the more walleyes it will hold. However, you may want to "test fish" a few smaller patches, particularly on a new lake, to see if the fish are using the weeds, and to identify the best patterns.

The darker and shallower the water, the more apt you are to find active walleyes during midday hours. In clear lakes, the bite may be early and late in the day. Still, don't quit if a morning bite quickly shuts off as the sun begins to penetrate the water.

Roaming 'eyes that hit fast-moving lures around sunrise often tuck into shady weed pockets as the sun rises. That's the time to pitch a light jig down into the greenery. Also, a brief feeding flurry at dawn or dusk is a pretty sure sign of good nighttime action.

Walleyes generally shift positions within weedbeds as the season progresses. Early in the year, active fish often cruise the weed tops, especially under low-light conditions. You can catch them on a

The Inside Edge

While most weed fishing focuses on the deep weed edge and pockets in the cover, never overlook the inside weedline. I've caught numbers of 5- to 8-pound walleyes on the inside edge, and always consider it when evaluating a weedbed.

In general, I've had my best luck on the inside during warming trends in spring and fall. A forgotten pattern also occurs during summer, when heavy boat traffic churns the surface, sending wakes crashing through weedbeds and against the shoreline. Walleyes often move into the stirred-up waters between weeds and shore to feed on baitfish and other forage.

To fish the inside edge, make long casts parallel to the weedline with shallow-running crankbaits. Tick the tops and edges of the weeds on the retrieve. Swimming-style jigs in the 1/16- to ⅛-ounce range are deadly, too, tipped with plastic, a leech or chunk of 'crawler. Fish the entire weed edge with long, parallel casts, making short underhand flips into pockets and slots as you go.

The best inside weed edges typically lie along quickly dropping shorelines, in at least three to four feet of water, although the fish may go shallower in turbid conditions, and at night.

Drift or use your electric trolling motor to search for irregularities like rock or gravel points jutting into the weedbed, fallen trees, edges where two types of vegetation meet, and pockets in the cover.

Top Spots For Weed Walleyes

Weedbeds that break sharply into deep water usually aren't as productive as those with slower tapers. Look for deep clumpy weeds (A) and low-growing fringe weeds like sand grass (B). Spence also targets irregular features such as weed-ringed rock piles (C), inside turns (D) and points (E). Early in the season, shallow flats dotted with patches of emerging weeds (F) attract baitfish. Walleyes follow.

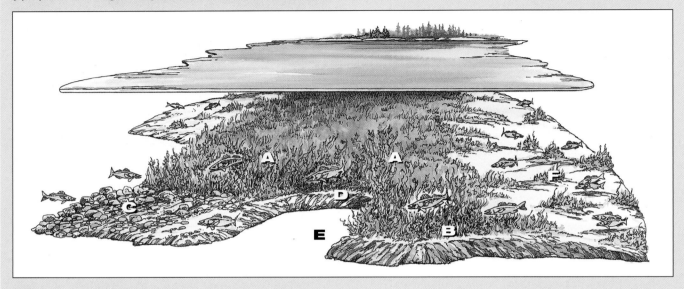

briskly worked jig dressed with plastic, or a thin-profile, tight-wiggling crankbait (a style that sheds weeds better than other designs).

When the weeds mature and thicken, most walleyes tend to move deeper. A distinct outside edge is very productive, as are holes or pockets in the vegetation. Weed clumps in the deep portion of a bed can be phenomenal. Walleyes can easily glide through while seeking forage, and take shelter from the sun by tucking tight to the vegetation clump.

It's not uncommon for the weed walleye bite to slow down or stall in mid- to later summer. In clear water, especially on lakes with a lot of boat traffic, the fish often become nocturnal or suspend over open water. In stained water, something different happens.

As the sun climbs higher in the sky and the water warms, a low-growing fringe of weeds sprouts just outside the deep weedline. It may be nothing more than a short version of the dominant weeds, sand grass or a host of other low-growing plants. The type of weed doesn't matter that much. The important thing is that new, low-slung cover has entered the vegetative mix—and walleyes love it.

When the weed fish seem to shut down in late summer, target the deep fringe, especially on flats and gradually tapering bottoms.

Isolated weeds in lakes where weeds are rare also become havens for walleyes in summer, as these vegetation-laden flats provide the only good cover for young-of-the-year perch and other forage. The weeds don't have to be deep, or even related to deep water.

Actually, I prefer weedlines on slow-tapering drop-offs over those that break sharply on a distinct edge.

In a deep, clear lake, only 10 to 20 percent of the walleye population may relate to weeds. In a shallower lake (less than 30 to 40 feet maximum depth), 80 to 90 percent of the fish could be weed related. But even when the lake has a low percentage of weed walleyes, it's often wise to try for them. Weed fish are typically shallower and generally easier to catch than deep, scattered walleyes. For example, you can find them in shady weed pockets

> **"When the weed fish seem to shut down in late summer, target the deep fringe, especially on flats and gradually tapering bottoms."**

under sunny conditions, you don't have to deal with suspended or extra-deep fish, and you certainly don't have to compete with other anglers as when fishing a popular piece of structure.

Weed Tactics

Like most other types of fishing, finding something different is generally the key to success in weeds. I look for spots with "character."

Points, cuts or cupped areas, corners of flats, clumpy weeds in an otherwise thick area, and thick patches in sparse weeds are all good examples. Walleyes also focus on areas where several different types of weeds mix, weeds growing on structure, vegetation intermingled with another type of cover, and the spot where wind or current hits the weeds. Whenever you stick a walleye in one of these areas, try to find similar locations elsewhere on the lake.

For penetrating vegetation, nothing works better than a jig. I used to fish a standard, $\frac{1}{8}$-ounce leadhead in easy-to-tear cabbage, then switch to a

Seasonal Progression

Walleyes use weeds differently as the season progresses. Fish cruise low-growing vegetation (top) early in the year. As the weeds mature (middle), they relate to both the inside and outside edges, as well as pockets within the bed. In mid- to late summer (bottom), some fish will remain in pockets in the weedbed and along the inside edge, but many also shift outward, onto new growths of shorter vegetation along the deep weedline.

weedless jig in clingy vegetation. It's a good plan, but now I fish Lindy's Timb'r Rock jig in both situations.

If the fish are inactive, tip the jig with a leech or minnow. 'Crawlers get ripped off too easily, especially in waters with lots of panfish. For aggressive walleyes, try a curlytail grub or tube on a slightly heavier head, and retrieve it with pops, hops or a brisk swim-fall cadence. In crisp cabbage or along weed edges, the faster retrieve and larger profile of a crankbait can be a better approach for active walleyes.

Slip floats are another option. They're easy to fish—unless you're too high-strung to sit in one spot and wait for a bite—and perfect for presenting live bait like leeches in a specific spot without snagging the weeds.

I use floats to suspend bait along distinct edges, to ride over low vegetation, and to pitch into holes in the cover. In all cases, I like to double-anchor just upwind from the target area.

To keep your bait in a specific spot or keep it fairly still, a long-stem, bulb-bottom "waggler-style" float is best. For a more up-and-down action, a buoyant, high-riding Thill Center Slider-type design works much better.

Some weedbeds lack distinctive features to zero in on. Here, slow-trolling the edge is the best way to go. My two favorite setups are an $\frac{1}{8}$- to $\frac{3}{8}$-ounce Lindy No-Snagg sinker rig with a weedless hook, and a sliding bullet sinker rig, also with a weedless hook. Put a small float three to four inches above the hook to elevate your bait and act as an attractor.

The best trolling areas are distinct weedlines, as well as long stretches of low-growing vegetation just outside a major weedflat. Let out as much line as possible (again, I prefer 10-pound, low-stretch superline). To work an erratic edge, use a slightly heavier weight and a little less line, so you don't miss too many fish-holding nooks and crannies. Once you locate walleyes, fish the area with jigs, cranks and slip floats to milk as many fish from the spot as possible.

To tap the night bite, slow-troll the weed tops with a shallow-running crank or spinner rig with a 'crawler on a double- or triple-hook harness. The best areas have a couple feet of open water over the weeds. Let out plenty of line, don't troll in a straight line, and tick the weed tops every now and then. If you need to get deeper, pinch a small split shot about 18 inches ahead of the bait.

Targeting walleyes in weeds is a different ballgame than fishing open water. In some cases, it's a lot more challenging, too. But the rewards are great, and the percentage of fish relating to vegetation increases every year. Isn't it time you got in on the action?

Ultimus ESOX

by Field Editor Spence Petros

We fished the small bay for more than an hour. Four anglers in two boats, casting a variety of bucktails, topwaters and shallow-running cranks— and not a single fish or even a follow. It was crazy. The bay always held a muskie or two.

Even my favorite spot, an 8- to 9½-foot-deep lip running just off a shallow weedbed, was dead. As I fired up the outboard to leave, a vision of past success flashed through my mind.

"Toss out a Suick on a short line," I told my partner. "We're going to troll our way outta here." We flipped our jerkbaits 30 to 40 feet behind the boat and began a trolling pass parallel to the slight breakline we'd been casting.

Why big jerks? Process of elimination. The muskies weren't active enough to come up and hit a blade bait trolled at or near the surface, and I wanted a slower presentation than a standard crank could produce. Plus, I felt we needed lures with enough quirky action to trigger a strike from reluctant fish.

We began our run with a boat speed of about 2 mph. I gave my lure fairly brisk pulls, ripping the stern-facing rod from a 1 to 3 o'clock position. My partner took a more subtle approach, working his bait with longer, gentler sweeps. We hadn't gone 50 yards when a 45-inch 'ski blasted his lure. The fight was short, but intense. Thirty yards later, a 47 incher crashed his bait. Two muskies in less than 10 minutes, from a spot we'd beaten to death casting. Behold the power of jerkbait trolling.

The incident, though memorable, was not unique. Trolling jerkbaits has helped me pluck several jumbo pike from heavily fished lakes. And one of my first 30-plus-pound muskies came while trolling a Bagley B-Flat Shiner over a slow-tapering flat peppered with sandgrass. The spot was totally ignored by other anglers.

And then there was an unforgettable muskie/pike trip in the early 1980s. A full 75 percent of my fish came on jerkbaits trolled along weed edges I'd already cast. That trip inspired me to write a jerkbait trolling article for *Fishing Facts* magazine, where I was an editor for 22 years. The piece triggered more big-fish photos from readers across the country than anything I have ever penned.

Since then, I've further refined the technique and find it more effective than ever.

What's The Attraction?

What I call "jerkbaits" aren't those skinny little 3- to 4-inch minnow lures that bass anglers toss. I'm talking about 6- to 12-inch slabs of wood or plastic that commonly weigh 2 ounces or more. Sheer size is one reason these baits produce so many trophy muskies and pike—big lures usually equal bigger fish.

The erratic manner in which jerkbaits are typically fished also triggers strikes from fish reluctant to hit a lure on a straight retrieve. There are several basic moves—slow pulls and pauses that cause the lure to glide from side-to-side; sharp jerks that send it darting downward; and sweeps that cause a tight swimming action.

Throughout the various presentations, the key to a jerkbait's success remains its erratic, darting action, which mimics an injured baitfish, causing muskies and pike to take advantage of the large, "easy" meal. And, as seasoned *esox* hunters know, changes in lure speed and direction are the best ways to trigger a following fish.

Being able to elicit strikes at slower-than-crankbait speeds has its advantages, too. If muskies or pike are tucked into a weed edge or pockets within the weeds, fish that aren't aggressive may not react to a fast-moving crank. But they'll often hit a jerkbait. A slow presentation also allows better lure placement along an edge, and makes it easier to deal with erratic weed growth.

Efficiency Factor

Most anglers casting a weed edge with jerkbaits position their boats over deep water and cast toward the weedbed. Lots of big muskies and pike have been caught with this approach, but it does have a downside: the lure is in contact with the edge for only a short period of time.

Also, if you're firing casts 10 to 15 feet apart, what about those "dead spots" between casts, where a fish might not see the lure? This is an even bigger problem in stained waters. If you tighten the distance between casts, the time it takes to cover an edge grows exponentially. Then there's the matter of getting your lure deep enough to attract fish holding near the base of a major weedline or over short fringe weeds that often exist a little farther out.

Another hitch with casting is that when you're fishing from a moving boat, you usually get at least a little bow in the line during the retrieve. This makes it difficult to work lures correctly, and tough to get a solid hookset when you finally connect.

Trolling solves these problems!

That's not to say pulling jerkbaits is the only game in town. Far from it. My strategy usually combines casting and trolling. Casting enables me to use a variety of lures and allows excellent placement.

Ways Of The Weeds

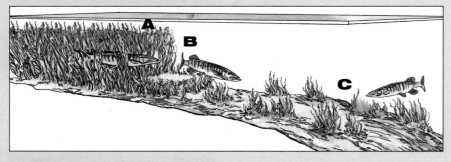

Different situations call for different lures and trolling tactics. Shallow-running, glider-type lures such as Bagley's B-Flat Shiner, Smitty Bait, Leo Lure, Jerko and Reef Hawg are perfect when two to five feet of open water covers the weed tops (A). The deep weed edge (B) and low-growing portions of the main bed are best trolled with deeper running lures like Berts, Vargas and weighted Suicks or Bobbies. Flats dotted with scattered clumps of sandgrass (C), lying between a major weedbed and deep water, are an under-fished haven for big pike and muskies. Zigzag a jerkbait three to five feet off the bottom.

Trolling gives me more control over a lure's running depth and speed.

One game plan that has produced many pike and muskies is trolling out of an area after casting it. After I cast an edge such as a weedline, chunk-rock bank or drop-off, I often make a trolling pass along it while I head to the next spot. This approach has a lot of benefits. First, the lure runs deeper. Plus, I can better follow the contour, check for suspended fish, trigger fish that may have only followed the lures I cast, and it gives me the option of choosing faster speeds. Many times, these trolling runs—which make up a mere fraction of my fishing time—produce the most and/or biggest fish of the trip. And under certain conditions, nothing works better than a trolled jerkbait.

Trolling has other advantages. Your lures get down to a depth where fish usually don't see artificials. It's also a lot less tiring way to fish than casting these weighty presentations—and you hook a much higher percentage of strikes.

When To Troll

The most productive times to troll jerkbaits are when the fish are within 12 to 15 feet of the surface. Although your lure may only run five to eight feet down, muskies and pike typically don't have a problem reacting to it.

Prime trolling locations include over and along weedbeds, small lips of a foot or two running along a bank or out into a bay (very overlooked), and wherever you encounter suspended fish—which often have crankbaits run under them.

You can start trolling jerkbaits over the weeds once the vegetation gets at least a third of the way to the surface. The muskie trolling bite commonly runs from this point well into mid- or even late fall, if you can locate green weeds.

On clear lakes, the best muskie action usually occurs early or late in the day, under low-light conditions or when brisk winds pound a structural element. In the muskie's northernmost range, though, I've had fish charge out of big pockets in weed flats under sunny, midday conditions to hit a shallow-running glider.

Pike can be caught any time they're within range of jerkbaits. It gets tough on deep, clear lakes during summer, when big pike drop into deeper water, often offshore. But even on such lakes, the action typically extends into July.

Start trolling jerkbaits again after the second cold snap hits in early fall. This happens anywhere from late August in Canada to early October in the pike's southernmost range. Cold snaps cause panfish to school in weedbeds; pike jump on the chance to zero in on bunched up forage. Windy, dark, cold days are most productive.

Large northerns are usually in range of a trolled bait in shallow to mid-depth lakes throughout the summer, at least under prime conditions—early, late, low light, cloudy or windy.

How To Troll

When you find several feet or more of open water over the top of a large expanse of weeds, you have an excellent opportunity to troll shallow-running, glider-type jerkbaits like the Bagley B-Flat, Jerko, Leo Lure, Smitty Bait or Reef Hawg. These lures don't dive much, but they have a great side-to-side gliding action.

Experiment with one on a short line to determine the best boat speed, length of rod sweep, and how long to pause between pulls to achieve maximum sideways glide. A good trick is to paint or tape a bright orange or chartreuse band along the top of the bait. Toss it 15 to 20 feet behind the boat and start working it. The bright color lets you see the type of action different moves give the lure.

To fish a jerkbait, point your rod toward the stern at about a 1 o'clock position. Pulls or jerks should take it to 2 o'clock—and no farther. If the rodtip passes 3 o'clock, you'll lose hooksetting power. To keep a shallow glider from digging too deep, keep your rodtip pointed at a 45-degree angle above the horizon. Amount of letback also governs depth. If you want the bait to run deeper, pay more line out.

Troll in a lazy S-pattern so the lure isn't always directly behind the boat. This is generally the slowest form of jerkbait trolling, since a sluggish pace gives the glider more time to swing to the side, and the fish a better chance to grab it.

Fishing The Fringe

Trolling jerkbaits is particularly deadly along low-growing fringe weeds adjacent to the deep weed edge. Pike and muskies lying on the fringe often refuse to rise to lures cast perpendicular to the edge, yet they often blast a deeper bait running parallel to it.

Spence's favorite jerkbaits include (from top left) the Varga, Reef Hawg, Suick, Bagley B-Flat Shiner, (bottom) Jerko, Bobbie, Bert and Smitty Bait.

If I run across a deep, wall-like weedline that lacks points or other "character," I often speed up until I locate an area with projections, low-growing fringe weeds or scattered clumps on adjacent flats. I don't like to waste a lot of time in low-percentage spots.

Most of the time, your jerkbait should run two to four feet above low-growing weeds. In clear water, however, fish usually don't have a problem hitting baits riding higher. Experiment to determine how deep each lure dives with a given amount of letback.

Sometimes a fringe top will suddenly rise a few feet, then drop back. Slow the boat to let your lure float toward the surface. When you think it has cleared the higher weed tops, resume your normal trolling speed and give the rod several hard pulls to get the lure down quickly. The pulls may also trigger fish lazily shadowing the bait.

The best jerkbaits I've found for the fringe have slanted fronts that make them dive, like the Bert and Varga. Weighted Suicks and Bobbie Baits are good, too. As a general rule, when beefing up a wooden jerkbait I usually place the weights underneath the lure's midsection.

One final situation that few anglers fish—yet one that has yielded many big pike and muskies—is a sandgrass-covered flat between a major weedbed and deep water. The short, crunchy, dill-like weeds are amazing fish attractors.

Jerkbait trolling is usually the best way to fish sandgrass. You can use the same lures you did on the fringe, except you have to let out more line, and troll in more of a lazy S-pattern.

Trolling jerks is also a great way to check out long, narrow bands of weeds that are too time-consuming to cast. For example, while the back of a bay is often rich in weed growth and fish, sparse patches along the sides can hold scattered pike and muskies as well. The quickest way to find 'em? You got it. Trolling is also a great way to fish shallow rocks battered by wind and waves.

It works for suspended fish, too. Years ago, I trolled a Suick over open water while two friends pulled cranks in the 8- to 15-foot range. The latter had been the hot pattern the previous day, and I wanted my buddies to get a taste of muskie fishing. We got three fish that day. Problem was, they all hit the Suick.

I guess there's just something about the darting, diving and rolling of a big jerkbait that triggers trophy fish. And by relying on your outboard instead of your arm, you can keep these deadly baits in the strike zone longer than you ever will by casting.

The Beauty Of Trolling

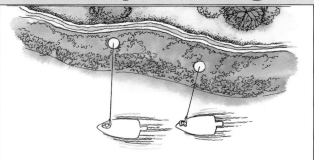

Baits cast to a weed flat quickly cross that all-important, fish-holding edge. Active pike and muskies holding in the lure's retrieval path may strike or follow, but less-than-aggressive fish won't, especially if they're a few feet from your bait. Trolling allows you to keep your jerkbait right on the edge, plus fish at depths and speeds difficult to obtain by casting.

Hand-to-Hand Combat

HANDLINING IS DEADLY ON RIVER WALLEYES.

by Steve Pennaz

Love 'em or hate 'em, tournaments do one thing well: they bring anglers together, and when that happens, you never know where things will lead. Case in point: The 2000 Wildlife Forever/MWC World Walleye Championship last June. I was standing near the weigh-in stage following the celebrity/pro-am portion of the event, when a low voice behind me whispered, "Eric Olson and Jason Przekurat are going to win this thing." I turned around, and there stood Rick LaCourse, a member of the NAFC Advisory Council and one of the leading walleye anglers in the country.

His presence was a surprise for a couple of reasons. For one, he wasn't fishing the tournament. Second, he lives in Ohio and this tournament was being held on the Mississippi River near Red Wing, Minnesota.

The fact that just moments before Olson and Przekurat had won the pro-am with an 8.8-pound walleye made it obvious they were onto something heading into the main event.

"They're handlining," Rick whispered. "And they're slaying 'em."

Let's back up a moment.

Handlining? The first question one must ask is why would today's fisherman, the beneficiary of years of accumulated angling knowledge, the one who has

access to tackle crafted from the latest space-age materials, the one who is fishing out of a sleek boat bristling with electronic gadgetry that his grandfather could only dream about, resort to an archaic technique so crude that you have to bring fish in by hand?

The answer, of course, is control. Once you learn how to handline, you can put your baits exactly where you want them and keep them there as long as you need to. What other method—jigging, trolling, slipping or casting—allows you to surgically dissect a piece of structure with such precision? The answer: None!

What Is Handlining?

Unless you live on, or near, the Detroit River in Michigan, it's probably safe to assume you've never heard of handlining walleyes. And even if you have, it's easy to discount the technique as a regional phenomenon practiced by anglers who value tradition above catching fish. The truth is, anglers who have been launching out of places like Erie Metro Park and Wyandotte know something you don't, and that is, handlining just may be the most deadly method ever devised for taking river walleyes.

The equipment used is simple. A spring-loaded reel filled with nylon-coated 60-pound stainless steel seven-strand wire is mounted on the gunnel, a foot or two in front of the angler. To the wire, the angler attaches a "shank," a section of solid or flexible wire to which several stationary leader loops are fastened.

At the bottom of the shank hangs a 1- to 2-pound (yes, pound) lead sinker that often looks like a huge bottom bouncer. The heavy weight is the key to the system.

Two or three trolling leads are attached to the leader loops. Most anglers use two because three can be a real handful. The bottom lead is approximately 15 feet long and mounted about 24 inches above the weight. The next lead is typically 25 to 30 feet long and attached 12 inches above the first lead. Staggering the two leads allows you to run two lures within inches of the bottom without tangling.

Stickbaits such as floating Rapalas in sizes 7 through 13, Storm ThunderSticks, Rebel Minnows, Bomber Long A's, Reef Runner Little Rippers and Ghost Minnows are all excellent choices. Avoid deep-diving baits. First, you don't need them; second, you lose control of your presentation because you have no idea how deep they are running. Avoid, too, sinking or neutrally buoyant lures. They also hang up. What's more, they don't wash in the current as well as floating baits.

Trolling upstream about 1½ mph, using either your main engine or a kicker, is your best option, but there are special situations we'll address later.

Avoiding The Big Wrap

Sooner or later, it's going to happen. Wrapping the wire around your prop, that is. And believe me, it's a mess you want to avoid. Besides putting you out of commission for a while, it's relatively expensive to replace the coated wire, shank and lures.

Enter Mac's Prop Saver, a piece of tough stainless steel that attaches to both your cavitation plate and skeg, and prevents the cable or line from tangling with the prop. Models are available for outboards from 5 to 50 horsepower, and sell for $69 to $89, depending on model.

To order, call toll-free: (888) 658-4700, or visit: www.propsaver.com.

The easily installed Prop Saver (on kicker motor, right), is a great way to keep a handline from tangling with a propeller. Serious handliners consider it a must-have item.

Handline How-To

Your biggest challenge when handlining is avoiding tangled lines. That starts the moment you begin fishing. LaCourse likes to let out the bait on the lower lead first, and once it's out and running properly, he lowers the weight carefully over the side and down a few feet. The second bait, which runs behind the first, goes in next.

When both lures are in the water and running, he lowers the weight to the bottom. When it hits, he lifts it up a few inches, then lowers it again after moving a few feet. This touch-lift/touch-lift sequence not only keeps your baits near bottom and in the strike zone, it gives them a surge-stop, surge-stop action that triggers strikes. It also keeps you from constantly hanging up on the bottom.

The first time I fished a handline, I was amazed at how sensitive the rig was. Determining bottom composition was easy, as was figuring out if baits were fouled. Strikes were aggressive, and bringing fish in hand-over-hand was as exciting as it was challenging. The spring-loaded reel kept the wire under control, but you had to lay the lead down in an organized fashion or you'd end up with a mess and a lost fish.

The Basics And Beyond

The basic handline rig, fished slowly upstream, is a very effective technique for river walleyes. It's the rig's flexibility, however, that

Rigging A Handline

While a self-winding reel makes handlining easier, it's actually the business end of the setup that makes the technique so deadly. The good news is you can use this setup while fishing with a rod-and-reel (see LaCourse "Rod-Lining" sidebar) or rig some sort of line storage device on your own. Here's the basic rig.

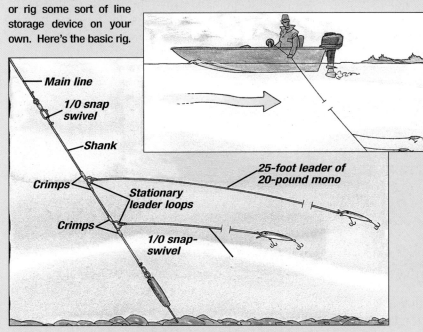

Main line

1/0 snap swivel

Shank

Crimps

Stationary leader loops

Crimps

1/0 snap-swivel

25-foot leader of 20-pound mono

Why Handlining Works

To understand why handlining is deadly on river walleyes, consider this typical scenario. You've located a school of walleyes holding at the base of an 18-foot hole, just upstream from the tailout. Like most walleye rivers, the current is moderately strong, keeping the fish tight to bottom. This eliminates casting as a possible way to present baits to these fish. So what options do you have? Here are the pros and cons of four popular methods:

1. Vertical Jigging

PROS— Easy to put baits in strike zone as you drift by slightly slower than the speed of the current.

CONS— Baits stay in strike zone for mere seconds.

2. Trolling 3-Way Rig

PROS— With enough weight, you'll follow contour to the fish.

CONS— Without heavy dropper weights, current will lift lures above fish. You can't keep baits in the strike zone.

3. Trolling Cranks On Lead-core

PROS— None.

CONS— No idea where your baits are in relation to fish, plus you give fish only one shot at lures they can see.

4. Handlining

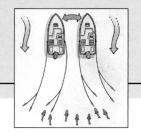

PROS— Setup allows you to present two, even three, baits to the fish at the same time, and heavy weights allow you to hold above fish and "wash" lures back and forth in front of them.

CONS— Can't buy equipment locally.

---

makes it more than just a glorified three-way rig. For example:

Lead Lengths—When fishing with a rod and reel, you are limited in lead length options. Go longer than the length of your rod, for example, and you face a difficult time landing fish. With a handline, however, you can use leads as long or short as you need to meet conditions.

That said, lead length selection is probably the most difficult part of the program to fine-tune, because there are so many variables. The best leader for handlining is a stiff monofilament or fluorocarbon in the 17- to 25-pound test range. The heavy line is easier to handle than thinner, limper lines, and it's more tangle-resistant, too.

You need to consider a number of things when selecting lead lengths. Everything from the lure used, bottom composition, water clarity and lead position on the shank plays a role.

To start, attach a 15-foot lead to the lowest clevis on the shank (about 24 inches above the weight). The second lead should attach about 12 inches above the first and run about 30 feet in length.

In clear water, you may need to lengthen each lead. You should shorten your leads if you are continually hanging up. Another option is to attach the leads higher up the shank. A rule of thumb used by experienced handliners: raising or lowering an attachment point by six inches will raise or lower bait by two inches.

If you are not hooking up with fish, continue to tinker with leader length and/or position. Finding the right combination is probably the biggest factor in success, assuming you are over fish.

Weight Selection—In general, not a critical problem. Use a weight that allows you to maintain a 45-degree angle between your line and the surface of the water. In most cases, a 1¼-pound weight works fine, but you may need to go as heavy as 2 pounds in heavy current and deep water.

Trolling Patterns—Here is where handlining really shines. You have so much control over your baits, you can run them wherever they need to go, even multiple times, and keep them in the strike zone 100 percent of the time!

Deep holes, eddies, washboard bottoms, rock humps, clam beds and channel ledges are all excellent holding areas for river walleyes, and each presents specific presentation

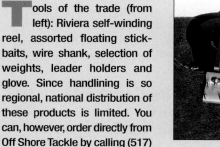

Tools of the trade (from left): Riviera self-winding reel, assorted floating stickbaits, wire shank, selection of weights, leader holders and glove. Since handlining is so regional, national distribution of these products is limited. You can, however, order directly from Off Shore Tackle by calling (517) 738-5700 or visiting www.offshoretackle.com. The Riviera handline reel comes complete with coated wire, shank with two leads and 1¼-pound weight for $149.00, plus shipping.

challenges, some that cannot be met with conventional gear.

Channel ledges are the easiest to fish, with or without a handline. You can vertically jig the structure while slipping downstream or long-line troll deep-running cranks or lead-core upstream and reach the fish. The key is staying in the strike zone and covering ground—walleyes are typically scattered up and down the length of the structure.

Rock humps, holes, washboard bottoms and eddies are tougher situations as all are relatively small, and the fish hold in specific, hard-to-reach areas. What's more, constant depth changes make long-line trolling impractical because you hang up too often, or miss fish holding tight to bottom.

Handlining, however, allows you to work your lures wherever you want. Find fish midway up the slope at the head of a hole? Then, hold just upstream and use your outboard to slide the boat (and your baits) back and forth in front of the fish.

Are they holding in the middle of the hole? Troll through them, then let up on power so you slip the baits back to them again, and again, and again. You can't do that while long-line trolling or vertical jigging. The best you can hope for is one good shot at the fish with each pass.

Landing Trophy Fish—You've just hooked your first 12-pound walleye, and besides a major adrenaline rush, you've got your hands full. Landing big fish is a challenge when fishing a handline.

You can do a couple of things. For one, consider replacing the hooks on smaller stickbaits with a set

Bruce DeShano, president of Riviera Tackle, with a handlined 9-pound 'eye out of the Detroit River. Landing big fish with this technique is a challenge. But then, who said it should be easy?

that's one size larger. Olson and Przekurat did that prior to winning the MWC World Championship (Rick was right!), going to size 6 VMC Vanadium Needle Cone trebles (V7541) on the size 9 Original Floating Rapalas they fished. LaCourse favors size 6 Excalibur trebles on his lures.

Secondly, don't pull a big fish up-current. Try slipping back to the fish or heading cross-current. When slipping, you run the risk of giving slack to the fish and/or tangling with the propeller. I like heading cross-current. Veer away from the fish at a 45-degree angle, then pull it to the boat. If the fish runs, let the line slip through your hands as needed.

A long-handle net is also a plus, as semi-whipped fish often rise to the surface a few feet behind the boat, then go nuts. A long-handle net puts these fish in range, and into your live well.

Handlining is a technique that generations of serious walleye anglers have relied on to put fish in the boat. It offers more benefits than most anglers realize, and is effective in walleye waters across the country.

Rod-Lining—The No Hands Way To Handline

NAFC Advisory Council member Rick LaCourse is one of the top walleye anglers in the country. That's not opinion. This former full-time Lake Erie guide travels across the country to compete on the Professional Walleye Trail (PWT), and as recently as 1997, won its prestigious World Championship.

A dedicated handliner, Rick started experimenting with the technique whenever his tournament travels took him to moving waters. It was as deadly as he expected. Then, in a move that continues to baffle LaCourse and many other competitors, the PWT banned handlining from its tournaments.

LaCourse was forced to abandon the technique, but not its benefits. He has re-created the basic setup, but instead of using 60-pound coated wire and a spring-loaded handline reel, he uses a stiff, 6-foot Shakespeare Ugly Stick and a baitcasting reel loaded with 50-pound SpiderWire. The shank, weight, lures and leads used are the same as when handlining.

When tournament rules prohibit him from using a handline (see reel in foreground), Rick LaCourse runs the business end of the handline on a rod-and-reel. The benefits are the same; however, fishing the rig on a rod is more difficult than handlining.

The trade-offs are immense. For one, fishing the rig is fatiguing. A 1-pound weight is a load to lift and drop when dangling from a rod, though surprisingly light on a handline. What's more, fighting a big fish is more difficult, too, because after you reel up to the shank, you have to drop the rod, lift the weight into the boat, then handline the fish to the net.

Is the hassle worth it? That's a question only you can answer for yourself. For LaCourse, it's a nonissue. His livelihood depends on putting fish in the boat, and he has found that, when fishing current, this rig puts more walleyes in the boat than any other.

Old Man's Fish

A LIFELONG DREAM DIES A SUDDEN DEATH.

by Kurt Beckstrom

When the fish took, it wasn't really a "strike;" more like the hint of a strike. Certainly nothing as violent as the sudden, line-jarring hit that had startled the old man out of his trance a half-hour before. That one had been a lean pike, going maybe 2 pounds, which looked about as hungry as it had acted when it took the bait. "It'll fry," the old man had thought as he punched the metal spike of his rope stringer through its jaws and cinched it down.

No, this strike felt more like the breath of a butterfly had disturbed the lip-hooked minnow. But it was enough.

The old man jammed the thumb-button down on his ancient Zebco 33, then quickly released it so line could feed freely from the spool as the boat continued its slow drift in the light June breeze.

He recalled how his boys, grown now, always teased him about fishing the old spincaster. They'd even presented him with a high-dollar spinning outfit a number of birthdays back. "The old one works just fine," he'd grumbled, as he placed the

sprint through 60 years of angling memories, none of which included a truly large fish.

His heart cramped when the first electrifying headshake wrenched the rodtip nearly to the surface. A second shake, more muscular than the first, bowed the rod even more, actually pulling the tip into the water. The line hummed like the high E-string on an acoustic guitar.

For a split second the old man's face registered a mixture of purified panic and absolute dread as he imagined the light leader parting. Then, the drag, like a neglected hex nut that just needed some rust knocked loose, broke free and began to give up line. Nimble fingers reached for the small outboard, tugged the starter cord and flicked the shift lever. The little boat idled toward open water.

The old man had been close to big fish before. Once his oldest boy, about 9 at the time, had done everything possible to lose an 8-pound walleye on a party boat plying one of the big, rolling lakes up north. For five bucks a head you could fish half a day with nine other anglers and the captain.

Through tangled lines, a dropped rod and a lot of shouting, the suicidal fish stayed hooked. And when the captain brought his long-handled net up over the side, all chatter and laughter ceased for a moment, then was replaced by rousing cheers and bellowed guffaws.

But the rest of the day, all the kid could do was complain about the kiss an excited woman angler had planted on his cheek. Not a word about the fish. "He just didn't understand the significance of what he'd done," the old man thought.

Then, there was the muskie. He, his wife and all four children were fishing perch from a rented pontoon boat. His oldest daughter, 15 years' worth of spunk and sass, was hauling in a yellow belly, when her light rod buckled. She shrieked in a way only teenage girls can, and the man jumped, thinking she'd been hooked herself.

When he reached her side and glanced over the rail, he saw the reason for her excited state finning lazily in the shallow water. "Oh, God!" was all he could choke out of his mouth. He could see the muskie was at least four feet long and that the ridiculously small hook was pinned in the side of its upper lip.

Incredibly, the girl brought the big fish close to the boat three times. On the fourth go, its head broke the surface, and it finally realized its peril. The tail, nearly the width of a kitchen broom, side-swiped once, twice—and the fragile line popped at the knot.

She turned, and with a big gum-snapping grin, chirped lightly, "Oh...it got away. Can you tie on another hook?" He did, but his trembling hands made the chore much more difficult than it should have been.

There had been other fish, too. Once, on this very lake when he was a young man and still full of

new graphite rod and machined-aluminum reel on pegs in the garage.

It wasn't just that the old Zebco still worked. He had fished the gift rig a couple of times on lone trips, but never got the hang of flipping the bail, fingering the line, and worst of all, reeling left-handed. "But they don't have to know that."

After 20 seconds, which seemed like 20 minutes, he slowly turned the handle until the button popped, clunking more than clicking into place. Three seconds later, the line tightened under the fish's weight and he set the hook. The boat rocked, starboard to port and back, from the force of the set.

The old man was surprised when the scarred, pistol-grip rod stopped solidly halfway through its arc, its tip bent crazily toward the lake's gently rolling surface. "Yes!" he whispered, as his mind did a wind-wild oats. Fresh from a European tour that had ended when Germany surrendered, he and his pals had driven five hours to fish the opener, starting at midnight. For 16 straight hours they'd sat in two rowboats at the mouth of the inlet and caught walleyes nearly nonstop on single salmon eggs impaled on long-shank hooks. Each of his three buddies had caught fish close to, if not breaking, the magic double-digit figure. He had to be content with numbers.

Actually, it was the best fishing the then young man had ever seen; he'd lost count of the 3 and 4 pounders he'd caught, but somehow a tinge of disappointment lingered.

Today, things were different. He was sitting in his own boat—a boat that a dealer had taken in trade and left for dead at the back of the lot. He'd brought it home, stripped it clean, painted and rigged it. It was high at the bow, and heavier than hell. And the little 15 tiller clamped on the transom could never get the tub on full plane.

But it was his, and the heavy fish lumbering directly below the hull was battling against his rod! Today was his day.

The fish was still green, but when it had made the mistake of allowing itself to be led away from the breakline, the old man knew that he'd eventually win the contest—barring tackle failure or angler error, of course.

There was little chance of a breakdown. The line was new, the knots good, the hook sharp and the little Zebco had showed up to play. Angler error was another matter.

His legs felt loose and jangley, like early Elvis Presley. His breaths came in short hitches. His heart beat rapid-fire, and the back of his head began to hurt. But his hands—his hands were eerily steady. Lift—drop/reel, lift—drop/reel. Stop and hold on a run! Somehow, they worked on their own, which was a good thing since his mind was fogged with excitement.

After the fourth run, or maybe the fifth, the old man brought the fish close enough to see a flash of color before it surged away again. Not color, really, just a white spot—a big white spot on the lower lobe of the caudal. But that was enough to tell him it was a walleye and not a pike, muskie or, heaven forbid, a carp or sheephead.

> ## "The heavy fish lumbering directly below the hull was battling against his rod! Today was his day."

After that run, it was over. The fish was still 20 feet down, but the booming headshakes had died to tremors, and it came up on the rod lifts like a gunnysack. Finally, it broke the surface, and the old man quickly scooped it up in the oversize net he'd bought years before, specifically for this day.

As usually happens in such situations, the real shakes didn't start until the critical moment had passed—as if the body continues to pump out adrenaline, but the crisis is over and the only way to burn it off is through uncontrolled twitches and jitters.

The walleye lay nearly motionless on the floor, only its mouth and gills slowly fanning. Yet, the old man couldn't steady his needle-nosed pliers enough to pluck the hook from its upper jaw. Holding the tool with both hands just made things worse. A spasmodic jerk caused the tip of the pliers to knock the hook free. The realization of how close to escape his prize had been brought on more shudders.

On his aching knees, and hovering over his prize, the old man stretched his tape measure—31 inches! Maybe more. Even lying on its side, the fish's belly drooped like it had been eating wet cement. A 10, for sure, and probably heavier.

It would go on his wall, of course, as an everlasting reminder of this fantastic scene. Every detail of the day, even what he'd eaten for breakfast, would instantly come to mind whenever he looked at the trophy. All his buddies, and especially his boys, and someday his grandchildren, would want to hear the story. This is what he'd been waiting for for so long.

The old man unfastened the stringer from the unused oarlock, and after a couple of tries, threaded the metal spike through the walleye's gill and out its mouth. With both arms, he scooped the fish up, leaned over the side and gently laid it in the water. He straightened up, passed the metal piece back through the oarlock and double-, then triple-knotted it.

He sat staring at nothing for he didn't know how long, enjoying the moment and knowing what it feels like to finally live a dream. Then, like a kid who knows there's a big stack of birthday presents hidden in the hall closet, he had to take another look just to make sure it was real.

"No!" he said as he peered overboard, the word coming so softly, he wasn't sure he'd actually spoken it out loud. The trophy walleye, with gillplates the size of tea saucers, had slid to the end of the stringer where the jaw-looped pike was pinned.

When it happened, it was quick, but the old man saw it in slow motion. The big walleye flared its expansive gills, and the pike's streamlined head slipped inside. One more flare, and its head protruded from the walleye's mouth.

That snapped the old man back to reality. Grabbing the net in one hand and the stringer in the other, he began to gently lift the two fish closer to the surface. He looked like an East Coast crabber using a chicken neck to coax his quarry within reach of the dip net.

But after the pike's head popped through, the rest of its body slid out as if it had been dipped in Crisco. The walleye was free, and the old man just stared as the fish of his dreams turned and swam away from the boat. It was only a foot or so down, and still within the big net's range. Slowly, the old man reached out the full extent of his arm and net. But the fish saw it coming and launched itself toward bottom, disappearing like warm breath on a cool morning.

Stunned, the old man kneeled there for a long time, hands gripping the well-worn gun- nel, trying to comprehend what had just happened. And when he finally did, his gray head and round shoulders sank and rolled forward in unison. They began to quiver, then shake, and finally lurch, but this time it had nothing to do with an adrenaline overdose.

The subdued reaction, which the old man considered a blatant outburst of emotion, was over in less than a minute. Without word or thought, he stowed his fishing gear, tugged the starter cord and pointed the bow toward the lodge's main dock.

Sitting now in the shade of his cabin, hours had passed since the dream fish had vanished. He'd told his wife the tale, and her years of experience in read- ing his moods told her that this wasn't a time for consoling. Better for everyone if she just took a walk—a long one.

Morning melted into afternoon as the old man sat brooding. All his life his daydreams had been filled with images of trophy fish—walleyes, muskies, pike, bass—striking, surging, leaping. And each daydream ended with a mental picture of the fish hanging on his wall, or as a glass-encased table-top mount. Each year, opening day had brought a promise of fulfilling those dreams, and season's end had broken every one of them.

"What happened wasn't fair," he thought, "even if it was because of my own stupid carelessness. Undeserving, wet-behind-the-ears anglers luck into wall-hangers all the time—always some kid, or a guy whose buddy talked him into trying it once. I'm no hotshot fisherman, but I've worked hard and deserve to catch..."

The word cut short his mental rant and hung, as if visible, in front of the old man's face. And in that moment the burden weighing down his shoulders and neck became a little lighter. And his eyes widened slightly as he recalled a truth that he'd repeatedly tried to hammer into his kid's heads during their formative years—that the real reward of doing a job well is having done a job well.

"At least I caught the fish," he said out loud, "even if I'm the only one who knows it."

At 5 o'clock, the sun leaning to the west, the old man rose from his chair. Not because he really wanted to, but because somewhere deep within his biological soft- ware a tiny switch flicked, signaling the evening bite was due. It was time to go fishing again. He half-heartedly strolled onto the dock where his boat was tied, and to where a woman, another lodge guest, stood look- ing out at the lake.

Eyes still on the water, she began rambling about the weather, the lodge owners, the cabins, as he undid the lines and shoved off. He was happy to be escaping the conversation without having to contribute more than a couple of muffled acknowledgments.

But as the starter cord recoiled and the outboard began to purr, she turned full-face to him and asked, "Did you hear about the guy who lost the big walleye this morning?"

"Yeah, I did," was all he said. Then, my dad slapped the shift lever, twisted the throttle grip and the boat began plowing its way back to his favorite breakline. >===<

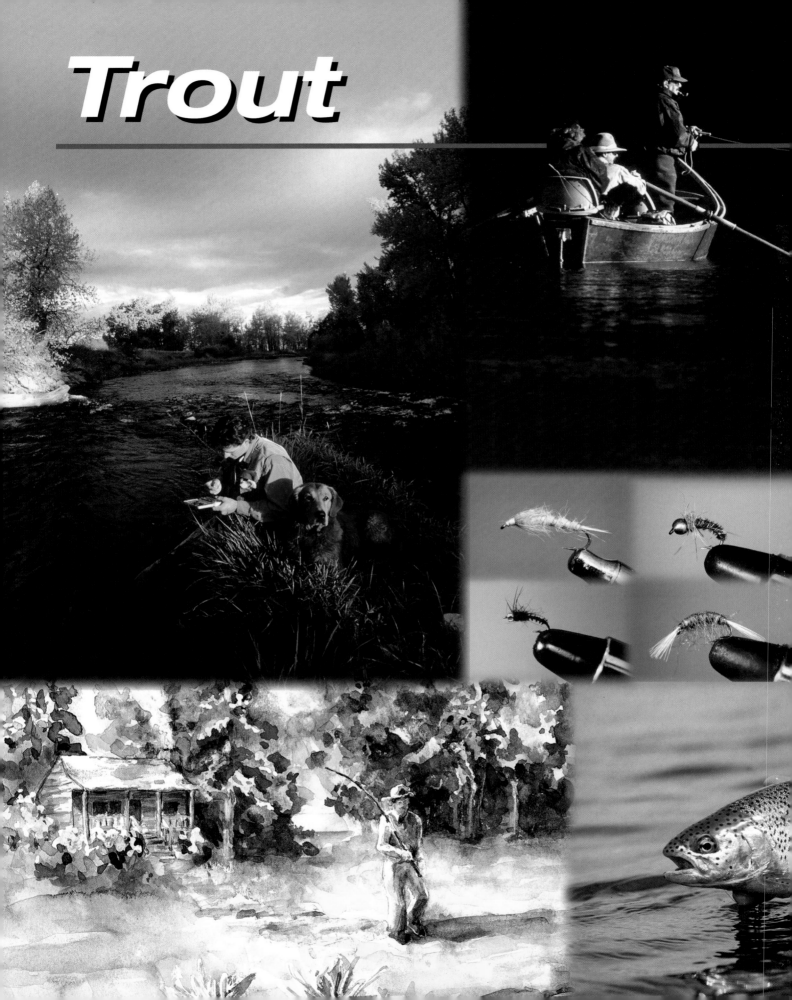

Trout

*T*rout are special. Not just because they're trout, but because they truly are wary, selective, cautious and suspicious.

Sure, you'll find some dumb ones (probably from a hatchery) now and then; but even after a few weeks in the wild water, these fish will acclimate and give even your best offerings the cold shoulder. And native fish, well, they're almost always tough; except when a hatch (or just the right set of conditions) has them on a feeding frenzy.

Here are stories to help you catch those tough trout. And a wonderful fishing tale about a man who loved trout as much as life itself.

Yes, trout are special. Not better than any other fish, but extraordinary because they fill a unique niche in the world of fish, and a special place in many anglers' hearts.

down down down down down DOWN!

FLY TECHNIQUES FOR TARGETING WINTER TROUT.

by Glenn Bamburg

Standing knee-deep in the frigid waters of the Roaring Fork River near Basalt, Colorado, I looked down when a tiny iceberg nudged my waders. Thick fingers of ice jutted from the frosty banks and the wind bit my face with the menace of winter, but the pool in front of me swirled freely and looked promising. I thought for a moment. Drifting a bead-head nymph through the hole might entice a hit from a bottom-hugging 'bow or brown...

Adjusting the strike indicator for a deeper drift, I flipped a size 18 Pheasant Tail upstream, right into the shallow riffles at the head of the pool. As the nymph touched bottom and skipped along the streambed, the yarn indicator twitched slightly on the surface. Lifting the rodtip, I felt the surging power of a Roaring Fork rainbow firmly attached to the business end of my leader—a joyous occasion repeated often that day.

Numerous spring creeks, tailwaters and free-stones remain open and accessible in winter. Unfortunately, many anglers fail to take advantage of the situation, opting to store tackle and tie flies, in wait for the warmer days of spring. However, fishing streams in the off-season can be exciting for those willing to battle icy currents. The reward: plenty of hook-jawed trout!

Flies To Try

Fly choice is always a matter of personal preference, but certain patterns imitate a variety of food items and are best bets during winter. Attractor patterns (above) include: 1. Gold Ribbed Hare's Ear; 2. Golden Stone; and 3. Olive Scud. Smaller patterns are fished either singly or as droppers. Recommendations include: 4. Black Biot Midge; 5. Bead Head Brassie; and 6. Bead Head Caddis.

Winter River Dynamics

The opportunities for midwinter angling vary greatly from stream to stream depending on regional location, elevation, severity of climate and state fishing regulations. A river's gradient, amount of sunlight striking the surface and tailwater releases from area dams also affect certain sections of streams. Most states now have at least a few wintertime trout fisheries, so check state regulations for a list of open waters near you.

"Whether our streams are open in winter is iffy," says Alan Czenkusch, aquatic biologist with the Colorado Division of Wildlife in Glenwood Springs. "Some are and some aren't. It depends on the weather, but tailwater releases from Ruedi Reservoir tend to keep the Fryingpan River open below the dam, as well as the Roaring Fork River from Basalt down to the Colorado, if it doesn't get real, real cold."

After fall turnover, water gushing from bottom-discharge dams like Ruedi Reservoir dips to 39 degrees or maximum density. Conserving vital energy, these tailwater trout seek refuge in deeper runs and pools, utilizing boulders, sunken logs, tree roots, undercut banks and any other current-breaking cover.

"Trout are cold-blooded animals," reminds Czenkusch. "They gear down like any other cold-blooded animal. When stream temperatures drop below 40 degrees, you're going to find them in that boundary layer of relatively low-velocity water down among the rocks. Rolling a fairly heavily weighted nymph through the deepest water you can find is the best strategy for catching them."

Prime holding areas include the heads of pools, pocket water, back eddies and current seams between faster and slower water. Fish won't hold in swifter flows. Instead, they locate in slack water next to good feeding lanes.

"Their feeding habits definitely slow down in winter," observes Czenkusch. "They just sit on bottom and something's got to come right to them before they'll eat it. If you drag a stonefly nymph past a fish's nose, he's probably going to bite it, but he won't chase it like in the summer. You may have to drift a hole several times before getting a strike."

The best wintertime angling normally begins at midmorning and lasts until 3 or 4 o'clock in the afternoon, depending on water conditions and weather. Peak activity varies from stream to stream, too, so check with local tackle shops or fisheries personnel for specific information on individual waters.

Small Is All

Although insect hatches diminish in icy currents, edible life-forms remain plentiful. Immature mayflies, caddis flies and stoneflies are constantly dislodged from their rocky homes and tumble downriver toward feeding trout, while some species of nymphs experience behavioral drift cycles and are available to the fish during certain periods each day. In many streams, midges, scuds, crane flies, sowbugs, dace and sculpins are also standard fare.

During the frigid season, some aquatic insects are at mid-

"A river's gradient, amount of sunlight striking the surface, and tailwater releases from dams affect certain streams."

point in their yearly life cycles and will not reach full maturity until spring or summer. Nymph patterns should be downsized to match the undeveloped larval or pupal stages.

"Basically, what I'll do is start off fishing small nymphs," says veteran guide Vance Watson of Englewood, Colorado, "but first I'm going to see what's in the stream by seining the water or flipping over rocks. Typically, there'll be some tiny Baetis or mayfly nymphs, midge larvae and midge pupae.

"Right now, I'm fishing a lot of size 20 to 24 Pheasant Tails, Brassies and Miracle Nymphs," he notes, "but I'll often fish a larger attractor pattern as my top fly to get their attention. I don't really anticipate they will take the bigger fly.

"I'm thinking they'll just get

The Puffball Nymph Rig

High-stick nymphing works great when the trout are right in front of you. But when they're 15 to 20 feet away, it takes a slight adjustment. With a puff-ball nymphing rig, each drift will offer many points of drag-free drift, even with longer casts. The idea is to run your tippet at a 90-degree angle to the leader and strike indicator. This way, the flies dangle and drift directly below the yarn.

Tying The Duncan Loop

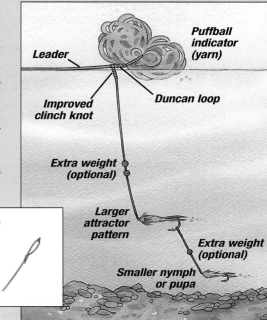

Leader

Puffball indicator (yarn)

Duncan loop

Improved clinch knot

Extra weight (optional)

Larger attractor pattern

Extra weight (optional)

Smaller nymph or pupa

Member Alex Hall: Winter Trout Specialist

Editor's Note: *In the NAFC Catch & Release Contest one year, Member Alex Hall from Pagosa Springs, Colorado, captured Top 10 honors for his massive 28½-inch rainbow trout caught in early March. Among his 66 other qualified entries, many of the most impressive trout were taken in tailwaters during the dead of winter. Here, he shares his winter trout system with other members.*

I love winter trout fishing for two reasons. First, there's less angler traffic. Second, the flows are low and steady, so trout are concentrated and the true giants are much easier to find. The key is getting down, but with the right setup and a little practice, it's not too hard.

I've experimented with a 90-degree hinge below a strike indicator, but I prefer a straight tapered leader with a strike indicator. A good all-around rig is a 5-weight, weight-forward floating line, 9-foot tapered leader and 3- to 5-foot section of 4X tippet. Place a small split shot, usually size 1BB, above the fly. Use a strike indicator on the leader, about 18 inches below the end of the fly line. Adjust the position of the indicator, as well as the length of the tippet, to compensate for any change in depth. As a general rule, if my tippet and leader total 14 feet, I feel I can get down to 10 or 12 feet.

During December, January and February, I fish egg patterns and midges. Sometimes, size 12 to 14 egg patterns are enough, but if the trout are fussy, I attach a dropper with a size 18 to 22 midge.

Presentation is key, and anyone who

has fished winter trout, or spent time on steelhead rivers, knows that with any deep drift, the window of opportunity is short. Sometimes, you'll only have a few seconds of drag-free drift—what I call the "sweet spot." The sweet spot must begin at the precise location where trout are holding.

To achieve the perfect drift, I quarter a long cast upstream and immediately begin mending. I continue to mend as the line floats downstream. The sweet spot comes when the fly is directly across the stream from me. Watch the strike indicator—any slight movement or hesitation signals a strike. When the line starts to form a downstream "U" the drift is over, so start again. Since trout will only move a foot or so to take your fly, this method demands repeated drifts through likely holding areas. It takes patience and practice, but the payoff is huge.

Member Alex Hall from Pagosa Springs, Colorado, dredged up this 22½-inch brown from the Gunnison River. His advice: Use egg patterns or small midges with long leaders to target deep winter trout.

Winter Behavior: What Trout Do

What do trout do in winter? Researchers at the University of Wyoming's Cooperative Fish and Wildlife Research Unit want to find out. Jason Hebdon headed one of two winter trout projects. His research focused on winter food availability in tailwaters.

Hebdon found that, while the average size of drifting organisms was very small, around 1/10 milligram, the average organism in trout stomachs was up to five times as large. It appears that during winter, tailwater trout seek "optimal forage"—food items that provide the most nourishment for the least amount of work. The food items were most often midge and mayfly larvae.

Also of interest to anglers is the role of water temperature. Hebdon found that trout feed little when water temperatures hover near 36 degrees, but with a warming trend, the feeding really picks up. For example, stomach contents in 36-degree water averaged 15 milligrams. But in 43-degree water, the average content was 102 milligrams; and in 50-degree water, the average jumped to 188 milligrams.

During winter afternoons, the sun can warm tailwaters as much as 10 degrees. Logically, the best time to fish winter trout is during sunny afternoons, when water temperatures rise into the low 40s.

The second project, by research associate Matt Dare, focused on habitat selection in Wyoming's Shoshone River tailwater. Using radio telemetry, Dare found that brown trout were always within a meter or two of cover—boulders, trees, cut banks. etc. Cutthroats were often near cover, but were also found in slow water that lacked cover. This was perhaps due, in part, to the fact that Wyoming stocks Snake River-strain cutts in the Shoshone, and the Snake system is known to lack cover. Still, if your goal is brown trout, stick to fishing obvious cover. If your goal is cutts, also be sure to cover large amounts of open, slow-moving water; specifically, the eddy lines, plus heads and tails of pools.

Tailwater anglers should pay special attention to the difference between feeding and non-feeding fish. Trout have two ways to survive winter. They can cease feeding and survive off body fat, or continue to feed through winter, hoping their net catch offsets the energy expended to obtain it. The angler should, of course, target "feeding" fish. Trout that hold in deep bellies of pools are likely employing the "waiting" method. Trout holding in the heads and tails of pools, or in shallower water, are more likely feeding and are the fish members should target.

—*Jon Storm*

their eye on the attractor, but actually take the smaller midge or nymph pattern below."

Other imitations include size 14 to 20 Hare's Ears, 10 to 16 Prince Nymphs, 6 to 10 Kauffman Stones, 14 to 18 Caddis Larvae, 12 to 16 Caddis Pupas, 14 to 18 Sowbugs, 12 to 16 Flashback Scuds, and 14 to 16 Blood Worms. Beadhead nymphs tied with tungsten, called "tungheads," are heavier than those with brass, so use tungheads when extra weight is needed.

Gearing Up

Leaders for clear, icy currents must be longer and of smaller diameter than those used during other times of the year. The newer fluorocarbon leaders and tippets are nearly invisible in water, giving anglers a needed advantage over the spooky trout.

"In winter, the water is usually a lot thinner," advises Watson, "so I'm going to fish a 6X or 7X tippet. I'll use a 10- to 11-foot leader as well, because I don't want the main line near the trout.

"Normally, I'll use a standard 9-foot leader tapered to 5X or 6X to the point fly, then add another 12 to 18 inches of 6X or 7X tippet down to the dropper fly."

When rigging two-fly combinations, attach droppers from the bend of the first hook, rather than from the eye, to avoid tangles. For deeper drifts, extra weight can be placed above either fly, but keep split shot and flies as far apart as possible for a more natural drift.

Staying in touch with the flies is easier when using strike indicators and here, yarn is the best since it's more responsive to subtle takes. Exact placement depends on water depth and where the fish are holding, but I generally attach indicators at 1½ times the water depth.

Rod selection is important, too. A 9½-foot, 5- or 6-weight fly rod is suitable for most winter nymphing. The longer length permits better line control when targeting narrow feeding lanes near the bottom, and keeps flies in the strike zone for a few additional, but critical, inches at the end of each drift.

Details On Dredging

Many anglers use high-stick nymphing techniques to probe winter trout streams. With this method, it's essential you take a casting stance directly to the side of a prime holding area. Shorter casts are more accurate, easier to control and make it much easier to detect light takes.

"Generally, the fish aren't much farther than nine or 10 feet away," estimates Watson, "and I'm casting upstream so the nymphs sink to the bottom. When the flies reach the fish, they should be at the lowest point of the drift, meaning closest to bottom. Then, I let them swing past me, because a lot of times trout think they're bugs rising to the surface and grab them. Basically, what you're trying to do is lift the rodtip immediately after casting.

"You want the least amount of line on the surface as possible, but enough that you can still make the correct presentation. Thus, you're holding the rodtip high and watching the indicator for any change in movement."

If trout are holding in water deeper than five or six feet, toss the nymphs farther upstream and throw a short roll-cast after the flies dip below the surface. This technique propels the leader and strike indicator back upriver, so patterns sink as deep as possible before reaching prospective feeders.

"The ideal situation is to spot a trout on bottom and continue making drifts until you get the nymphs directly in its feeding lane," stresses Watson. "Even then, you'll generally have to make several presentations before it takes the fly."

High-stick nymphing is less effective at distances of 15 to 20 feet, and here, a change in tactics is needed.

Ideally, you want the weight and flies to hang straight down and drift naturally at any distance, but that's rarely the case. Most terminal tackle has a turnover point where it's near bottom and drag-free for a little while, but not for long.

A technique known as "puffball" nymphing allows you to dead-drift nymphs from greater distances, even in deeper water.

To build a puffball rig, cut several strands of yarn, shape them into a ball, then use a Duncan loop to attach the puffball to the end of the leader. Tie tippet material to the leader with an improved clinch knot or Duncan loop and draw it down snugly against the puffball, allowing the tippet and nymphs to hang at a 90-degree angle.

Increase or decrease tippet length as water depth changes. One or two split shot can be used to plunge nymphs to the streambed. When fished properly, puffball indicators create a series of turnover points where nymphs drift freely without drag. To accomplish this, cast upstream and toss a tight roll-cast or stack mend directly at the indicator, flipping the terminal rig back upstream. From this angle, the nymphs sink quickly and tumble naturally.

More stack mends are thrown as needed, creating a succession of turnover points and drag-free drifts. As the indicator passes in front of you, shake out excess line to extend the presentation. Watch for strikes anytime during the drift, but especially after each turnover point.

Streamers are another option. "Occasionally, I'll streamer fish in winter," tips Watson. "It's always a good possibility in a river that has large brown trout because a lot of these fish gladly take a big meal over eating 500 midges.

"I'll dead-drift a streamer much like a nymph," he instructs, "but when it reaches the point where it

Even in the dead of winter, most tailwaters are trout hotspots. Downsize your flies and refine your presentation to target these willing biters.

begins to swing downstream, I'll give it a couple of pulls back upstream. This subtle movement seems to get more strikes."

Work streamers in and around boulders where trout hole up to avoid current and absorb solar heat from sunlit rock surfaces. Favorite patterns include a size 8 to 12 Woolly Bugger, Leech, Yuk Bug, Sculpin or Zonker.

Stay Safe

"I recommend using either korkers or studded soles in winter," warns Watson. "You need to be careful because felt soles ice up when you're out of the water. So wear boots with plenty of traction."

When entering a stream, wade sideways to the current rather than broadside. Less water strikes the body from this angle, making it easier to maintain balance. Never use rocks as stepping stones—they may be unstable or slippery. All movement should be slow and deliberate. Always fish with a friend who'll not only provide camaraderie, but will be there to help if anything goes wrong. You can also use the buddy system when crossing difficult stretches.

A wading staff improves balance, helps locate pitfalls along the streambed and quickly serves as a rescue pole if someone falls in. Bring extra clothing, matches, candles, hot drinks and high-energy snacks to combat hypothermia in case of emergency.

Dredging up winter trout may not be for everybody, but the action can be exciting and rewarding for those who are willing to brave the elements. Contact your state agency to get a handle on winter fisheries in your area. The action is red-hot and it's the best way I know of to cure the winter blues.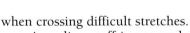

> "In winter, the water is usually a lot thinner, so I'm going to fish a 5X or 7X tippet with a 10- to 11-foot leader."
>
> —Vance Watson

My Marabou Kit

A retired Montana trout guide pays homage to the flies that saved so many days.

by Paul Updike

That mid-October morning, the air had a hint of winter riding its currents. I was guiding two college roommates, together for the first time in 20 years. Al, a general practitioner from New England who was used to fishing small streams, chose the front of the drift boat. His old college buddy, Vince, a surgeon from the Midwest who fished Great Lakes steelhead rivers, took the back. I, of course, was on the oars and carrying my unfailing marabou kit—a collection of Woolly Buggers and Marabou Muddlers that are prime fare for big fall trout.

Our plan was to spend a full week of fly fishing three of Montana's best rivers; the Beaverhead, Bighorn and Yellowstone.

Things started slow. Fishing the Beaverhead, I had both of my anglers fishing a nymph. Cast after cast, drift after drift, yielded nothing but sore shoulders and the frustrating thoughts of big trout ignoring our perfect placements.

The sun flickered in and out of the big white cumulus clouds against the dark blue Montana sky. The Beaverhead River had the fish; we needed a change in tactics.

I beached the drift boat and tied a size 6 brown Woolly Bugger and size 4 multicolor Marabou Muddler on the two visiting doctors' 10-pound tippets. As I started to close the lid on my marabou fly kit, I paused, staring at the big, bold, bushy flies. Even expert fly casters on their first trip down the Beaverhead can lose between one and two dozen flies. My marabou kit is a large plastic fly box crammed with dozens of the pulsating flies. Would they come to my rescue once again?

I pushed the drift boat back into the swirling current and Al, on his first cast, was fast into a red-spotted brown of 2 pounds. Vince, in the stern, plopped the Marabou Muddler into a brush-lined pocket and stuck an identical fish.

I sat back for a moment, watching the clouds and the partners fighting their fish, and quietly said to myself, "Thank you, marabou kit." The kit had saved another day, and in the cool October air, with the insect hatches of summer all but gone, the big flies strapped with wraps of lead, chenille and feathers were destined to do duty once again throughout a week of classic fall fishing. Big flies for big fish, I like to say, especially in cooling water, and there are few trout flies bigger than the size 2, 4 and 6 streamers in my marabou box.

After releasing those first two fish, we glided downstream, targeting the winding river's brushy pockets with precision casts. We found several hungry, 1- to 4-pound brown trout.

Another guide boat in front of us was busier watching us than fishing. I could tell, even from a distance, they were nymphing. Like a stubborn old codger, the guide refused to switch and his clients suffered for it. By the end of the day our boat, fishing marabou flies, would outfish them four to one.

Marabou Methods

From the moment of their first cast with the marabous, the doctors had done as I instructed: cast within an inch of the bank and employ a stop-and-go retrieve. The fly, I told them, should make three 6-inch hops when they pumped the fly rod. The most important step is to stop the fly for a couple of seconds. This allows the trout to catch up to it. Secondly, the fly should make short hops, measured in inches, not feet. Do this for 6 to 8 feet, I told them, then cast again.

I also explained that brown trout love undercut banks and the stop-and-go retrieve brings savage strikes in the fall, and on rainy summer days. Yes, there are times I'll encourage clients to dead drift. Letting the marabou fly drift naturally, with a couple of 6-inch hops, imitates a dying minnow, grasshopper or stone fly. This works when a more active retrieve won't.

Sometimes, I cast across the current and let the fly line develop a belly to drag the fly across the surface. This is deadly with a size 6, unweighted, brown-and-yellow Woolly Bugger. Trout slash this grasshopper presentation in late summer and early fall.

I once put on a show for my fishing buddy, Tim Shaw, of Virginia. I had 21 strikes in a single run. Tim came up to me on this otherwise slow fishing day and said, "Puh-lease show me what you are doing." Tim now carries a box full of brown-and-yellow Buggers.

I'll use a 9-foot, 7-weight fly rod with a weight-forward size 7 floating line and a short, 7-foot leader in 8- to 12-pound test.

The only time I use sinking or sink-tip lines is while float-tubing lakes. The marabou kit rules on trout lakes. If it's big fish you're after, then try the marabou flies in lakes.

On To The Bighorn

The Beaverhead is a place you'll never want to leave, and we didn't want to, either, but we had motel reservations for the next three days on the Bighorn River, which boasts an outstanding fish-per-mile population.

The current was steady and deep green below the Afterbay Dam as we started our 13-mile float. The doctors asked which fly they should start with. Of course, I suggested a size 4 brown-and-yellow Woolly Bugger.

My suggestion was well received by a deep-bodied, 3-pound brown that charged from an undercut bank to get at Al's Bugger. Several more browns attacked from the bank to engulf the tail-dancing flies.

We were halfway through the float and, although we had good action, had not hooked one of the Bighorn's jumping rainbows. So I gave Al a size 4 black Woolly Bugger and Vince, a size 4 white Marabou Muddler.

We entered the swift-running "car body" pool, so named because the whole outside curve is lined with old car wrecks. I called out a deep pocket in back of the '54 aqua-blue Ford and Al planted the black Bugger up against the car trunk. There was a large swirl on the third pump of his rodtip and 5 pounds of crimson rainbow took to the air. "Look at that jump," screamed Al. "There's another one!" shouted Vince. Four jumps later and after the boatside struggle, we released this beautiful fish.

The black Bugger took 6-inch hops across the bottom in a slow-moving backwater eddy. A 3-pound rainbow caught Al by surprise and nearly stripped the rod from him. Six jumps later we released him and he swam back to his home.

Traditionally, the Bighorn Streamer had always been tied with brown and yellow hackle. So for a change, I tied a Woolly Bugger with brown

Spring to fall, summer to winter, marabou flies have the versatility to save most any kind of fishing day.

and yellow marabou the first year the Bighorn River opened for public fishing. It is now one of my favorite flies and takes fish all over Montana.

A pair of mallards flushed as we rounded the curve and the boat slid into the head of what I call the "big rainbow" pool. The pool has been very good to me, yielding a 5-pound-plus rainbow on many trips through. The water turned a deep, dark green as it flowed beneath an undercut bank.

Vince, in the stern, placed a white Marabou

Muddler in just the right spot, waited for the fly to sink and then started a slow, jerking retrieve. Twenty-four inches of deep red rainbow put three feet of air between him and the water with the Muddler in the corner of its jaw. Doc had too tight a grip on him, however, and the fly shot by his ear with the velocity of a .22 long-rifle bullet. The beauty of the jumping fish and the parting fly will be remembered on a cold winter's night, by the warmth of a fireplace with a glass of good bourbon.

Tying The Woolly Bugger

The Woolly Bugger is a simple fly to tie. I like to use 10 to 15 wraps of medium lead wire on a 2X, long nymph hook in sizes 6, 4 and 2. Cinch the lead to the hook with a generous amount of thread and glue thoroughly. Next, tie in two marabou feathers for the tail and glue. Then, tie in a 6-inch piece of copper wire, a grizzly hackle and the chenille. Wrap the chenille forward and tie off and glue. Now, wrap the hackle and tie off, then wrap the copper wire over the body, cinching the hackle to the body. Form a head of thread, tie off and glue. Another option is a bead or cone head, with fewer wraps of lead.

I like to glue each step; it takes longer to tie but the fly will last much longer. My main colors are black, brown, olive and brown-and-yellow. The combination of black marabou tail and olive chenille body, shown above, is a favorite.

The multicolor Marabou Muddler in the same sizes, and similarly weighted, has orange, yellow, brown, and black marabou in it. It's a deadly fly.

Whenever I think a big fish is present, I use the white Marabou Muddler, which I also tie weighted. My customers use it in a size 6 or 4, but I fish only the size 2. This fly has taken many 6- to 10-pound brown trout in October.

Black-and-Olive Woolly Bugger

Brown-and-Yellow Woolly Bugger

White Marabou Muddler

Brown Woolly Bugger

Multicolor Marabou Muddler

Yellowstone Ending

The two surgeons had one day of fishing left so we headed for spawning browns on the Yellowstone River. We put in a couple of miles downstream of Livingston where the water varied from pools and undercut banks to class-four rapids. I got my exercise at the oars that day. The Crazy Mountains had a fresh dusting of snow above 4,500 feet. The combination of the new snow, mountains and golden aspen...truly the work of a great artist.

We used the marabou kit exclusively on this last day.

The fishing started out slowly and picked up in the afternoon. Putting a full bend in the oars, I beached the raft at the tail end of an island, and the doctors walked up to the head of the gravel-lined side channel. The opposite bank was thick with overhanging brush. The channel was blanketed with copper-color gravel, preferred by spawning brown trout.

Each caster side-armed a size 2 white Marabou Muddler up tight to the bank and retrieved in short, sharp jerks. The Marabou Muddler accounted for nine browns up to 6 pounds released from this one channel.

The doctors were busy giving each other advice as the fish tore up the channel, while I was checking out a big whitetail buck's tracks in the sand.

Thank you, marabou kit.

For big trout, don't be afraid to use a big fly.

Appalachian Troutman

MARK CATHEY LIVED A GOOD LIFE.

by Jim Casada

By the standards of many, Mark Cathey was a ne'er-do-well. Yes, other than occasional secretive adventures connected with the manufacture of "corn squeezin's," seasonal work as a logger to obtain the scarce commodity he styled "cash money," and guiding visiting "sports" who came to catch wild mountain trout, Cathey never held a meaningful job. Many of his high country neighbors considered him "quair," a local expression applied to someone who danced to a distinctly different drummer.

Yet, this staunch son of the Great Smokies became the most innovative, ingenious angler the southern Appalachians have ever produced.

Only the mists of time's memory know precisely when Cathey became a devotee of the long rod and whistling line, but well before the turn of the 20th century he was an accomplished dry fly fisherman. That alone would have earned him distinction as a troutman, for this was a time when most fished for the wild brookies and introduced "California trout" (rainbows) with bait. Even those who used the new-fangled fly rod stuck to "casts" of two or three wet flies.

Cathey's use of dry flies set him apart, as did the original patterns he tied. But how he used the deceitful little creations of feather and fur garnered even more attention. Long before the icons of America's trout-fishing establishment adopted the technique they described as "fishing the dry fly as a living insect," Cathey went astream daily to perform his deadly "dance of the dry fly." Holding his rodtip high, he would waltz the fly on the water's surface in an exact imitation of an insect struggling to escape the film. Trout found it irresistible.

Cathey was also a real character. Once, a big-city angler came to Cathey's hardscrabble home place and hired him as a guide. Outfitted with the sort of expensive equipment unknown to most highlanders, the "sport" promised to be what Mark called "a project." In particular, he stared in wonder at the man's waders, the first he had ever seen, and at the foot-long Bowie knife adorning his belt.

The visiting angler proved to be a study in ineptitude. Despite Cathey's best efforts the man caught nothing. Meanwhile the stoic guide patiently endured a ceaseless flow of sarcasm, disparaging remarks about the region's residents and suggestions that the stream was devoid of trout. Finally, exasperated with hours of verbal abuse, Cathey stepped into a pool, proceeded to land half a dozen nice trout, and muttered: "Still reckon there ain't no trout here?"

Late in the afternoon, the visitor managed to hook a tiny trout, which Cathey later said was "hell-bent on suicide." Greatly excited, the fisherman reeled madly until the wiggling fish was at the tip of his 9-foot rod. "Now what do I do?" he yelled in desperation.

Cathey couldn't resist the opportunity. "Well," he drawled in his high-pitched voice, "I expect you'd better draw that Bowie knife, climb that bamboo pole and stab him to death."

On another occasion, Cathey was fishing with a bunch of friends while camped in a remote cabin on one of his favorite streams, Deep Creek. The breakfast

cereal Raisin Bran had just been introduced, and one of the party had brought a box along.

The first morning in camp the friend poured a bowlful and topped it off with milk, which had been cooling in a nearby spring. He offered Mark some and the erstwhile fisherman dug right into his portion. With almost every bite though, he would turn away from the table and spit. Finally, when asked what he thought of the cereal, Cathey commented: "It's passin' fair food, but I do believe the rats have been at it."

Then there was the time Cathey acquired a complete set of false teeth. The last thing he did before climbing into his bunk was carefully place them on an exposed 2x4. Shortly afterward, a fellow angler who also had a plate took his out and placed the false teeth a few feet away. As soon as both were snoring peacefully, a mischievous member of the group switched the plates. Amazingly, the next morning each man inserted the other's false teeth and ate breakfast. Immediately afterward, the pair left the cabin, and when their companions followed them outside, they found Cathey and the other unfortunate soul on opposite sides of the building, pocket knives and false teeth in hand, trying to whittle them to shape.

Cathey fished scores of days every year over portions of seven decades. Then, in the fall of 1944, he failed to return home from a late-afternoon jaunt with his dog. A search party was organized. Hours later, they found him slumped against the stump of a massive chestnut tree, his faithful canine companion's head resting in his lap. Fittingly, he was buried within casting distance of another hallowed name in the annals of the Smokies, Horace Kephart, author of *Our Southern Highlanders* and the man often described as the "Dean of American Campers."

A massive granite boulder marks Kephart's grave, but it is the poignant epitaph adorning the simple stone over Cathey's mortal remains that catches the eyes of passers-by:

Mark Cathey, 1871-1944
Beloved Hunter & Fisherman,
Was Himself caught by the Gospel Hook
Just before the season closed for good.

The inscription looks northward toward Cathey's home waters, the misty blue, stair-step ridges of North Carolina's Deep Creek and its feeder, Indian Creek. Soaring peaks and deep hollows fade into the distance as they lead to lofty Clingman's Dome, the second highest peak in the Appalachian chain.

Mark Cathey loved this remote, rugged country, and as we look back on his world—one we have sadly lost—realization dawns that here was a man who was truly blessed. He may have held no regular job and was sometimes demeaned as "trifling," but his easygoing existence as an Appalachian troutman was assuredly one well worth living.

Cats, Crappies & Salt

Here are three topics of high importance to NAFC members.

Catfish (if they could) speak for themselves. Many of us love to chase catfish, sometimes to the exclusion of other species.

And who can argue with a crappie? If he could, he would say, " I am the greatest gamefish. There are lots of me, I can grow to slab proportions, and once I'm through spawning, good luck trying to catch me."

Finally, with so many of our members living close to or within a drive of an ocean coast, saltwater fishing is important to the NAFC crew, too.

So here is a little fishing potpourri!

OF CATS AND CRAWS

by Keith Sutton

It was May and spring floodwaters were receding along Arkansas' lower White River when Jim called me. "We need to go tomorrow," he said, "or they'll be gone. I'll pick you up at 5 a.m."

The call was expected. I had been watching the Clarendon gauge on the river and knew my chance to see my first "crawfish run" was near.

We met at the appointed time—Jim Spencer, my son Josh and I—then drove to the river. After motoring a few miles downstream in a jonboat, we tied the craft to some old cypress steps on the riverbank, made our way up and walked to a small oxbow off the beaten path. A bit of water still flowed through the runouts connecting the river and oxbow lake, but in a day or so, as the water continued falling, the connection between river and lake would be severed.

Only days before, the woods around the lake had been swamped beneath 12 to 18 inches of water—the result of high water that comes, on average, three years out of five in this region. As the White River dropped, however, the water pulled out and left behind wet, muddy, leaf-strewn ground. But even now, with the water gone, the ground was hard to see, for thousands upon thousands of crawfish covered the damp earth. You couldn't step without mashing them beneath your feet—huge rusty-red crustaceans with pincers like Maine lobsters.

"Look, Dad!" Josh screamed in excitement. "They're everywhere! There must be a million of 'em!"

We had toted a 100-quart cooler to the lake's edge, and each of us carried a wire fish basket to store our catch. Walking through the woods, we gathered crawfish—a dozen here, a dozen there—and when our basket was full, we returned to the cooler and dumped in the catch. In less than an hour, the cooler was overflowing.

"This is the best of two worlds," Jim said. "We've got catfish bait and dinner, too, all in one cooler."

Crawfish Connection

Now, it may sound odd to begin a catfish article with a discussion of the crawfish run, but read on, because in this neck of the woods, the fortunes of catfish and crawfish are inextricably linked.

See, catfish like to eat crawfish almost as much as we do. That night, fishing with crawfish tails in the runout between river and lake, each of us caught a dozen or more cats, and before the sun rose, we had polished off more than 10 pounds of spicy fresh-boiled crawfish apiece. I decided then and there, those many years ago, that catfish, crawfish and bottomland rivers formed a minor trinity.

I had known for years that catfish migrate into flooded spring woods to eat crawfish. As a youngster, I often accompanied uncles on fishing junkets into the woods, tying yo-yos and limblines to green branches along the edges of inundated forests, and baiting them with the tails of crawfish caught in homemade dip nets. As we'd paddle through the woods making our sets, big cats shot this way and that, spooked by our approach. We'd see their wakes, sometimes the tip of a fin or tail, as they scurried away through the shallow water. By that sign, we knew our timing was right. Cats were in the woods gorging on the annual banquet nature provided, and by morning, we'd be weary from catching and cleaning fish.

There was no doubt about the inspiration for this catfish celebration. The catfish we caught—blues, channels and flatheads—were literally stuffed to the gills with crawfish. Often, a fish would take our bait even though several crawfish could be seen protruding from its gullet. Their stomachs were distended like beer bellies with dozens and dozens of crawfish. Eating more was an impossibility, but the catfish still tried.

Woods fishing is one of the oldest, yet most obscure, forms of catfishing. Few cat fans are familiar with the tactic today, but earlier in this century, it was widely practiced in the lower Mississippi River Valley.

D.S. Jordan and B.W. Evermann were among the first to write about this unique sport in their 1923 book, *American Food and Game Fishes*.

As they relate the practice, "During the spring rise in the Mississippi hundreds of square miles of the adjacent country become flooded, and then the catfish leave the rivers, lakes and bayous, and 'take to the woods'.

"Here the fishermen follow them, and 'woods' or 'swamp' fishing is resorted to. Short 'brush' lines with single hooks are tied to limbs of trees here and there through the forest, in such a way as to allow the hook to hang about six inches under water. The trees selected are usually those along the edges of the 'float' roads, and, that he may readily find his lines again, the fisherman ties a white rag to each tree to which he has attached a line.

"The lines are visited daily, or as often as practicable, and the fish are placed in a live-box, where they are kept until the tugboats from Morgan City (Louisiana) make their regular collecting trips. Then they are transferred to very large live-boxes or cars carried in tow by the tugs, and are taken to Morgan City, where the fish are dressed, put in barrels with ice, and shipped to the retailers in many States of the Union."

In *Catfishin'*, published in 1953, Joe Mathers also commented.

"Brush line fishing (also referred to as 'woods' or 'swamp' fishing) is employed by fishermen along the Mississippi and its large tributaries," he writes. "As the spring floods come, these rivers overflow their banks and flood the surrounding lowlands. The blue catfish especially characteristically leaves the rivers, lakes and bayous and moves into these flooded areas. The fishermen follow them..."

Because the ground in a river floodplain is low and flat, a rise in river level of only a few inches can flood literally thousands of acres of bottoms. As the water rises and the woodlands become flooded, a new food source—terrestrial crawfish— becomes available to the catfish.

Crawfish are abundant in most bottomland hardwood forests, but during most of the year they live on land, where they are inaccessible to catfish. During overflow periods, however, the crawfish are forced to live in an aquatic environment, and catfish come to them like kids to a candy store. Flatheads, blues and channel cats all join the feeding frenzy, moving from rivers, lakes, bayous and sloughs into the shallow water that now inundates many acres of bottoms. They feed here as long as the water is high enough to swim in—sometimes for several months.

Ready, Set, Catch

It would seem, with so many actively feeding fish gathered in shallow water, catching would be quite easy. That is not the case. Fishing in flooded woods is difficult in the best of circumstances, and because the catfish are widely scattered, catching them on rod and reel is iffy.

Catching them with setlines is another story. This is the limbliners' season, and as soon as the bottoms become inundated, the period of fun begins. Hanging setlines from low branches produces extraordinary numbers of catfish, particularly toward the end of flood season when the waters are warm.

Some limbliners make special sets with a piece of rubber inner tube tied in the middle of each line to act as a shock absorber, which prevents thrashing catfish from pulling free. Others tie their sets on springy green limbs that function in a similar manner. Still others fish with yo-yos—the spring-wound Autofisher rigs popular in many parts of the South. Often, dozens of sets are placed; each checked at regular intervals to remove the catch. This is an extraordinary time characterized by extraordinary fishing.

Runouts With Rods

Limblining is not for everyone. If you're a diehard rod-and-reel angler, you'll want to pay particular attention to the period of this phenomenon known as the "runoff." This occurs when a river "falls out of" a connected oxbow, usually in spring or early summer when overflow waters recede from the river bottoms. There comes a point, when the water has fallen low enough, that the only connection between an oxbow and its parent stream are small chutes or "runouts" created by low points in the area topography. In some cases, only one runout exists; in others, several. All runouts, however, serve up incredible catfishing for savvy anglers.

The key to runout fishing is timing. The best fishing occurs during the few days before the river falls completely out of the lake. Water constricted through these runout chutes increases in velocity. Crawfish and other forage items are pulled by current into the rushing stream of water and adjacent areas. When this happens, catfish gather in great numbers.

Some hold near cover at the head of the runout, in the lake. Others position themselves at the runout's tail, where the rushing water meets the river. All feed ravenously on the bounty before them, and any bait—crawfish, nightcrawlers, cutbait, live fish—drifted through or along the runout area is likely to be taken.

In the close confines around runouts, use a 5½- to 6-foot medium-heavy rod with a whippy tip and stout butt section. This will allow you to flip a bait in just the right spot with fewer hang-ups.

A float rig works great here, with the float positioned so the bait rides just off the bottom. Cast above the runout and let the rig drift back through, or drift the rig through current in the runout tail. Live crawfish or crawfish tails are top baits in this situation—for both rod-and-reel and setline fishing. But because these pre-spawn catfish are feeding ravenously, they'll accept almost any offering from nightcrawlers and chicken liver to live bluegills and cutbait. If the catfish seem persnickety, try peeling crawfish tails before putting them on the hook.

For runout fishing to be successful, you'll have to learn the river-gauge level at which the parent river will overflow into each oxbow. When gauge numbers are higher than this "magic number," you know the river and oxbow are connected. When gauge numbers are lower than the magic number, the river level is so low it doesn't connect to the lake. Runoff conditions exist when the river level is just slightly higher than the magic number, and it's during the first few days of

this short period when runout catfishing is at its best.

The best way to obtain the "magic" gauge number is to inquire at local bait-shops or ask area anglers. You can then find the current gauge number printed in local newspapers or by calling government hotlines, then plan a trip during the peak period.

While at the baitshop, also inquire about local regulations. This is especially important on border waters with differing rules concerning setlines.

Although the popularity of woods fishing has declined in recent decades, this is still a topnotch tactic for catching lots of catfish. If you live in the lower Mississippi River Valley, or anywhere else these floodplain-river ecosystems exist, give woods fishing a try this spring when the big rivers have overflowed their banks. When catfish are in the woods, it's a sure bet they'll be biting. 🐟

Cat Conservation: The Crawfish Connection

Fishermen have known for decades that catfish feed heavily on crawfish in floodplain-river ecosystems such as those found in the lower Mississippi Valley, but only in recent years have fisheries researchers studied this phenomenon. Don Jackson and Joe Flotemersch, researchers at Mississippi State University, studied the unique relationship between terrestrial burrowing crawfish and channel cats in channelized and nonchannelized sections of Mississippi's Yockanookany River.

Some of what they learned is old news to ardent woods anglers. For example, they found that, "Adult channel catfish aggregated in locations where the river channel and adjacent floodplain were coupled and subsequently foraged heavily on crawfish." Sound familiar? It should. This is the typical runout fishing scenario described in the accompanying article.

However, the most important information discovered during this study was not previously known. Jackson and Flotemersch learned that peak use of crawfish occurs prior to egg occurrence in channel catfish. And because the crawfish are excellent sources of essential amino acids and fatty acids, they are likely significant resources for egg development. In other words, if

the rivers didn't overflow, and the catfish couldn't reach the crawfish to feed on them, the catfish would not produce as many eggs. As a result, these floodplain-river ecosystems would not produce the astounding numbers of healthy cats now available to anglers.

For this reason, all of us who enjoy catfishing in big bottomland river ecosystems should be concerned about flood control and navigation projects that utilize channelization, dredging and construction of levees and wing dikes. Such activities can "disconnect" floodplains and rivers, and hurt catfish stocks.

A proposed U.S. Army Corps of Engineers navigation project in my home state of Arkansas will do just that if opponents don't manage to get it stopped. The Corps says that maintaining a 9-foot-deep, 200-foot-wide channel along the lower 258 miles of the White River, as the agency proposes, won't affect the area's ecology. But fishermen, hunters and conservationists are already convinced it will and are protesting loudly. Catfishermen like me have joined the fray, knowing full well that a bottomland river that doesn't overflow can never realize its full potential as a catfishing hotspot.

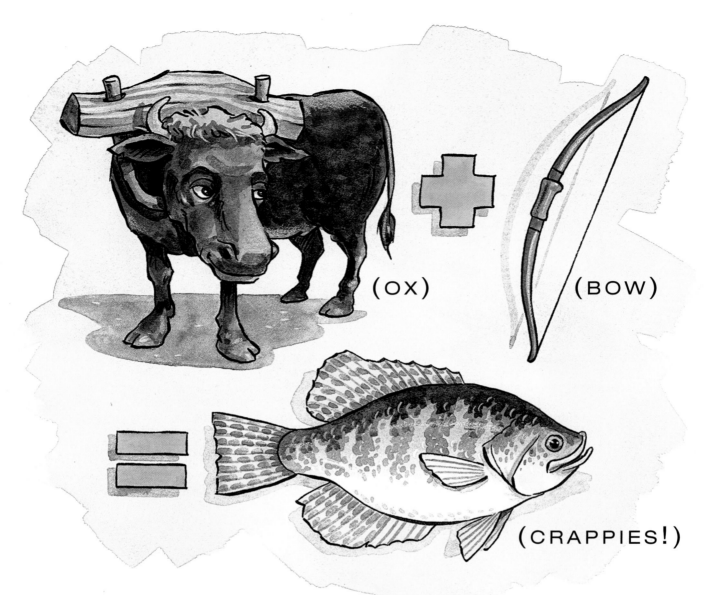

(OX) + (BOW)

= (CRAPPIES!)

by Keith Sutton

Word has it the crappies are tearing it up on Hook-A-Slab Cut-off, a big oxbow lake down in the south of the county. All week, a friend at the pool hall has been bragging about the cooler full of crappies he caught last Saturday. The fishing report in yesterday's newspaper said several 2 pounders were weighed, and limit stringers have been common. You heard similar reports this time last year, but never found time to make the long drive. No such misfortune now, though, so you hitch up the boat, pick up your fishing pal Bubba, and at dawn, the two of you catch your first glimpse of this 1,000-acre natural lake.

Everything looks perfect. It's been raining to the north for several days, but the skies here are just overcast. You're a bit surprised there aren't more folks out fishing, but hey, that just makes things all the better.

As the sun sets, you arrive back at the boat ramp. "I just don't understand it," Bubba says. "A few days ago, Mack was over here and loaded the boat with some dandy crappies. We get here and nothing...not even a nibble."

Has something similar ever happened to you? For many anglers who have never fished an oxbow lake, catching crappies can be like breaking a secret code. Even the very best lake and reservoir anglers often fail to solve the oxbow crappie puzzle. Try as they might, it seems impossible to achieve consistent success, and many go away frustrated, vowing never to fish an oxbow again.

But contrary to the opinions of some, the only real "secret" to oxbow crappie fishing is preparing yourself with an in-depth knowledge of oxbow dynamics. What the fellows in our opening story didn't know, for example, was that upstate rains had caused the adjoining river to overflow into the oxbow 48 hours prior to their arrival. The sharp rise in water level, unnoticeable to our fishing duo, gave crappies a bad case of lockjaw. Few fishermen were on the lake that day, because most regulars knew the crappies

Discerning The Difference In Oxbows

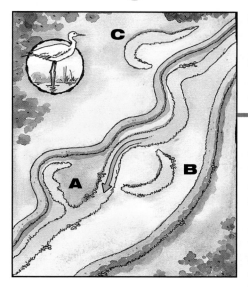

There are three major types of oxbow lakes. A river-connected oxbow (A) retains its connection to the river and experiences rapid changes in water levels. A disconnected oxbow that's still within the floodplain (B) will still experience water level fluctuations, but the changes aren't as drastic. An oxbow that lies outside the floodplain (C) will maintain a fairly stable water level. However, these oxbows silt in and die much more quickly than those within the floodplain.

weren't likely to bite until conditions stabilized.

Rapidly changing water levels are just one of several factors oxbow anglers must figure into the crappie equation. To better understand the variables that influence oxbow crappie fishing, let's examine the origins and physical attributes of oxbow lakes. Knowing what to look for, and when, and where, will increase your chances for success.

Oxbow Origins

A lowland river left to its own devices will writhe and twist in its valley like a head-shot snake. The river erodes earth away in one place, only to deposit it somewhere else, and though a river may always look the same to a casual visitor, it's never the same two days in a row.

Over the years, a lowland river plows a new channel here and abandons an old one there, always following the path of least resistance. Sometimes, when a meandering stream erodes the shores of its broad bends, loops of water are severed from the main stream. The ends of the loops are blocked by sediments deposited by the parent stream, and a crescent-shaped lake is left behind. The shape of these lakes resembles the U-shaped piece of wood on an ox yoke, thus the name. Oxbow lakes are also known as "cut-offs" or "river lakes."

When an oxbow gets cut off from the river, its character immediately begins to change. Sediment carried in from seasonal flooding builds up on the bottom, and the old meander scar becomes shallower and relatively flat-bottomed. Water-tolerant plants like cypress, tupelo, buckbrush and willow take root along the lake's edges. In years of drought, some shallow oxbows dry up, allowing plants to gain a foothold and encroach still farther into the lake.

All these natural processes, from the cutting off of a new oxbow to the building up of bottom sediment to the gradual extension of woody vegetation, are stages in the death of an oxbow. The process may take 500 years or more, but left undisturbed, all oxbows will eventually revert to wetland forest.

During this long process of dying, oxbows provide fantastic crappie fishing. The annual cycle of winter/spring flooding that gradually chokes these lakes with silt also figures heavily in making them the outstanding crappie fisheries they so often are.

Oxbow lakes occur across the Southern part of the U.S., but are most common along the Lower Mississippi drainage. However, Texas' Brazos River, for example, or wild rivers throughout Georgia, all create oxbows ready for fishing.

Oxbow Types

Perhaps the most important step in solving the oxbow crappie riddle is understanding that not all oxbows are created equal. There are, in general, three types of oxbows. Each reacts differently to changes in water levels, and the crappies react quite differently as well. Some oxbows remain connected to the parent stream, for example, while others are isolated. Some lie within the floodplain of major rivers and streams; others lie entirely outside. Differing conditions on each type of oxbow dictate the manner and amount of planning necessary to enjoy a productive fishing trip.

• Connected oxbows—Oxbows that remain connected to their parent river during all or part of the year normally provide the best potential for big crappies. When the river floods, inflowing nutrients enrich the water and help sustain

Up North Crappies: The Backwater Connection

Time was, northern rivers created strong numbers of oxbows, especially the Missouri, Upper Mississippi and Ohio rivers. But navigation and flood-control projects tamed and straightened the rivers, and northern oxbows are now approaching extinction. However, big rivers in states like Iowa, Wisconsin, Ohio and West Virginia are still home to vast networks of backwaters, and although not oxbows in theory, their dynamics are similar.

John Pitlo, a fisheries research biologist with the Iowa Department of Natural Resources, is involved in backwater research. He explains their connection to crappies, and the forces that threaten these unique fisheries.

"Backwaters can offer up tremendous crappie fishing, especially those with prime spawning habitat. In spring, target crappies around any wood that's available—snags, stumps, laydowns and shoreline brush are prime territories. After the spawn, as water temperatures warm and water levels drop, crappies usually move closer to the river, often locating in side channels with slow-moving water. However, in high-water years, the crappies may stay tucked back in still water through summer.

"Make no mistake, today's backwaters are in serious jeopardy. Control projects on rivers mean backwaters are continually being lost to siltation. So too, tamed rivers seldom flood to historic levels and isolated backwaters are often left to die. Those backwaters

thriving communities of forage, upon which the crappies feed. This yearly overflow cycle also provides temporary, but important, spawning habitat.

Unfortunately, severe water level fluctuations also make river-connected oxbows the trickiest to fish. When the river rises, the lake rises; when the river falls, the lake falls. Changing water conditions dramatically affect fishing, and anglers must monitor water levels closely to pick the most productive days.

There are no hard-and-fast rules for fishing river-connected oxbows—fish are caught under all conditions. But as a general rule, crappies seldom bite when the water is on a fast rise. Fishing runout areas—the cuts connecting oxbow and river—can sometimes be outstanding during a fast fall. But the best fishing on these oxbows is usually when the water level is steady, or slowly rising or falling.

On river-connected oxbows, crappie anglers should also know the depth at which the river moves in and out of the oxbow. This information is usually available at local baitshops or from area anglers, and once you know it, you can monitor the river level in local newspapers to plan a trip during peak fishing periods.

Connected oxbows do occasionally dry up and lose their fish populations. Many oxbow fishermen believe the annual flooding cycle in river-connected oxbows is actually a restocking process, and the floodwaters import a new batch

of crappies each year. But telemetry and netting studies have proven this isn't so. There's enough fish movement from river to lake, or from one lake to another, to restore a fish population to an oxbow that has dried up over a hot summer, but the mass influx of catchable-size crappies that many anglers envision simply doesn't occur.

What apparently happens is, annual floods stimulate the existing fish population in a river-bottom oxbow to go on a feeding binge. The feeding binge puts them in excellent spawning condition, and because the oxbows are so fertile, heavy spawns usually follow each winter/spring flooding cycle. This past year, for example, was exceptionally dry, and many oxbows dried up for the first time in nearly 70 years. In two to three years, these oxbows will likely offer unparalleled fishing for outsized slabs.

• Disconnected but inside the floodplain—Many other oxbows are no longer connected to the river proper, but still lie within the stream floodplain. These lakes, too, are subject to flooding and rapidly changing water levels during wet months, and here again, crappie anglers should scrutinize water fluctuations while planning a visit.

Dissecting An Oxbow: Universal Hotspots

Most oxbows share similar shapes and features. At right is a typical river-connected oxbow. Be sure to fish runout chutes (A) whenever water is falling at a rate of three to six inches a day. When crappies are in the shallows, target heavy cover like cypress trees and button willows (B). If water temperatures climb above 70 to 75 degrees, target the deepest water in the oxbow, which is almost always found along the old outside river bend (C).

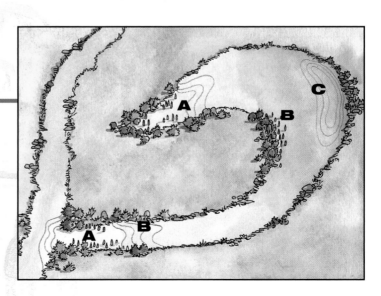

that become overly shallow, and experience a heavy growth of vegetation, are especially prone to winterkill."

Pitlo notes the importance of backwater conservation. "These areas are nurseries for crappies, as well as bluegills, bass and larval walleyes and sauger. They also provide the only habitat for these fish to survive winter. To help stem the rapid loss of backwater habitat, Congress has authorized the Environmental Management Program (EMP) on the Upper Mississippi. About $10 million a year is directed to the river to rehabilitate backwaters or other degraded habitats."

While the news on backwaters is largely bad, fisheries that winterkill are capable of recharging. New crappies that move in and spawn often do so without competition, and the resulting year-class can be phenomenal. If you know of a backwater that has experienced winterkill, jot down a few notes, then plan to visit three or four years later. You may just discover a bonanza slab fishery known only to you.

Disconnected oxbows share many similar characteristics with river-connected oxbows, but can take longer to recover after exceptionally dry periods. These oxbows tend to be shallower and generally receive floodwater only three out of every five years. With a lack of river access, many are off the beaten path and relatively unknown. Find and fish even the smallest ones for a unique experience.

• Outside the floodplain—Some oxbows lie entirely outside the river floodplain, completely isolated by levees or dams. These lakes usually provide the most predictable fishing opportunities, since water fluctuations are less dramatic and exert less influence on overall fishing conditions. Consequently, they may be the best oxbows to fish when water conditions are unfavorable elsewhere.

If it's big crappies you seek, however, you'll probably be disappointed. The absence of an annual overflow cycle leads to decreased fertility, and quality crappies—1½ to 3 pounders—are seldom found. These lakes also die the quickest, some lasting only decades. The rapid runoff from agricultural lands increases siltation, which makes the lakes shallower and often too warm.

The general oxbow guidelines outlined above can be helpful, but don't neglect to do additional homework before fishing. Some isolated oxbows offer astounding fishing for outsized crappies, and some river-connected lakes may produce few, if any, quality fish.

Prepare yourself by contacting local baitshop proprietors or fisheries biologists and asking a few basic questions. Is this a good crappie lake during this time of year? What size crappies are likely to be caught? Can you offer pointers on picking the best fishing days? Can you suggest where I might call for an up-to-date report on fishing conditions? The more you know about a lake before you visit, the better your chances for success.

Finding Crappies

Finding oxbow crappies isn't unusually complicated. One thing to remember is that even though most oxbows are relatively flat and of uniform depth, the outside bend of the lake is almost always a little deeper than the inside bend. This can be important when water temperatures rise above the crappies' preferred 70- to 75-degree comfort range.

When the water gets unduly warm, crappies tend to concentrate on the deeper side of the lake, where the temperature is more to their liking. In most oxbows, the amount of deep water is very limited, so you don't have to look far to find fish.

When crappies are in the shallows, they invariably relate to some sort of cover. Cypress trees skirt the banks of many oxbows, and working jigs or minnows around their broad bases and knees is a good way to catch crappies. Buckbrush and willows are also prevalent in many oxbows, and stringers of crappies are caught in the thickest cover available. Other prime fishing spots include fallen trees, beaver lodges, sunken Christmas tree shelters, lily pads, weedbeds, shoreline riprap, stump fields, boat docks and duck-hunting blinds.

If you're on an oxbow when flood waters are receding, try fishing around runout chutes between the oxbow and river. These are crappie magnets that attract fish with the promise of an easy meal. Look for areas where outflowing water is constricted, such as sloughs and natural cuts, then work a minnow, jig or jig/spinner combo around woody cover. Key your efforts on periods when water is falling three to six inches a day—a faster fall makes it hard to locate fish.

One final note: when you're considering where to go, think small and visit lakes off the beaten path. Lightweight jonboats or canoes are ideal fishing craft, and on small oxbows, an outboard is unnecessary. Carry in a canoe or jonboat and bring a sculling paddle.

The splendid bottomland scenery will take you back to a time when our country was still wild and uncharted, and you'll experience a feeling of wonderment and tranquility no man-made impoundment can impart. When the crappies are biting, there's only one way to describe it. It's heaven on earth.

Pier Paradise

WALK TO SALTWATER SUCCESS.

by Bob McNally

Each year, thousands of saltwater anglers flock to fishing piers in pursuit of such sought-after species as tarpon, king mackerel, sailfish, cobia, jacks, redfish, snook, seatrout, flounder, striped bass, surf-perch, Pacific mackerel, steelhead, salmon and sturgeon, along with many others.

And they're successful. In fact, anglers fishing from piers have caught a number of International Game Fish Association (IGFA) world-record fish. Perhaps the most amazing of all was the record Walter Maxwell set on June 14, 1964, at the Cherry Grove Pier near Myrtle Beach, South Carolina. With 130-pound-class tackle and a 16/0 reel, Maxwell fought a massive tiger shark for nearly five hours before beaching it. The shark measured almost 14 feet long, had an 8½-foot girth, and weighed 1,780 pounds! It still is the largest tiger shark ever caught on rod-and-reel.

Elvin Hooper also caught his IGFA 30-pound line-class record redfish of 90 pounds from a pier at Rodanthe on Hatteras Island, North Carolina. And Hooper's feat was no fluke. Other redfish records have been caught from piers, and each year anglers swarm to North Carolina's abundant Outer Banks piers to waylay giant migrating redfish, bluefish, striped bass, flounder and others. It's a sport that gets in the blood, no matter what your angling background.

The same is true in other coastal areas when big fish migrate through a region. Every spring, for example, cobia journey along the upper Gulf of Mexico coast. At times anglers along Florida's panhandle and in parts of Alabama and Mississippi catch "ling fever." While boat anglers cruise the beach, pier fishermen have their innings. "Board walkers" often catch more and bigger cobia than do anglers bobbing on the surface.

At places like Panama City Beach and Clearwater, Florida, and Orange Beach, Alabama, cobia can sometimes swim so tight to breaking surf it's too dangerous for boaters to get within casting range. I've seen fish swimming inside the surf line that boat anglers just 50 yards away couldn't see, much less get a lure to.

Good Timing

Naturally, angling action is not always hot at every pier all the time. In fact, one of the aspects freshwater anglers have the most difficulty understanding is that marine species'

Pier anglers catch giant fish all the time. This 90-pound redfish, caught in 1973 from a pier in Rondanthe, North Carolina, by Elvin Hooper, still stands as the IGFA's 30-pound line-class record.

migration habits are completely different from those of their sweetwater brethren.

Spanish mackerel and bluefish, for example, may show at a given Atlantic Coast pier for only a few weeks, or even just days, during the spring. Then, they head north on a "run" that can cover hundreds of miles in just a couple of months. Other species like kingfish, jack crevalle, bonito, striped bass, cobia and others migrate similarly.

The point here is that you can't catch fish from a pier when the fish simply aren't there. Fortunately, runs of different species of gamefish usually occur through the seasons, with Spanish mackerel available today, for example, bluefish next week, seatrout or redfish after that, and so on.

Water temperature, baitfish (which also migrate long distances), tide phases and other factors have much more bearing on saltwater pier fishing success than they do in freshwater. In addition, severe storms, high winds and swift tides shift sandbars and other underwater migration routes fish use in the surf near piers.

Improve The Odds

Experience is the best teacher when it comes to learning to time runs or identify productive tide phases. But you can give the process a healthy kick-start by talking to pier operators, other anglers (the regulars affectionately call themselves pier rats) and bait/tackle shop owners. Such inquiries will yield information about such things as "when Spanish mackerel run close to a pier," "when the blues are in," "what time of year sheepshead are around, or kingfish, snook, pompano..."

Also, keep an eye peeled for fishing reports in local newspapers, and on the Internet, as well. There are countless Web sites devoted to specific saltwater piers where you can get the latest scoop on the hot bites, tide information and more. Some even offer real-time photos that show the current wind and tide conditions.

Consider The Variables

Angler Debi Johnson of Naples, Florida, is a bona fide pier rat. She's spent most of her life treading the boards of the local pier, and has even taught pier fishing techniques to local youngsters for 12 years. Debi was also the lead angler in the pier fishing segment on the NAFC's "Success Without A Boat" video.

When she walks the planks, Debi first considers all the variables, and recommends you do, too. Here's her take on what a smart angler considers.

Time Of Day: Sunrise and sunset.

Moon Phase: Full is best—always.

Tide Phase: A moving tide is better than slack water; and a rising tide is better than a falling tide.

Location: Fish move; so should you.

Water Temperature: Varies with the species targeted.

Wind Direction: Fish into the wind.

Water Clarity: She likes some color; not too clear or too stained.

Water Depth: Always look for troughs and cuts in the bottom, but don't think you have to fish the deepest water available. Many of her fish come from five to eight feet of water.

It helps to be observant, too. Visit your chosen pier(s) often to learn what goes on from week to week, or even day to day. If you find it unusually crowded, there's a reason. You should make a point of jotting down the tide phase, wind direction and speed, water clarity, moon phase (dictates tide strength), weather conditions, baits and lures being used, and especially, where the anglers who are catching the most fish are standing along the pier. None of these things are chance events, and wise anglers keep a log of such conditions.

The best tide phases are usually when the water is moving, often the early stages of flooding or ebbing tides. But this isn't always the case. And only by checking a tide table and watching which way the water "runs" will you know what the tide is doing.

Wind speed and direction play an important part in tide flow and its velocity, which greatly influences baitfish and gamefish location. By noting the wind, and its relationship to tide, you're adding important information to your mental computer.

Where To Fish

Tide phase and wind direction also affect water clarity. How clear the water is often determines the type of fish that will come within casting distance, how they'll feed and what they'll strike.

Clear water is best for most species, especially sight feeders like mackerel, jacks, seatrout, bluefish and snook. Bottom feeders like black drum, redfish, croakers and whiting can hit well in off-color water. Fish that feed near pilings, like sheepshead, flounder and spadefish, aren't as affected by dirty water, either.

To be consistently successful, take your cue from the conditions and be prepared to modify your game plan accordingly. Clear water, for example, may prompt you to cast spoons or grubs for seatrout or jacks. But if the water is murky, bottom-fishing with live mullet or shrimp may produce best for flounder and redfish. Color changes or "breaks," where dark, dirty water meets clear, are choice spots often available to pier fishermen.

Weather is vitally important, too, with the best action frequently coming just before or soon after a violent storm. Wind, waves and tides slamming into a pier typically form an undulating bottom around pilings, as well as sloughs that run perpendicular to the pier, parallel to the beach. Varied bottom depths and gouged-out sloughs form underwater highways for marine species.

In saltwater, however, such bottom structure frequently shifts due to changing tides, current and wind direction, and this can alter baitfish and gamefish location.

Experience has taught pier regulars just where the best sloughs and holes are located—during a given tide phase, at a certain time of year, for a specifically sought fish species. On some days, for example, the "up-tide" side of a pier may be most productive; on others, the "down-tide" side will yield the most fish. Be observant and watch what other anglers are doing.

Some piers feature rock piles, concrete slabs or jetties that reinforce the pilings. These can be important fish magnets, as rocks are a haven for baitfish. Bottom feeders like drum, flounder and sheepshead are commonly found around such structure. Hard-hitting predators like 'cudas, snook and seatrout are likely to be there, too.

Piers are the great equalizer. Board walkers can enjoy as much, and at times more, success than boat anglers.

Little Piers, Big Opportunities

For every large ocean pier, there are at least two or three small, inshore piers, docks or jetties that extend into salty bays and estuaries, rivers and creeks, sounds and inlets. And while such smaller docks may not draw the crowds the big piers do, they can be outstanding places to catch a variety of gamefish.

Anglers commonly catch snook, seatrout, striped bass, snapper, bluefish, flounder, mackerel, redfish, sheepshead, black drum, tarpon and a host of other species from small structures that are frequently overlooked by marine fishermen. Often marina piers, where boats for offshore fishing are headquartered, are major gamefish magnets, especially at night or in the early morning when human activity is low.

Docks and jetties around seaside restaurants and old wharf areas can provide shore-bound anglers with outstanding fishing. Just as you can't tell a book by its cover, you can't tell how good one of these spots may be until you fish it. Have no preconceived notions about what you'll catch or what its size will be. Work every smaller structure as though it attracts heavyweight sportfish, and don't be surprised if it does.

Small piers, docks and jetties outnumber large fishing piers 4- or 5-to-1, and they account for very impressive catches, both in size and numbers. Don't overlook the small stuff.

After Dark

Never overlook nightfishing. Often the very best action from notoriously nocturnal feeders like sharks, snook, striped bass, tarpon and seatrout occurs after the sun goes down, especially on piers with lights that cast a glow into the water. Vertical jigging, or soaking live or dead bait, at the edge of the halo of light shining near a pier often brings solid strikes from heavy fish. Tarpon, stripers and snook hooked at night are difficult to land because they're masters at weaving your line through and around pilings. For some species like sharks, it's best to position your bait well away from the pier so pilings don't come so much into play.

Pier Gear

Virtually any type of tackle, from heavy, big-game outfits to ultra-light spinning rigs can be used successfully by pier anglers, at least some of the time. The heavy stuff is reserved for sharks, stout drum, salmon and other giant fish that run far and fight hard. Midsize casting and spinning tackle is serviceable for striped bass, kingfish, cobia, snook, tarpon, steelhead, surfperch and others, while light-action spinning, or even fly gear, can provide anglers with top sport for ladyfish, weakfish, bluefish, jacks, flounder, pompano, sheepshead, whiting, croakers, spots, grunts and more.

Many commercial fishing piers have bait and tackle shops nearby. Usually the baits needed to catch local species (sand fleas, shrimp, smelt, anchovies and mussels to live mullet, bloodworms and mud minnows) can be purchased on-site.

All piers have regional favorite lures for different species, and wise is the angler who has a selection handy when "walking the boards." But a standard selection of jigs, flashy spoons and plugs should serve any pier angler well.

If you're new to pier fishing, and you choose the right pier, you can actually rent all the equipment you need for a day on the boards. Some charge a flat fee, say around $10, for daily gear rental; others may charge a half-day, or even an hourly rate. Add that to the typical $4 to $6 admission charge (state- or city-owned piers typically charge no admission), and it's still very affordable recreation.

On top of that, you may not need to purchase a fishing license when angling from a saltwater pier. In states like Florida and California, a permit is not required. In others, it is. Check the regulations before venturing out.

Serious pier fishermen usually tote their angling paraphernalia in a wagon or cart of some type, since it can be a long walk from the parking lot to the fishing area. Wooden or plastic carts are best, since they don't rust as readily as metal ones.

Along with rods, reels and tackle, carry a bait bucket, lunch cooler and a hoop net or pier gaff for lifting your catch from the surface, which might be 50 feet, or more, below the pier deck.

For the few bucks admission, saltwater piers may just be the best fishing bargain in America. Where else can you enjoy the sea, watch the sun sail serenely over the water, catch enough fish for a meal, and maybe even land a fish that'll break a world record?

The King

YOU BOW WHEN IN HIS PRESENCE.

by Howard Tripp

The small trickle of sweat began somewhere beneath my cap. It worked its way slowly down my neck and under my collar, only to be absorbed by the already damp shirt on my back. Thick, humid tropical air wrapped itself around us like a warm, wet blanket. Dark, tannic-stained water lay still like a perfect mirror for lazy white clouds. Only the muffled sounds of distant birds and my own thoughts penetrated the silence.

This calm was a lie, and unlike my wife, Julie, I wasn't buying into it. While she saw a postcard scene of tropical relaxation, I sensed an unseen tension that hung like burned ozone in the aftermath of a too-close lightning strike.

Silently I searched the surface of the tea-colored water for any sign of life.

"It's starting," a voice whispers, not my own. "There's some current on that point. The tide's starting to move out."

"Is that good?" Another voice. A woman's.

"Yes, they will be here soon," the first voice replies.

"Look! There's bait moving." My own whispered voice surprises me.

Over the years of pursuing outdoor adventure, I have learned that there are moments of sweet agony that come in the anticipation of pleasure or danger. Where countless hours of fantasy and planning meet expectation at the brink and hoped-for goals seem too much to hope for. They are interminable moments that cling painfully at the precipice and are so addictive and so unbearable that they become, in fact, more intense than the pleasure or the goal itself. Time stands still and you see, hear and remember everything in high-definition and surround-sound.

For me, this was such a moment.

The backcountry of the Everglades is the only place in Florida that hasn't fallen prey to developers hell-bent on turning every square inch of "unproductive" Florida into an endless row of strip malls, condos and trailer parks. Panthers and bears still roam here, as well as deer, 'coons, 'gators and manatees. For humans, its remoteness has always been its allure. Pirates, smugglers and 'gator hunters all have used it to safeguard their activities.

Generations of fishermen have also come here, most searching for trophy tarpon, redfish and snook. Many, like myself, come in search of something even more elusive and precious than trophies. Escape. I am drawn here in the hope of experiencing something as close to the way God created it, instead of the way that man has changed it.

I have been here many times and it is without a doubt my favorite fishing spot. On this trip I have brought my number one fishing partner for the last 18 years, my wife, Julie. It is her first fishing trip here and I am anxious to share it with her.

Our headquarters is Everglades City and the adjacent port of Chokoloskee (pronounced Chuck-a-lusky). These sleepy outposts lie at the end of the road on the northwest corner of Everglades National Park. Chokoloskee has a colorful past as a frontier town and is still pretty rough around the edges.

We are fishing with Robert Collins, arguably the best artificials-only guide in southwest Florida. A quiet-spoken man in his 40s, Robert knows every river and flat that drains the 'Glades into the Gulf of Mexico.

If you have never fished the 'Glades, the number and size of the fish here will leave you jaded for life. It is an unbelievably competitive environment, which breeds powerful, aggressive, ruthless predator fish.

It is November and only a handful of locals are about. We leave the dock as dawn approaches. The heavy humidity softens the light, creating a pink, hazy glow in the eastern sky. In this glorious light we ride in Robert's flats boat, weaving around several mangrove islands before finally breaking free into the open ocean. Other than our wake, barely a ripple stirs.

As we continue southward, we pass fishing spots long familiar. Spots with great names like Pavilion Key, Huston River, Alligator Cove, Seminole Point and Lostman's River. These large rivers drain huge expanses of the 'Glades. They flow through complicated chains of bays and lakes, all of which are interconnected. It is virtually impossible not to become disoriented in this mangrove-lined maze, yet Robert confidently guides the boat ever deeper into the secret places known only to men of his craft.

We spend the morning hooked up with small jacks, snook, ladyfish, seatrout and reds. To Julie's chagrin, 'gators by the score swim mere feet from our boat and squadrons of leopard rays glide in and out of sight.

Midafternoon, we make our way into a vast interior bay. It is here that we plan to rendezvous with destiny. All day we had anticipated the perfect combination of circumstances. With the outgoing tide, fish begin to pull out of the shallow, flooded backcountry and seek refuge in slightly deeper channels. Disoriented bait caught up in the building current get swept like lambs to the slaughter, and this triggers every predator within the ecosystem.

This is where we wait in ambush, armed only with bass-size tackle.

"There they are." Robert's voice is all business.

"Where?"

"Nine o'clock, moving to 12. Sit down, we're moving." The outboard chirps to life and we idle toward the fish before Julie and I can react. All eyes are riveted forward. Even Julie can feel the tension now.

Handing her my Fenwick rod, I gently push her to the front of the boat. Just as suddenly as it had started, the outboard goes silent. Our momentum carries us forward. "Be ready," I whisper, "It's going to happen any minute."

A rolling flash of silver and white. "Go, go, go! Cast! Cast!"

"Where? Where?"

"There, there, go, go!" And then she sees them, too. Instantly the MirrO-Lure fires through the air, only to land behind the moving tarpon. "Quick! Reel in, cast again."

"I know. Now stop it, you're making me nervous," she says pointedly. Sometimes I have been accused of being too intense, too competitive. This may be one of those times.

There are now numerous large tarpon rolling around us. Julie casts again. This time the plug lands perfectly in front of a traveling fish. That's when things get out of hand. A violent explosion of water erupts, stopping Julie's retrieve cold. A momentary look of terror crosses her face while a shriek of fear and excitement rips from her throat as six feet of silver explodes into the air, nearly ripping the rod from her hands. The tranquil deception of this jungle is finally exposed.

Now Julie knows the truth. The king has arrived. The tarpon again launches itself into the air. "Bow, Bow, Bow!" I scream. She bows perfectly, rod lowered and extended, giving slack and protecting her mono from the impact shock of the fish landing on her line. At 30 feet, re-entry sounds like a VW dropped off a pier. For 20 minutes, the fish puts on an amazing aerial display. It ends suddenly and the real fight begins.

Legs spread, knees bent, rod butt tucked into her stomach, Julie slugs it out. Long, powerful, unstoppable runs melt the 15-pound-test mono from the shiny Ambassadeur reel. Each run is followed by a furious pump-and-wind retrieve that never seems to net enough line back to show any real progress. At the 30-minute mark, an exhausted Julie asks, no begs, for me to take the rod from her blistering hands. I refuse. Instead, Robert and I coach her.

"You can do this, honey. Just hang on. You will regret it later if you quit now. It will be over soon, and you will be so proud." I know the right things to say; after all, I had coached the birth of our four children.

At the 40-minute mark the fight becomes personal. Her resolve stiffens and her competitive juices kick in. Tightening the drag, she clamps down on each new run. "No!" she declares. "You're coming in now."

And it did. Fifty minutes into the battle, she eases the whipped tarpon to boatside. Slipping a small gaff into the bony jaw, Robert hoists the 71-incher over the gunwale and onto the deck. We snap a few pictures, then release the mighty king.

High-fives all done and drenched in sweat, Julie melts onto the front deck, grinning from ear to ear.

With happiness in my heart, I thank Robert for bringing us to this magic place. As we leave the realm of the silver king and glide across flat seas in the warm rays of the late-afternoon sun, I say a silent prayer. I thank God for making the 'Glades, for providing for their protection and especially for a wife who loves to fish.

Fishing Strategies

*Y*ou can't go fishing without a plan. Well, you can— *but you can't fish effectively.*

It's fine just to go fishing and have some fun. But when it's time to be serious about catching fish, the strategy you put to work will make all the difference in your success.

As we said in the introduction to this book— there is nothing wrong with wanting to catch some fish!

That's what this chapter is all about. Here are stories on fishing's big picture, to help you put together a better plan every time you hit the water.

You wouldn't go fishing without rod, reel and terminal tackle. You shouldn't be on the water without a strategy either.

Rigs, lures, locations ...
Advanced Trolling

DAHLBERG ON TROLLING SMART.

by Larry Dahlberg

As a youngster, I remember trolling as being some sort of last resort. As a passenger, the only time it didn't seem aimless was when we were headed toward the boat landing. I even recall an early revelation of sorts that occurred while trolling about 40 years ago: "When you're trolling, the only one fishing is the guy driving the boat." I know now, even that is questionable sometimes.

But it doesn't have to be.

I know lots of anglers who are instantly turned off by the mere mention of trolling. To many, it might be considered the polar opposite of fly fishing. Maybe they had the same early revelation I did. But, truth is, those anglers who are yearning for a fish they can cast to might save lots of time and catch more fish by first locating a bunch by trolling, then resorting to their more preferred methods.

The beauty of trolling is the efficiency with which it allows you to cover water, both horizontally and vertically. Whether you are checking water you already know, or trying to fish and evaluate new water at the same time, trolling is often simply the most efficient means.

Looking at trolling in the broadest sense, you can boil it down to two categories: 1. Precision trolling for fish tightly related to structure and/or cover; and 2. Not-so-precise trolling for fish that are suspended over open water and not closely related to cover or structure.

This might seem like a tidy, simple little picture that can be followed by a formula for certain success, but it's not. The problem is, fish don't always do what they're supposed to do. Dahlberg's second immutable law of angling: The fish are where they are, not where you wish them to be.

A good troller needs substantial mechanical and strategic skills. These skills include the ability to: 1. Accurately define the borders of the structural element or basin being fished; 2. Control the boat so the lure goes where it is supposed to; 3. Keep accurate track of what has been covered and what hasn't; 4. Make observations while trolling that weigh the relative value of each spot against the next; and 5. Identify those features that are currently holding active fish or have the most potential to hold fish at another time.

Obviously, accurate observations are critical and your observations are only as accurate as your electronics allow. You are at the mercy of your depthfinder. Buy the best you can afford.

Precision Trolling

Some of the earliest precision trollers I know of were the Mississippi River rats who dragged L&S Bassmasters on metered lead-core line. The guy running the boat knew where he was going and how much line to let out in order for the lure to get to the bottom. As the depth changed, he would call out "colors" to his fishing partners so they could let out or retrieve line to compensate.

Some of the problems with this method were the sheer weight of the lead line and the size of the reel needed to hold it. Plus, it was tough to avoid snags even if you were very hip to the program. Also, because of its relatively large diameter, lead-core has a great deal of water resistance. Achieving the desired depth or speed often required the lure to be so far behind the boat that it became hard to keep track of.

The father of true precision trolling is Buck Perry. A physics professor by trade, Perry developed a series of lures called Spoonplugs that are actually swimming/diving plates. Each size is designed to run at a given depth with a given amount of line out.

Perry recognized the problems of maintaining close control of the lure, and even developed a metered no-stretch line to help overcome the problem. Unfortunately, it had the same approximate formula as the nylon used for toothbrush bristles. When even greater depths or tighter control were required, Perry recommended using wire line instead of mono.

Partly because it has weight, but mostly because it has a very small diameter and zero stretch, wire can get a diving crankbait to remarkable depths with the absolute minimum of letback. You can use wire to scrape the bottom in 60 feet of water or more with a lot of line out, or you can use it to bang a crankbait against bottom along a 20-foot weedline with the lure practically under the boat.

Wire gives you absolute precision and control, although when a big fish nails your lure, it'll yank you out of your tennis shoes if they're not laced up tight.

Likewise, if you try to horse a fish on wire, you may pull the hooks free.

Other thoughts on wire: Use seven-strand, not Monel, because it's thinner and less likely to kink. Use the reel with the largest diameter spool you have, and leave the clicker on all the time. Finally, wire cuts—use a roller-tip rod.

The relatively new superlines are a good choice, too. Their capabilities lie almost right between mono and wire.

Because water resistance is such a big factor in determining how deep a bait will run, it's best to use the smallest snaps and swivels you can, or to avoid using them entirely. When tying directly to a lure, use a split ring or loop knot, or you'll kill much of its action.

I assume because it's not legal to troll in bass tournaments, not many anglers troll lures for bass anymore. In my experience, there's no more effective way to put a whole bunch of big fish in the boat than to grind diving lures into the bottom at a rate faster than anyone in the world can crank. This is especially true in natural lakes, after bass have finished spawning and have set up on weedlines or main-lake structures. Those who've tried speed-trolling know it can be deadly on pike, muskies, stripers, walleyes and trout as well (see "What Do We Really Know About Speed?" page 108).

Figuring out the best speed to trigger fish is important, but the most critical factor is getting the lure tight to the best cover on the structure. This means super-accurate mapping and marking.

I used to use dozens of marker buoys placed exactly on every point, inside bend and especially on spots where the primary breakline and weedline occur together. Now I use GPS. You'd think that the process would be simpler with GPS and loads of waypoints, but I've never been able to maintain the same accuracy with GPS as with actual physical markers.

Boat Control

Another critical factor is boat control. Precision trolling is almost impossible with a non-tiller boat because the turning radius is too long and throttle control requires a spare hand.

Most of the time, when you want to scrape an inside corner, you have to overrun the corner, then turn the boat sharper than 90 degrees, while at the same time gunning the throttle to keep the lure moving and get the boat back where it needs to be. This is also difficult with large-

Split-Tail Rig

The split-tail rig is a saltwater standard with great potential for freshwater predators such as big bass, muskies, stripers, pike and lake trout. Although it looks complicated, the process is simple once you get the hang of it.

Starting just behind the dorsal fin, run a fillet knife along the spine to the tail and split the tail, side to side (A). Break or cut the backbone where it connects to the tail and insert a deboning tool, available from saltwater tackle shops and catalogs, (B). Remove the spine (C). Next, use an awl or ice pick to punch a hole in the top of the head, centered between the eyes and nostrils, that exits beneath the jaw (D). Insert a 4/0 to 7/0 long-shank hook in the mouth, so the eye lines up in the hole you just made, and the point protrudes from

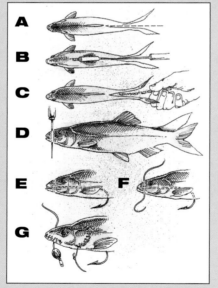

the belly just below the gills or pectoral fin (E). Run a 45-pound wire leader through the head and hook eye (F). Loop it through a narrow-diameter egg sinker, crimp it on really tight and sew the mouth and gills shut with dental tape and a mortician's needle (G).

If short strikers or solid hooksets are a problem, rig a stinger on a short wire tether off the lead hook. The second hook may stick out either the top or bottom of the bait. The trick to both single- and double-hook rigging is getting the bait to "swim" without spinning. If it spins, cut a small notch in the flesh ahead of the hook bend(s). To save time on the water, debone baits ahead of time at home. Cure them in saltwater a few hours before freezing to firm up the meat.

Digging Deep

Line weight and diameter help determine how deep a given lure will run. If you need maximum depth, or want to troll 15- to 20-foot ranges with minimum letback, wire line (A) slices through the water column better than other options. Braided and fused superlines (B) are easier to spool and fish than wire, and reach nearly as deep. Due to its large diameter and resulting water resistance, nylon monofilament (C) is the poorest choice for depth-dredging. However, if you want to troll a diving crankbait shallow, without snagging bottom or cover, heavy mono can keep the lure out of trouble.

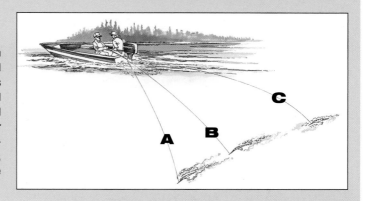

horsepower tillers because they do not have a tight enough turning radius, either. I've seen tillers built for commercial use that allow much tighter turns, which would solve this problem, but as far as I know they are not available to the angling public.

Fact is, for precision trolling it's hard to beat a 14-foot aluminum V-hull with less than 30 horses pushing it.

Don't hesitate to make several series of "strafing" runs at different angles when fishing points and small, isolated spines off larger structures. And again, above all, make sure the lure is ticking bottom.

Backtrolling is popular among Midwest walleye heads, but it totally baffles the rest of the world. The boat is pointed in the front; anyone with even the slightest bit of sense can see it's made to go forward.

Actually, backtrolling was invented by Al Lindner back when he was a walleye guide. The logic behind it was so Al could get his leech to the walleyes before his customer did. Just kidding. Obviously, it's a way to decrease both speed and also reduce the turning radius of the boat.

If you're locked in to a large boat with a big motor, it will be more difficult to be super precise. It's especially hard with a console rig. One solution is to tie a drift sock to the nose of the boat. Use the shortest amount of rope you can. This will allow you to turn the boat in about one-tenth the distance you'd be able to without it.

When fish are tight to cover, total precision is the key. Anytime your baits are running off of it, you're wasting time. If I can't troll an inside corner as precisely as I'd like, I often bomb right through it until my lure gets gobbed in the weeds. At least then I know I've presented it in the right area.

Your follow-up is critical, too. Most people are unwilling to crank up, spin around and dig through a specific area immediately after passing through a first time. Too often, fishermen make slow, wide, lazy turns in areas where total precision would be more effective.

A precision troller could be compared to a bird dog with his nose to the ground, following a scent trail. Instead of his nose to the ground, he has his face buried in the locator as he zigzags along in an effort to keep the boat on a specific contour line.

Open Water

Open-water trolling requires a different set of skills and mindset. It's more like mowing a field than it is like weed-whipping around the bushes. I like to think of it as rubbing the silver off a lottery card.

There are hundreds of open-water techniques, many of which employ rather ingenious devices. Downriggers. Side planers. Diving planes. An added complication of open-water trolling is the fact that the fish are most often suspended, so getting the lure to the right level is critical.

It's difficult to monitor the exact depth a lure is running because it isn't ticking off the bottom to give you a reference. When fish are suspended in deep water, the challenge becomes three-dimensional, and you have two more edges or breaks to monitor; temperature and also, possibly, oxygen.

Many serious trollers rely on the book *Precision Trolling* by NAFC members Dr. Steven Holt, Tom Irwin and Mark Romanack to help them determine the running depths of specific lures with different speeds and amounts of letback. It's a very useful tool for open-water trolling.

Often, fish species we associate with cover and structure use "open water." The best place to look when this occurs is usually off the edges of the structure, sometimes as much as several hundred yards, typically at the same depth as the primary breakline. This is especially true of fish with nonvented bladders like bass, pike, muskies and walleyes.

A GPS unit is extremely useful for this kind of fishing. It allows you to keep exact track of the grid you cover and it gives you great repeatability. Plus, marker buoys aren't very efficient in water much deeper than 20 feet because they drift, are hard to see, get in the way of your lures, and are a pain in the butt to wind up in deep water.

If you spot good concentrations of large fish suspended off structure, but can't get them to bite, it's usually a good idea to return later to see if they've moved back to the shelf to feed.

Usually, fish that normally relate to structure move off for one of two reasons: 1. They've been spooked off the shelf and sought security in open water rather than cover; or 2. They moved out to feed on some organism that's presenting an easy opportunity.

This could be mayfly larvae or other insects coming out of a soft bottom and rising yo-yo fashion to the surface prior to hatching. Or, predators may be attracted to baitfish that are eating insect larvae or zooplankton in the upper surface layer.

A big spread of lures is usually advantageous when open-water trolling. That is, if you can negotiate it without becoming totally tangled. This applies both horizontally and vertically. Some of the most amazing spreads I've seen were developed more than a generation ago in the Finger Lakes in New York by commercial fishermen who used hook-and-line methods with very thin spoons to catch salmonids. Although it's not practical or legal for the average fisherman today to pump down 20 lures or more at once like the commercials did, the details may be of interest.

One is the concept of trolling lure "sets." What this means is rather than putting out a whole mish-mash of different lures to give the fish their choice, they trolled identical spoons. When they wanted to change, they changed them all.

The benefit? Not all lures work best at the same speed. When you're fishing identical lures, if you dial in the right speed for one, it's right for the entire spread. With a variety of different lures, it's unlikely they will all operate at optimum efficiency at any one given speed. It could be also argued that "sets" more closely emulate a school of bait, but I think the speed thing is more critical.

What is the "right" speed? For spoons you want a nice side-to-side wobble. You don't want them to spin. A good way to keep track is to run one lure right beside the boat, near the surface so you can see it. Vary your speed until you're comfortable you've got a feel for the range the spoon will tolerate. Obviously, you can do the same thing with other types of lures.

Tuna and marlin fishermen in saltwater have perfected open-water techniques that allow them to cover miles of water with great efficiency. Average trolling speeds vary from 8 to 12 mph! The system involves using a spread consisting of four to six lures and various hookless attracting devices. Most often,

at least two of them are run on long outriggers that project from each side of the boat. Outriggers get the lures away from the prop wash, and give the baits action as they flex with the movement of the boat.

Most of the lures are designed to run on or very near the surface. The most effective ones alternate between plowing along the surface and diving to a foot or so. As they do, they leave a bubble trail behind them called "smoke," visible from a great distance underwater, which gives large predators the same impression as a school of fleeing baitfish.

I have no doubt in my mind this technique could be modified slightly to be deadly on a variety of freshwater species, especially in very clear water.

One of the most interesting and ingenious means of attraction I've seen anywhere is used by commercial fishermen off the coast of South Africa, who use powerful pumps and nozzles to shoot bursts of water into the air. The water falls to the surface, creating both

Trolling Triggers

- Change of speed
- Change of direction
- Bottom contact
- High speeds
- Lures that have a hitch in their giddy-up (erratic action)

sound and physical disturbance. The theory is that this brings in predators because it looks and sounds like a school of bait, and arouses the curiosity of a fish looking for dinner.

Another deadly saltwater concept begging for discovery by the freshwater crowd is the split-tail rig. This tactic involves splitting the tail of a dead baitfish, removing its spine and sewing in a keel weight and hook (see Split-Tail Rig sidebar, page 104).

A bait properly rigged in this fashion swims like it's alive and can be trolled at almost any speed. I've rigged suckers and large chubs this way and found both very effective on hard-to-fool fish. I shudder to think what a split-tail rainbow (where legal) would do for bass and stripers in Western reservoirs and lakes where fisheries agencies stock trout. Baits rigged in this fashion can also be cast and worked like jerkbaits.

A modification of the most popular way to catch sailfish is also extremely effective on brown trout and rainbows when they are near the surface in spring and fall. One method involves rigging dead smelt on a hook and trolling them just below the surface behind planer boards. An old friend of mine, Larry Presnell, demonstrated this to me almost 15 years ago on Lake Michigan browns.

It was murderous.

The other method, which I saw employed to catch 20-pound-plus rainbows on Lake Pend Oreille in Idaho many years ago, involves 4-inch-long tube flies pulled behind side planers.

Dahlberg's Trolling Lures:

Bass . . . . . . .Down Deep Fat Rap, Bomber (the original!), HellBender

Muskies . . .Magnum Saltwater Rapala, Bagley DB-06, Swim Whizz, Reef Hawg, Suick

Walleyes . .Shad Rap, Jointed Rapala, Wiggle Wart, spinners and 'crawlers

Trout . . . . . . .Evil Eye spoon, large dodgers, J-Plug, Magnum Flatfish

The flies are made by stretching a Flash-abou Minnow Body over a flat piece of plastic, onto which a thin, plastic tube has been glued. A shock of Big Fly Fiber is tied to the front. The "fly" is designed to actually plane on the surface and makes a tiny, v-shaped wake.

It doesn't wiggle. It doesn't flash. It doesn't move from side to side. Nonetheless, those giant 'bows came up and powdered it with more consistency and gusto that anything else we put behind the boat. I suspect that in the crystal-clear water, the fish are pretty hard to fool. A bait that skims the surface appears as a silhouette, making it more difficult for fish to detect that it's artificial. Plus, because it makes a wake, it actually has more attracting power than a lure traveling just under the surface.

Special Presentations

All trolling, whether on structure or off, is much more than tying on a bait, tossing it in the water, putting your rod in a rod holder and putzing along at high idle. I rarely use a rod holder in freshwater. With the exception of times when you need a fleet of planer boards to cover a wide swathe of open water, you're better off in direct connection with your line. This is especially true when grinding uneven bottom or fishing structure or cover along a winding contour line. Only by holding the rod and constantly adjusting the amount of letback can you hope to keep the bait in the right position. Too, you can feel if debris fouls your lure.

If you troll structure with a few buddies, it's absolutely crucial that the guy running the motor is the hippest to the area you're trying to fish—and that he fishes while steering the boat. You can't really tell what's going on with the lure or changes in depth, bottom content or current unless you're controlling the motor and hand-holding a rod at the same time.

Another big benefit to holding the rod—it's easier to pump the rodtip every few seconds to trigger strikes from fish that are following the bait but are reluctant to hit. I do it continuously.

Erratic movement trips predators' triggers. I learned this long ago in northern Canada, when I could see lake trout shadowing my spoon but they wouldn't strike. First one fish tagged along behind the spoon, then another and another, until I had a veritable parade going just behind my treble. I'm sure the

Trolling isn't Dahlberg's first choice of fishing methods, but under many conditions and for a wide variety of fish (shown with giant lake trout), it's the deadliest.

lakers would have followed me all the way back to camp—had I not jerked the rod ahead. The instant the lure sped up, a fish attacked. Same pattern worked all day, and continues to work today.

Sometimes a slow glide-pause-glide cadence with a super-size jerkbait will outfish other presentations for lure-shy fish like big muskies, pike and stripers. Trouble is, to get a jerkbait to run more than a few feet below the surface, many anglers weigh it down with enough lead to sink a battleship. That kills the pause.

To achieve running depths of 10 to 15 feet without ruining a bait's action, I put a 20-foot section of 45-pound-test lead-core about an arm's length ahead of the lure. You need a "soft" line in between the lure and the 'core so the lure can glide or rise when it stops or slows down after you stroke it.

Walleyes scattered along the top and edges of a flat are also prime targets for trolling. You can catch them by fishing the break with a spinner rig behind a heavy pencil sinker (up to 3 ounces or so, depending on depth). But if you really want to do some damage, try a technique I call the "Walleye Picker."

It works best with six anglers in the boat. All six fish three-way spinner rigs, but differences in rod length and rig weighting keep everyone from getting tangled up. The two up front wield 5- to 5½-foot rods, and 2 to 3 ounces of weight. The middle guys hold 7-foot sticks and use 1 to 1½ ounces of weight. The cleanup crew gets 7- to 9-foot rods, ¾-ounce weights and snell floats.

Despite being last, the rearward lines are often the "luckiest." They have the lightest sinkers, so they're farther behind the boat. Plus, the inside line will stall on a turn (hence the float, which keeps the bait off the bottom). As a result, they pick up a lot of bites from walleyes that aren't aggressive enough to chase the lead spinners.

I must admit, it would drive me crazy to troll all the time. But messing around with different approaches and studying the techniques used by anglers for different species all over the world makes it extremely interesting—and also satisfying, when all the elements fall into place. One last suggestion, if you get hooked on speed-trolling because of its effectiveness, be sure to scrape the bugs off your teeth before you go home. 🐟

WHAT DO WE REALLY KNOW ABOUT
SPEED?

There are times we need to speed things up.

by Capt. Chip Porter

Speed is one of the great false boundaries in fishing. I say false because tradition, not the fish we pursue, created the limits that govern the trolling and casting presentations of millions of anglers.

Do these speed limits make sense? Could we catch more and bigger fish by trolling and retrieving our baits faster than we ever thought possible? Speed may not be the next radical breakthrough in fishing, but judging from the success of anglers living in the fast lane, it's a subject that deserves a closer look.

Major Myths

If one were to look at the source of most fishing knowledge, it becomes apparent that much of what we "know" was gained in reverse of proven scientific methods. Whereas science will try to remain open-minded in its search for answers, fishermen tend to have the answer first, pass it down over several generations to solidly implant it in our heritage, then wait for someone to disprove our conclusions. The problem with this methodology is that we never learn what is really true, only eliminate things proven to be false.

Before we disembowel the speed myth, it's imperative that you open your mind. Don't carry with you the lore of generations past, grizzled and wizened though it appears. Instead, ponder how Jules Verne wrote *20,000 Leagues Under The Sea* 100 years before the advent of the submarine, and you'll be somewhere nearer a mind-expanding Timothy Leary explanation of fish and speed.

Fast Bass

Tournaments, especially at the highest levels, give us the opportunity to pit our best fish-catching theories against the greatest minds in fishing. Bass anglers who call themselves "power fishermen" know the benefits of speed, but do they really know the upper limit, or are they limited by their tackle?

For example, top pro Mark Menendez recalls a tournament where the wind started to buck early one afternoon. He abandoned his dock-fishing pattern in favor of a windswept main-lake point.

"I was at Lake Martin in Alabama, whipping a Riverside Counter Attack spinnerbait and cranking a 7:1 reel as fast as I could. The fish were attacking the spinnerbait so wildly that I had to add a trailer hook to increase my hookups," he says. The net result?

Truth About Reel Speed

Casting or spinning, two factors govern how fast a reel picks up line—gear ratio and inches-per-turn (IPT). For greater speed, conventional wisdom says to go with the reel that has a higher gear ratio—7:1 versus 3:1, for example. There is, however, more to it. Speed also depends on the reel's full-spool diameter. A high-speed reel with a thin-diameter spool can actually be slower than a lower-geared model with a larger spool. For example, Abu Garcia's Cardinal Agenda 6 spinning reel has a 5.8:1 gear ratio, compared to the 6.3:1 ratio of the company's Ultra Cast T Pro 3000. Yet, the Cardinal wins speed trials hands down. It retrieves 37.15 inches of line with every turn of its handle, versus 22.25 IPT for the Ultra Cast, thanks to a full-spool size of 2.04 inches. The Ultra Cast's spool measures just 1.125 inches.

If the manufacturer doesn't supply the IPT number (few, if any, do), figure it out yourself by measuring the amount of line it collects when you turn the reel handle one revolution. Or, if you know the gear ratio and full-spool diameter, use the following formula: spool diameter x 3.14 x gear ratio = inches per turn. Once you know a reel's IPT, you can determine how fast your bait will move based on retrieve speed. If you crank three turns per second with a 24-IPT reel, your lure will travel six feet per second, or roughly 4 mph. That's significantly less than the top end "burst speed" fish use to capture escaping prey.

—Dan Johnson

Menendez scored over 20 pounds of spots in 40 minutes, the largest an ounce shy of 6 pounds.

"I wish I could have made that bait go faster," he grins. "I'm sure I would have made more casts and caught more fish."

Putting the hammer down for bass generally calls for a few modifications or specific baits. My favorite speed lures are finely tuned lipless rattlebaits like the Rat-L-Trap and Cordell Spot. To fish a spinnerbait deep and fast, use a willow-leaf blade and pinch a dog-eared sinker to the lower arm. If you're jigging, bump up the weight a notch.

Few know the benefits of keeping an open mind about presentation better than Field Editor Spence Petros. He's a champion at "staying loose" and trying various methods until he hits a hot pattern. It's no surprise, then, that he often breaks the speed limit when fishing bass.

"My first experience with high-speed fishing was years ago on Taylor Creek Reservoir in Florida," he says. "I was trolling a Spoonplug down a man-made channel between two basins. My first passes produced nothing, so I kicked my speed up a notch, then another. When that failed, I cranked in my lure while the boat was traveling about 5 mph. Bang, a nice bass hit. I ended up catching a bunch of good fish by fishing, maybe 6 mph, from an area where I couldn't catch anything by fishing slowly."

Petros admits the conditions that day were ripe for aggressive fish—the tail-end of a week of warm, stable weather. But, he's had similar experiences in conditions most anglers wouldn't dream of fishing a fast-moving lure.

"One March, I was fishing pre-spawn bass on an Illinois Lake. I was finessing plastic worms and slow-rolling spinnerbaits in a shallow bay that typically warmed up fast—but the water was still in the high 40s. Plus, there was a major cold front and the weather was rotten.

"I struck out until I saw a 12-year-old kid casting a Rapala from shore. He worked it fast and was catching bass."

When Petros fished a minnow bait quickly, the bass responded.

"I caught more than a dozen fish from 2 to 4½ pounds," he says. "Every few fish, I'd try a worm or slow-roll a spinnerbait, just to see, and caught nothing. It proves you should never pigeon-hole presentations to specific conditions."

High-Speed Steel

Bass aren't the only fish that occasionally like it fast. As first broken here in the pages of *North American Fisherman* three years ago ("Trolling On The Cutting Edge," July 1998), Great Lakes anglers have applied red-line tactics for spring and summer steelhead, which many anglers consider our fastest freshwater predator.

While trolling speeds of around 2.6 to 2.9 mph are common for most salmonids, some top steelheaders targeting open-water temperature breaks cruise these surface slicks at speeds of 7 mph and up.

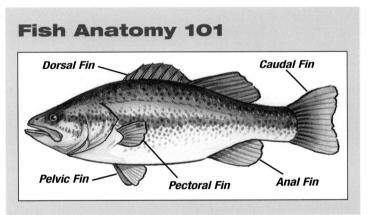

Fish Anatomy 101

Dorsal Fin
Caudal Fin
Pelvic Fin
Pectoral Fin
Anal Fin

Built For Speed

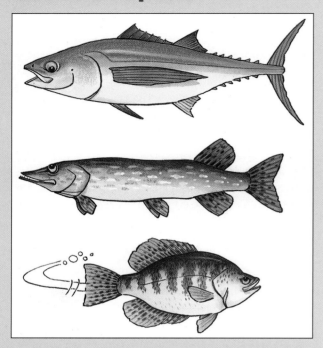

Much of a fish's top speed and mobility are determined by the shape of its body and fins. For example, the narrow, muscular posterior (peduncle) and thin, sickle-like caudal fin of the tuna (top), a high-speed cruiser, create powerful swimming strokes and offer little drag in the water. Fish with long, narrow bodies like northern pike (center), are mid-range on the speed spectrum. Their elongated frame and broad, powerful tail are good for quick bursts of speed, but they lack a high, sustained top end, and are not highly maneuverable in tight quarters. On the station-wagon end of the spectrum, fish in the centrarchid family, like the crappie (bottom), have broad, compressed bodies that offer great maneuverability, but poor top-end or sustained speed. The broad tail and peduncle, however, are good for quick, powerful bursts attacking prey or avoiding predators.

The trick is finding baits that run fast and true. Dodgers or spoons aren't options at speeds over 4.5 mph. Neither are most crankbaits. The Rebel Fastrac is the most productive speed lure I've seen to date, although the tight-vibrating Cordell Spot holds its form well, too.

My typical high-speed steelie spread consists of two flatlines off the stern, and four lines on Yellow Bird side planers off each side of the boat. The outside line will have about 80 feet of letback, a ⅜-ounce bead-chain sinker and 6-foot leader.

As I move inside, each Bird will have slightly less letback (down to maybe 15 feet on the inside line), along with an extra sinker to add depth. Flatlines trail 100 to 150 yards behind the boat.

Riders On The Storm

We all know that a falling barometer usually creates a feeding opportunity of gigantic proportions. Muskie expert Jim Saric, a man who in Y2K boated 10 gargantuan fish over 50 inches, explains.

"Anytime a peak feeding window exists, I want to fish my best spots quickly and thoroughly. The fish will be eating everything in sight, so all I need to do is put a bait in front of them."

A prime time to exceed the speed limit is when muskies and other predators are cruising a large structural element. "Under these conditions, you can't move a bait fast enough," says Saric. "Even with today's equipment, we're not capable of reeling a bait faster than a fish that wants to attack it."

Extra speed can be achieved by trolling, as long the lures don't blow out. DepthRaiders, Jakes and the Bagley DB-06 are all good options for muskies. Some trollers, like muskie expert Dale Wiley, custom build baits that handle speeds most anglers consider excessive.

"I hardly ever go less than 5 mph," he says. "Most days it's upwards of that."

That's straight ahead speed. Wiley can cite hundreds of examples of when, by turning the boat, he increased the speed of his outside bait and caught fish.

Speedy 'Eyes

Then there's the walleye, a fish that many anglers consider lazy. The myth here is that walleyes are slow, lethargic and need to be finessed into biting. Top pro John Campbell, past winner of Masters Walleye Circuit (MWC) Team of the Year honors and currently number three on the all-time walleye pro money list, has made a living out of blowing by other competitors. Literally.

"At times I kick up my speed, particularly during warming trends when the water goes higher than 60 degrees," he says. One such example occurred during an MWC tournament on Big Stone Lake along the Minnesota/South Dakota border.

"My partner and I were trolling twice as fast as the other competitors," he recalls. "We were in a shallow basin, doing 3 to 4 mph with crankbaits on planer boards. The area was crowded with boats, so making radical turns—further increasing speed on the outside lures—was the order of the day."

Campbell and his partner boated 63 walleyes, many on the outside lures during sharp turns. The speed of those baits was completely off the scale of what most walleye fishermen consider acceptable.

"Thing was," he continues, "water clarity was only about five inches. Yet, when we blew baits past the fish, they homed in and overtook them."

Walleyes hit fast baits in clear water, too, Campbell says. "The same thing happened during a tournament on Lake Huron's Saginaw Bay. It was pretty much the same situation, only the water was gin clear. I was trolling faster than the other guys, twisting and turning, and triggering bigger fish than anybody else."

Like Campbell, I've enjoyed similar success speed-trolling walleyes. My go-to lures are 24A Bombers and Smithwick Deep Rogues. You can also

Cruisers And Accelerators

Compared to birds and some terrestrial animals, fish are slow. Most fish that anglers seek with fast-moving plugs—trout, bass and a long list of saltwater creatures—can sustain swimming speeds equal to about 0.5 to 2 body lengths per second. That means an 18-inch fish can maintain a sustained, energy-efficient speed of anywhere from .5 mph to slightly more than 2 mph, while a 36-inch fish swims at speeds between 2 and 4 mph. Note: this is not a bait-catching sprint.

"Burst speed" is more relevant to capturing prey. Burst speed—how fast a fish can move for 10 seconds—is usually about five to 10 body lengths per second. So an 18-inch fish can run down prey at speeds between 5 and 10 mph; a 36-inch fish has a theoretical burst speed somewhere between 10 and 20 mph! That's upwards of four times faster than anyone can reel with equipment available today. Although fish have various gaits that help increase efficiency when swimming at different speeds, they have to give up a few things to get others. For example, tuna—the speed champs of the fish world—are designed for high-speed cruising. The circular body (cross-section) maximizes muscle mass with minimum surface area—thus, less frictional resistance. But speed is gained at the expense of maneuverability and acceleration.

"Accelerators" have broad caudal fins and a deep, elongated body, or at least a relatively deep profile along the posterior third of the body. Fish like trout, pike and bass are good accelerators.

To catch prey, or to avoid being prey, fish are concerned with high-speed maneuverability—what biologists call "agility." Agility results from the body pushing against the water. Therefore, a deep body and broad dorsal, anal and caudal fins mean more agility. A short, deep body like that of a bluegill also means a tighter turning radius, plus faster stops and starts.

How fish swim, where they live and how they feed are closely interrelated. Most accelerators feed by hiding at the edge of cover and ambushing their prey. Agile fish often live deep in cover where their maneuverability allows them to capture small food items and escape less-agile predators.

"Cruisers" give up acceleration and agility for speed. These fish need open water and prey that can be "run down" in structureless habitat. However, some of the cruisers' prey are deep-bodied fish with good acceleration and agility. In response, fish like tuna and striped bass often team up to corral agile baitfish, canceling the agility advantage.

—*Dr. Hal Schramm*

---

add weight to a spinner rig and switch to an "open-water" willow-leaf blade, or beef up leadhead size from ⅛ to ¼ ounce to pick up the pace.

When To Speed Up

How fast should you fish bass, stripers, muskies, trout, walleyes and other gamefish? Depends on the situation. The last thing I want is all half-million of us NAFC members tearing up the water at 10 mph all the time. But there are times when faster is better.

Aggressive fish are top candidates for speed presentations, and there's no magic involved in determining their mood. If you cast a jig along a 10-foot weed edge and a bass inhales it five feet off bottom, you're probably dealing with aggressive fish. The same thing is true if a bass swallows your crankbait to the knot.

Sometimes tough-bite situations call for a little speed, too. When a major front hits and you're facing high, clear skies and sluggish fish, cover water and play the odds—sooner or later your bait will cross paths with a fish that's ready to turn on. Cover enough water and you'll catch more than the guy who fishes one spot all day.

When someone can finally come to the table and tell us how quickly an 8-pound bass or 30-pound striper can travel (see "Cruisers And Accelerators" side-

bar above), I believe it's going to blow our minds to the point of completely rethinking our tackle, baits and techniques.

Red-lining isn't the approach in every situation. Some days, slower is best. On others, speed is more effective than sluggish presentations. Push the envelope.

Rome wasn't built in a day, and neither was the lore handed down by our fishing forefathers. The scary thing is that parts of Rome are still standing today. We need to revisit what we "know" and put those ancient conclusions to the test. We may be fishing too slow. In fact, in many cases, I am sure of it.

PSST...Do the little things right and you'll catch more fish.

Spence Speaks

Note: For the past 29 years, Spence has taught thousands how to fish through his seminars and classes. Having sat through some of them myself, I know the value of his messages. His seminars taught me things that I had not learned during a lifetime of fishing. Because of him, I have successfully changed some of my fishing mechanics.

This feature is not going to blow you away. The average NAFC member fishes 72 days a year, nearly double the average angler, and an article on fishing basics seems absurd. Then again, revisiting your fishing fundamentals is not a bad thing. You may find, as I did, that you could benefit by making some adjustments.

—*Steve Pennaz, Executive Director–NAFC*

Boat Control

Spence says: Get in the right position to catch more fish!

It's not a glamorous topic, but boat control is one of the most important facets of fishing, particularly when you're targeting specific pieces of cover or structure. Here's how I typically approach common fishing situations.

MOVING IN—Good boat control starts with motoring into your fishing spot. For example, when approaching shallow cover, do so perpendicularly to prevent boat wake from washing over fish. Shut down your outboard short of the cover and run your electric motor the final few yards.

DRIFT, IF YOU CAN—If you can fish a spot by silently drifting, do it, especially if you're targeting big fish. To slow drift speed, use a drift sock. My second choice is a controlled drift where I make periodic corrections with my electric motor. If I need to use the electric a lot, I keep it running at a low, steady hum. This will spook fewer fish than short, powerful bursts—especially in close quarters.

ON EDGE—Fish into the wind when working along edges or tough-to-work pieces of cover and structure, especially those that are submerged. That way, when you need to make a quick adjustment in boat position or your tackle, you can simply kill the motor and fall back, rather than drifting past or over a potential hotspot.

More Facts:

1. Look for areas where the wind is blowing directly into the weedline, which tends to concentrate the fish.

2. I typically fish about half a cast length from the weed edge and make long, quartering casts to the cover.

3. Toward the end of each cast, say, when a bait that's running at nine feet moves up to seven, give the lure a sharp, upward rip. This often converts follows into strikes.

4. To feel the weeds and get rock-solid hooksets, I use low-stretch superline—either a braid or FireLine.

5. When fishing points and inside corners, I often fire casts into deep water to check for suspended fish.

6. After casting a weedline, I often turn around and troll it at 2.5 to 6 mph, occasionally sweeping the rod to help trigger strikes. You'll often pick up bonus fish that casting missed.

Improve Your Hooksets

Spence says: Correctly position your feet and you'll catch more fish!

Unless you're using a circle hook, a solid hookset is critical to success, especially with hard-mouthed species or when you need to drive a hook through a thick plastic bait. And, like any other technical aspect of the sport, there's a right and a wrong way to do it.

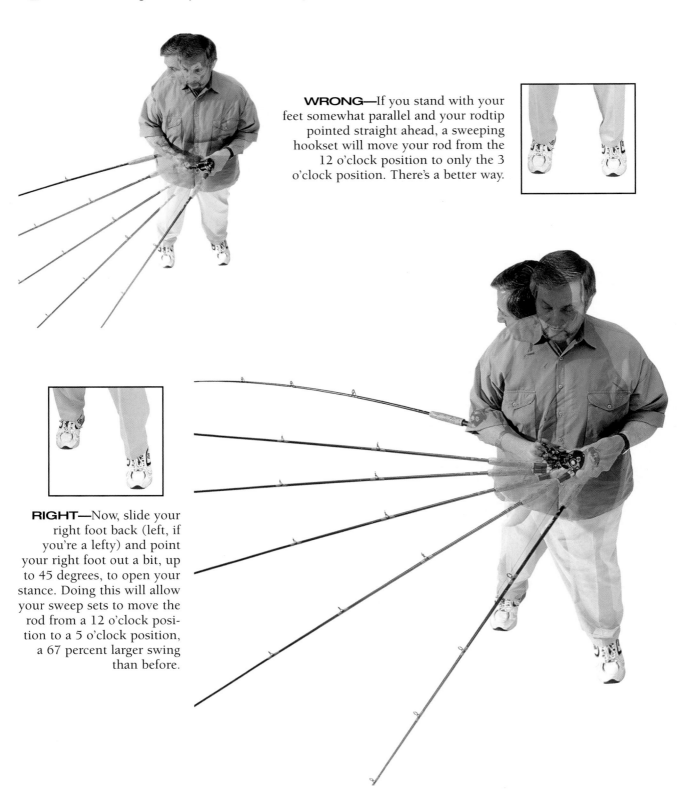

WRONG—If you stand with your feet somewhat parallel and your rodtip pointed straight ahead, a sweeping hookset will move your rod from the 12 o'clock position to only the 3 o'clock position. There's a better way.

RIGHT—Now, slide your right foot back (left, if you're a lefty) and point your right foot out a bit, up to 45 degrees, to open your stance. Doing this will allow your sweep sets to move the rod from a 12 o'clock position to a 5 o'clock position, a 67 percent larger swing than before.

SET—Most of the time, I use a sideways "sweep" set as it not only tends to bury the hook in the corner of the fish's mouth, it also keeps the fish's head down, thereby reducing the chance it will jump. In general, I set only once, but I will set again if I feel my first set didn't do the job.

More Facts:

1. Match hooksets to the line, rod action, lure and species of fish. For example, if you're fishing with monofilament, use a long, hard, sweeping hookset.

2. When fishing a low-stretch superline, use a forgiving rod with flex in the tip, and tone down your hooksets. Avoid the temptation to cross the fish's eyes.

3. For solid hooksets while trolling with mono, screw the reel's drag down tight (near the line's break strength); with superline, use a looser drag setting.

Sharpen Hooks Right

Spence says: Sharp hooks mean more fish.

Sharp hooks are critical to solid hooksets. Some premium, high-carbon hooks hold their points well (and may actually be damaged by sharpening), but most hooks—especially large ones—need occasional touch-ups. The following two-file method gives me the sharpest point in the shortest amount of time.

INSIDE JOB—Using a flat-sided file (Luhr-Jensen and South Bend both make good ones), sharpen both sides from the top to create a V-shaped, knife-edge cutting surface.

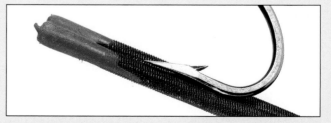

FINISHING TOUCH—To remove any burrs that could hamper your hookset, sharpen both sides of the point up to the barb with a double-cylinder file.

Snap Casting

Spence says: This makes casting almost effortless, even with big baits.

Snap casting works with moderately stiff spinning or casting rods with at least 7 to 8 inches of butt below the reel seat. The technique is less tiring than one-hand or sloppy two-hand casts, plus it gives you lower trajectory, more distance and better accuracy.

LOCK AND LOAD—Grasp the rod butt with your left hand and wrap your right hand around the reel seat. Open bail (spinning) or hit free-spool (baitcaster). Swing the rod back to about the 10 o'clock position using your right arm (for right handers) and begin forward motion.

BOMBS AWAY—As you drive the rodtip forward with your right arm, simultaneously pull the rod butt toward your chest using your left hand. Release the line before you reach the 2 o'clock position.

More Facts:

1. Avoid lofty, rainbow-arched casts, in which the bait hits the water hard, creating lag time before the retrieve can take up the slack.

2. When fishing casting tackle, shift the rod from your casting hand to retrieve hand before the bait lands.

3. To increase accuracy and soften splashdown at the end of the cast, lightly feather the line with your finger (spinning reels) or thumb (casting reels).

4. To further limit the delay between landing and retrieve, engage the reel just before the lure hits the water, then either lift the rodtip or begin reeling.

5. Keep the reel's spool almost full. A half-empty spool reduces distance and accuracy.

6. If pinpoint casts are necessary, choose a rod with a little flex in the tip. Stiffer sticks tend to spray lures around targets, which can dramatically reduce your success.

Fighting Fish

Spence says: Backreeling is often your best bet in freshwater.

A properly set drag is essential, especially when fishing saltwater species capable of lightning-fast runs. When targeting most freshwater species with spinning gear, however, I generally backreel. Doing so reduces line twist and friction, both of which reduce line strength. Backreeling also gives me more precise control during headshakes, runs and jumps.

SHORT BURSTS—Control quick, brief runs by palming the rotating reel handle. Be ready to stop the reel handle immediately when the fish quits taking line, to avoid tangles.

GOING THE DISTANCE—When a big, powerful fish makes a long, hard run, it's easier to control the situation by applying the brakes with your fingertips.

Get The Facts:

1. Fish lightly hooked on the side of the mouth facing you must be played gently. Lighten the drag or even freespool line during runs. Take line in only when you're sure the fish isn't going to make a run.

2. If the fish is hooked on the opposite side of the mouth, keep your rodtip low and the pressure on.

3. Never reel a fish close to the rodtip. Make sure the line from the tip to the fish is at least the length of the rod.

4. Lead fish into a landing net headfirst, unless exposed hooks are likely to tangle in net mesh (if so, take fish from side).

5. Always rinse your net after landing a fish. Nets stored with slime on them may attract mice that gnaw on the mesh.

Keeping Notes

Spence says: A journal helps you develop successful patterns.

K eeping a journal or fishing diary is a great way to hone your ability to capitalize on ideal conditions and avoid repeating past mistakes. Years of entries have helped me identify seasonal peaks and must-fish conditions. Plus, my notes also suggest the best presentations for each situation. For example, my fishing log helped me understand that pre-spawn bass in my favorite local waters will often knock the paint off fast-moving lures. Once the water temperature reaches the low 60s, however, slower, finesse presentations are usually necessary to catch the bigger females. Without my journal, I would never have recognized this pattern.

WRITING RIGHT—You don't have to be Shakespeare to write a journal. Simply jot down pertinent information about each fishing trip, including: date, time fished, water clarity, water temperature, weather conditions, fishing methods, areas fished, species caught and other useful details.

There are many peak-fishing situations, and even more that make fishing tougher. The trick is to keep an open mind, keep records until you get the feel for things, and be as mechanically perfect as possible on the water. In the end there is no one big secret; success is just a matter of doing a lot of little things right.

To attend a Spence seminar, visit: www.spencepetros.com.

Tricks for Small Rivers

DAHLBERG, THE QUINTESSENTIAL RIVER RAT, SPILLS HIS HARD-WON RIVER SECRETS.

by Larry Dahlberg

In much of the country, a small to medium-size river offers the last refuge to an angler trying to escape the crowds. Often, it's the kind of place where you have dozens of spots that you, and you alone, fish. It's my favorite scenario.

Rivers are tricky, though, so it pays to have a few tricks of your own. For instance, most river fishermen limit themselves to just a few key holes. What I call key holes are the largest, deepest ones in the river. This approach runs hot and cold. The key holes are always capable of holding good numbers of resident fish. Most load up with migratory fish during seasonal transitions as well.

The problem is, even on relatively "untouched" rivers, the key holes get fished hard. In most cases, the resident fish get more and more plucked over as the season wears on. Some fish are taken home and eaten. Some die from post-release mortality. Those that are caught and released again and again get smart to the program. The hole gets tougher and tougher until a seasonal movement, or monumental change in water level, reshuffles the deck.

And let's face it, most of the time, most of the fish are dispersed throughout the rest of the river system anyway.

A better strategy is to look at larger sections of river, with the thought of fishing greater numbers of smaller pockets and finding ways to access the places that are lightly fished. A good distance-per-day figure, if you're just floating and fishing banks, is about 12 miles per day. That's a lot of casts, but well worth it!

Using a map, I like to find stretches with the most bends, or S-curves, per mile. I also look for the narrowest areas in a given stretch, since they're usually the deepest, which along with sloughs and oxbows, can be very important.

Boiling it down, there are seven basic types of places to fish in a small to medium-size river: outside bends; inside bends; pools/holes/runs; tailouts; tributaries; sloughs and oxbows; and islands. Each type of habitat takes on importance under various water conditions and throughout different seasons.

Outside Bends

Outside bends are places where the current flow, or channel, is forced against the bank. These could be rock, sand or clay. They can appear quite flat (especially in low water) but are more likely steep, or even feature a reverse undercut. Some of my favorites bristle with log piles, roots or other obstructions. Others have rock points or large boulders projecting outward, creating feeding lanes and eddies. Always start at the very top of an outside bend and work it all the way downriver until it begins to get shallow.

I prefer to fish outside bends during normal and low-water conditions. In times of high water, I usually avoid all but the very top end, where there can be a small eddy of water, just above where the water begins to get deep, that collects baitfish attempting to find refuge from the increasing current.

Current naturally picks up on outside bends and as a result, most anglers move too quickly past these prime banks. Boat control is critical. The natural effect of the current will be to suck you closer to shore. Compensate for this by using a bow-mount trolling motor, or some other method, to keep the bow oriented upstream and pointed just slightly out from parallel. You want to be moving slower than the current so you can get a cast tight to the bank and next to every piece of cover. You'll catch more fish by presenting your lure or bait so it travels at a slight downstream angle. I like to use jigs, fast-diving crankbaits, topwater lures and minnow baits in these places.

To fish deep brush piles and avoid getting hung up, you may have to cast above the cover while keeping the boat stationary, then let the current swing the lure or bait in a quartering motion to the cover. Be sure to slow your retrieve to a crawl, or stop it altogether, as the lure begins to swing. Use a long rod to help keep your line off the water.

Minn Kota's Autopilot electric is a great aid to a river fisherman because it keeps the bow oriented properly without having to think much about it. Another good trick is to use a section of old inner tube for a drag anchor off the bow. Just tie one end shut, put a bunch of rocks in it and tie a rope on the other end. It will keep the boat oriented, and by lengthening or shortening the rope, you can control your speed. When

The River Patrol

When I was a kid, the biggest, fastest boat on the upper St. Croix River in western Wisconsin was my dad's Grumman sport canoe with a 7½-horse motor. Anything larger was suicidal because of all the snags and boulders. After spending 1,500 hours a summer for over a dozen years on the river, poking around with a push-pole and running small motors, I decided to get a 13-foot Boston Whaler with a short-shaft 35-horse. Later, I went to an even larger motor. I'd paid my dues, and in my lifetime had never as much as sheared a pin.

With this boat I could access the upper 50 miles of river above the camp where I guided. It enabled me to reach places that had seldom been fished at the prime part of the day.

At about this same time the river had been designated a National Scenic and Wild River. With that designation came canoers and campers. Although I was always polite, and never even came close to sinking any of them, they would always give me dirty looks (and sometimes worse) when I motored past. Even though I had the only motor of any size on the entire river, some paddlers thought the state should institute some sort of horsepower restriction, and deposited suggestion slips toward that end.

I argued that the river could protect itself, as was evidenced by the fact no one else had a fast boat. I knew I was fighting a losing battle and was losing sleep over what to do. One night I was startled from my sleep with an idea. I rushed to the hardware store that morning and bought a small paintbrush, can of black enamel and some stencils. I carefully stenciled RIVER PATROL on the side of my Whaler. Instead of giving me dirty looks and obscene gestures, the canoeists now smiled and waved, and checked to see if they had enough boat cushions. Sometimes I'd have to remind them to pick up their litter, or do a better job of extinguishing their campfires. They would rush to do so without complaint. I didn't get another horsepower grievance in the entire time I lived there.

Here comes Dahlberg—be sure to put out those campfires! With some paint and a little river-rat ingenuity, Dahlberg avoided conflicts with the anti-motor crowd and maintained his access to miles of river.

Tribs—When Water Is High

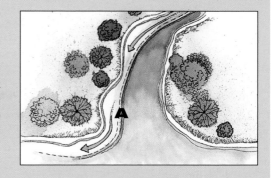

Main River Flooded...

When heavy rains hit the upper stem of the main river, but the tributaries still run clear, the heavy current from the main river can act as a "dam" and back water up into the mouth of the tributary. To escape the current, fish will move into the tributary (sometimes as much as a mile or two), and where the clearer water enters the main river. Focus on the clearest water you can find, both in the tributary itself and where it enters the river (A).

Flooded Tributary...

If a big rainfall hits the drainage of a tributary, but the main stem of the river receives less rain or none at all, the tributary might flow so hard it backs up water from the main river, creating an upstream pool (A). Fish the choppy water created by the backflow (B) and upstream (C) all the way up to the first shallows.

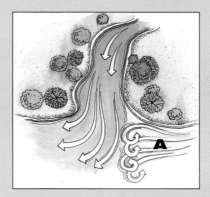

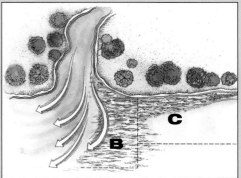

you're finished fishing, dump out the rocks, roll it up and store it.

On outside bends, the largest brush piles will usually have the deepest water under them and hold most of the fish. If you can't get fish to chase lures, try anchoring close to the bank, above the brush pile, and use a slip-sinker rig, jig or jig-and-spinner combo to walk live bait such as 'crawlers or minnows under the cover.

Rocky outside bends are a better bet during high and rising water. Their fishability increases if they have lots of irregularities to break the flow of the current.

Inside Bends

Inside bends aren't nearly as consistent a pattern as their outside-bend opposites, but sometimes they do pay off. Silt will often accumulate in these areas, which can create a flat with vegetation on it.

Inside bends that are just off the flow of current are usually better than those with no adjacent flow. In rivers where distinct sandbars form near current on inside bends, your odds are usually better. Fish will sometimes move from the deeper opposite bank to chase baitfish. Some species may even use these areas to spawn. I usually check them when the fish aren't where they're supposed to be. Nineteen times out of 20, however, inside bends will be a waste of time.

> *"Look at larger sections of river with the thought of fishing greater numbers of smaller pockets and finding ways to access the places that are lightly fished."*

Islands

Island banks that are oriented so the current runs against them can often be regarded in the same way as outside bends.

The heads of islands (upstream end) often have cover extending well upstream, sometimes a hundred yards or more. This is especially true of islands that were formed by sand building up on logjams and brush piles. This submerged cover could hold anything. In low, clear water I've seen giant schools of catfish in places like this. I've also caught hundreds of muskies from this kind of spot, not to mention walleyes and smallmouths.

Using The Grid System

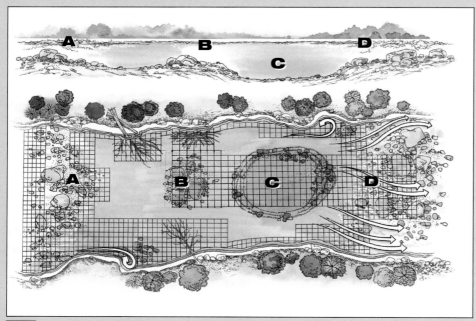

The diagram above lays out a typical hole in a small to midsize river. To fish it effectively, Dahlberg envisions a grid system over each key area, then tries to pass his bait or lure through every quadrant of that grid using multiple casts. He uses a 7½-foot rod to better control the presentation.

Four key areas include the head of the pool (A) where Dahlberg anchors and casts spinners or cranks, which he allows to swing in the current. In the middle section (B), Dahlberg again anchors, working precise drifts and retrieves though each quadrant. An upstream presentation is often best. The belly of the pool (C) takes less precision, but be sure to focus on the middle sections. Anchor, and always repeat any drift sequence that results in a strike. The tailout (D) often holds aggressive fish. Anchor upstream, then cast down and across, using the current to swing your bait through key areas. Of course, also fish the shorelines and be sure to probe any wood and eddies.

from anchor positions well to the outside, the second closer in. Pay special attention to current seams where the waters meet.

Tributaries are especially important during high water. If large amounts of rain fall in the upper stem of the river, but not in the drainages of a given tributary, the current from the main river might actually act as a dam of sorts and back water up into the mouth of the tributary. In this case, the tributary will usually be clearer than the main river and fish will hold back up inside it (sometimes a mile or more) and where the clearer water line makes its exit. In cases of extreme contrast, this clear water tail might hold fish for a great distance downstream from the tributary.

If the main rainfall hit the drainage of the tributary, and the main stem of the river has less rain or none at all, a different effect takes place. The tributary might flow so hard it backs up water from the main river, creating a pool above where it enters. Depending on configuration, there may be an eddy below it, too, which should always be checked, but odds are the water color will be bad.

I've had some of my best fishing after near flashflood conditions by running many, many miles of water and focusing exclusively on tributaries both large and small. We're talking 50-fish days catching smallmouths on topwater flies.

Often it takes a few days for fish to get oriented after the water takes a big jump. In extreme conditions, where water stays very high for a long period, you may even want to run the entire fishable length of the larger tribs. Focus your efforts on where the water clarity is best. Also, don't forget to check tributaries of tributaries.

The downstream point of an island always forms a natural current break. Fish usually hold along the sides, or downstream side, of where it breaks off. Often a patch of vegetation will form here as well.

Islands are significant most of the time, but take on a special importance during periods of high water, especially if the water isn't too dirty. Always add a few island stops to your route when tributary hopping during high-water periods.

Tributaries

Although tributaries are always important, they take on a special significance during the spawn (particularly for walleyes) and during very high water. Plus, if they are colder than the main river, they can be very important during the hot summer months. Use the same tactics you'd use other places, and again, anchor position is critical.

Start on the main river, above the mouth of the trib, then continue to move down at small increments. You may want to make two passes; the first

Pools And Runs

Depending on depth and current flow, these areas will usually hold fish during all water conditions. In super-low water, the fish may concentrate where it's deepest or where the most cover exists. In high water, they might be jammed in an eddy or tucked behind big boulders. Depending on the river (or section you're in), a deep pool might be only four or five feet deep, or it might be 15 feet deep. Depth is relative. The biggest and deepest have the best odds for catfish. They'll also hold sturgeon, muskies and the largest specimens of other species.

I like to carefully define the edges (inside, outside, top, bottom), visualize a grid over the surface, then position and reposition the boat with an anchor so I can swing my lures through every quadrant of the hole. Experiment by changing presentation angles. Some spots will produce best if you fish them from inside out; others, outside in. Usually you won't find fish spread all over. They will be in specific, consistent spots relating to cover in the form of boulders, ledges or wood. Once you pop a few fish and they slow down, try radically changing your lure color. Usually you'll get an extra fish or two.

If lures don't produce, try Texas rigging a live 'crawler or fish a large minnow on a short snell with as light an egg sinker as you can get away with. Fish it almost like you would a lure. Cast it, let it settle to the bottom, then slowly swing it through the area. This method is faster and usually much more productive than just tossing a bait out and hoping a fish finds it. Once you've located a pod of fish by casting, you may want to reposition directly above it in order to reduce your likelihood of snagging.

In super-low water conditions, I like to fish the fastest water at the top ends of pools, holes and runs. It's even better if there are sharp ledges and rock breaks for the fish to tuck under. You might have to anchor in dicey water or pull your boat up on a rock to stay in position. You may also have to make very short casts, or drop your bait just upstream from your target. Fish (especially walleyes) are sometimes very spooky in these areas when the water is low and clear. If I know a pool holds fish, I'll often park my boat above it and sneak down quietly on foot.

Not all pools are obvious, especially those found in long, relatively shallow stretches. The faster and more broken the surface water, the less depth it takes for a fish to feel secure. Look carefully for pockets and pools hidden between riffles in long, shallow stretches. They hold smallmouths and walleyes most of the summer.

Tailouts

Tailout is the term used to describe the tapering, shallower lip that occurs downstream from a deeper hole. Tailouts are always key areas for feeding fish. They have the potential to hold any species. I like to position so I can make long casts and swing my offering from one edge to the other. Spinners and crankbaits are great for this. Topwaters are a good choice, too, depending on the species you're after. If you're looking for cats, you'll want to be soaking bait in the tailouts of all the deeper pools.

Most tailouts have one or more funnels where the main flow of water is directed. The edges and center of the funnel are usually the best spots.

Sloughs And Oxbows

The mouths of sloughs and oxbows are always important places (see "Oxbow Crappies," page 90), especially if they are adjacent to other holding water. They have the same significance as tributaries during high-water periods.

Depending on their depth and configuration, sloughs and oxbows may operate like small, independent lakes and be significant much of the season. In almost every case, they are important spawning sites for some species. They are also important in the fall when cooler temperatures force the resident baitfish out into the main stem of the river.

Special Places

Small and midsize rivers offer peace, solitude and great fishing. You won't be able to locate fish by using your binoculars to spot the flashing and splashing aluminum nets. Most likely you won't even have access to a hydro map. But once you've defined the various sections, you'll be able to select the stretches that offer your best odds. They're intimate places that require time and careful observation. It's truly a discovery process, a process in which you may discover as much about yourself as you do about the river.

"Experiment by changing presentation angles. Some spots will produce best if you fish them from inside out; others, outside in. Usually you won't find fish spread all over."

LARRY'S WORLD

Enter the mind of perhaps the best angler on the planet.

by Larry Dahlberg

The world of angling is like a sphere perforated with a billion keyholes. Anglers gather at these keyholes, peering in for a glimpse of some truth that might help reduce the percentage of time they spend on the water in a disconnected existential drift hoping random chance will bestow good fortune upon them.

They are arguing. At one keyhole they're shouting, "Blue! The world of fishing is blue."

At another keyhole they're saying, "We catch more fish than you and we say the world is green."

They are all correct in their observations, but it could be said that they are looking only in two dimensions. In order to get a 3D view of what's going on in that sphere, one must peer through as many keyholes as possible.

This takes great effort. Does it pay dividends? Yes, but one caveat: Much more often than the statistical odds would dictate, the gods smile on an unwitting angler when he or she least expects it. It happens. We've all been there.

Unfortunately, if you're reading this, odds are if it hasn't happened already, it won't happen for you (see Dahlberg's Immutable Law of Angling). You are a hardcore fisherman. You have a boat and lots of gear. All the right stuff. You want it too badly. You deserve it. (The zen: "Inducing a big fish to bite is like picking up a wet bar of soap. The harder you try to grab, the farther it flies.")

The best way to make your own luck in fishing is to be thorough and efficient. Every great angler I've fished with in both fresh- or saltwater has an approach that involves three basic elements: strategy, mechanics and tactics. If you look at it broadly, all kinds of fishing can be broken down into those elements.

Start With Strategy

Strategy is your plan. It's based partly on the knowledge you have from previous success and partly on your current observations.

Some of the first questions I ask when developing a strategy:

What is the size of this lake or river? How much of it can I actually cover? How deep are the basins or channels? How far apart are they? Do shelves extend into them? Where did the fish spawn? Where are they now in relation to the spawn cycle? Is the water temperature fluctuating greatly from night to day? How clear is the water? What cover is available? At what depth do the deepest weeds root?

What about sand, rock, gravel, mud, steep cliffs, narrows, natural barriers, tributaries or changes in water color? Which way does the wind usually blow? Does it always blow like this? Where do you think the most or biggest fish are right now? Where did you catch your last fish? Do you have pictures of what you've caught? When did you catch them? How did you catch them? What time, what tide? How deep? Are there commercial fishermen here? What do they catch? Can I see their fish? May I talk with them?

How fast does our boat go? How much gas do we have? How far will that take us? Is gas available there? Can we take more gas? If I travel beyond that set of islands will those soldiers shoot at me? (I have asked this!) How far can they shoot accurately? Do they have a fast boat? Where can we get extra gas and an additional motor?

Putting together a solid strategy requires many questions and solid "no voodoo" type observations. It requires breaking these observations down into bite-size pieces while not losing sight of their relationships to one another.

The mechanics are much less existential. They aren't about questions, they're about possible solutions to prove or disprove assumptions you've made based on observations. Your mechanical skills determine the success with which you physically execute your strategy.

Mechanics

Day 1. If we use both motors simultaneously we can outrun any boat here, plus I won't be tripping over the spare and getting black goo all over my fly line. Given the fuel we can carry and our speed, the basin north of the islands is as far as we can go. We'll take off at dawn tomorrow, but right now let's mount the transducer on your boat and get it set so it reads at top speed.

Next day. It's foggy, but my GPS says the peninsula sticks out over there about a quarter-mile. Let's run this underwater point. We can check the depth and contours against the chart we bought.

Look at all the bait.

Look at those big hooks at 45 feet under the bait. Let's spool up with wire and egg sinkers, and drag an orange Rap past 'em.

When I hit neutral, let out your line. Use the clicker so you don't backlash but still thumb it. Let me know when it hits bottom. When we take off, let out just enough line so you keep bumping. I've got the transducer tilted forward a little so it'll look deeper on the screen, but we'll also see the suspended fish sooner in case we have to reel up and put the lure in their faces.

You don't have to set the hook because wire line is nonelastic.

That roller-tipped rod is so stiff you have to absorb the shock with your arms. I've added 5/0 4X hooks so they don't open up easily.

Double back. The points and inside turns on this underwater flat are so close together that all we can do is buzz the points and corners—lots of wasted effort. If we put a drift anchor off the bow and travel in reverse, we can hover right over the spots and turn on a dime. We'll jig spoons on top of them. When the line goes slack or you feel a tap, set the hook and reel like crazy.

Fish On. Let's move out over deep water so he doesn't cut you off on the ledge if he sounds. Short stroke him. Lift crank, lift crank. Don't stop at the top. Immediately after you lift, drop your tip and take one or two cranks as fast as you can. Without hesitating, pump back another foot or two and do it again. If he wants to run, let him run against the drag but don't reel. You can add a little heat with your thumb if you put your glove on.

I'll tail it so it doesn't get beat up in the net. Let's spin the boat upwind and move those rods. Where are the pliers? Hit the free spool and keep your thumb on the reel in case I can't hang on to him.

Nice fish!

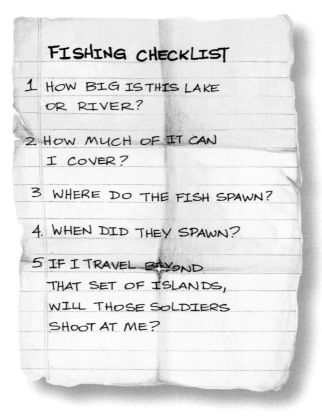

FISHING CHECKLIST

1 HOW BIG IS THIS LAKE OR RIVER?

2 HOW MUCH OF IT CAN I COVER?

3 WHERE DO THE FISH SPAWN?

4 WHEN DID THEY SPAWN?

5 IF I TRAVEL BEYOND THAT SET OF ISLANDS, WILL THOSE SOLDIERS SHOOT AT ME?

In summary, knots and rigging, boat control, fish fighting, choice of equipment and the skill with which you use it make up the mechanical aspects of fishing. All of these are things you can both practice and, more or less, control.

Tactical Decisions

Tactics are where most of the voodoo sneaks in. What lure? What color? What size? What should I do first? Here's how I approach it.

All fishing situations take one of two forms: Fish you can see or fish you can't see. In a totally foreign body of water, my strategy (and this could vary depending on species and season) is to look around in each of the different kinds of areas available to see what I can with my eyes. I like to visually scope out as much water as I can during my initial reconnaissance. I'll usually start looking shallow around major structures and working my way out over flats and edges until I can no longer see the bottom. I prefer to do it when the water is calm and the sun is shining. Viewing from a 10-foot stepladder secured to the bow of the boat with turnbuckles is more effective than viewing from lower angles.

Sometimes you get lucky and stumble on a mule. If you can physically see the fish, catching it becomes purely a matter of tactics and mechanics. Attract it, trigger it, hook it, land it. Avoid the psychological and physical pain of having to find a fish by making him bite.

As I said, if you can actually see the fish you're after, everything boils down to tactics and mechanics. The only challenge is to get the bait/lure/fly to the fish without scaring it. A fish that knows you're after it cannot be caught, another Immutable Law. If you spook the fish, don't cast again. Leave it alone until it settles down. You may have to come back in several hours.

Before it bites, watch the fish closely. How does it react to your presence? How does it react to your offering and what you're doing with it? Watch the gills. Watch the fins.

Speed, size, sink rate, color, angle, flash, buoyancy, bottom contact, action and sound can all play a part in triggering the fish. As the fish's mood changes, the triggering factors often change as well. Be quiet. Be sneaky. Be accurate. Come across in front of him and angling away. One good shot is all it takes. Read the fish.

There are many tricks, and the fish will teach them to you if you are observant. (Read "Lunkers Love Nightcrawlers," and other early works of Bill Binkelman for some interesting and pioneering underwater observations about how fish react to live bait.)

Fish You Can't See

If you can't see the fish, you've got to employ some kind of strategy for searching. The key in this is first accurately defining the options available to the fish. In natural lakes, I like to first locate the main basins, followed by locating the main structures related to them. Classify the relative sizes, depths and cover available. You'll need this information to search methodically and to establish patterns.

In rivers and reservoirs, I like to get a feel for where the channel is located and where and how deep the holes are. I also like to locate all natural barriers and tributaries if there are any. It's usually helpful to get a feeling as to the relative vertical drop, and note the places where the vertical drop goes from fast to slow or vice versa. I like to see at least 40 or 50 miles of water.

If possible I'll try to cruise the water from an airplane before getting in the boat. With the map in my lap and a GPS, I'll make notes. Mostly what I'm noting are physical features that appear unusual or differ-

ent. Giant rocks, gravel, sand, points, underwater shelves, flooded terrestrial cover, and wind-funneling geographical features.

As far as your specific approach, as I see it, you've got only about four options: 1. Trolling 2. Drifting 3. Flogging 4. Picking a spot and sitting on it.

Whatever you're going to do, look at all the spots. Give each a relative value based on how much life it can support.

When you fish each spot, be sure to clearly define the area first. It has a beginning and an ending. Pay attention to all the points and inside corners along the upper and lower edges of the drop-off. Note any variation in the steepness of the drop-off and how far it continues to drop into deep water before leveling out. Look for cover. Mark the edges and corners. I often use balloons for this.

Be precise. If you haven't read Buck Perry's book on spoonplugging, read it. One keyhole maybe, but it's pioneering work on using an efficient system to fish and define "structures."

Depending on depth, how large or detailed the area is, and how much time you have, systematically cover all the options with whatever tactic gives you the best efficiency. For me, especially on larger bodies of water, speed trolling and clanging into the bottom with the lure (sometimes using mono, at other times wire) has been universally effective. In blue-water environments, smoking a

"DAHLBERG'S IMMUTABLE LAW OF ANGLING"

Your odds of catching a big fish are inversely proportional to how much you actually deserve it.

Larry Dahlberg

Preventing A Fish From Rejecting A Bait Or Lure

Predators are famous for following and fading off artificial lures. Something wasn't right. Too big? Too Flashy? Moving too slowly? Here are a couple of good thumbnail rules for triggering predators.

1. The larger the lure, the easier it is for a fish to determine it's fake (this is especially true in clear water).

2. Most of our attempts to imitate a specific organism would be more successful if we worried more about what it "does" rather than exactly what it looks like.

3. Many times, rather than trying to "fool" a large predator by attempting to imitate some natural food, it's better to appeal to the fish's built-in "natural selection" instinct.

4. If you're fishing a twitch-type lure with a stop-and-go retrieve, take special note of what the lure does when you stop it. A lure that rises in reverse when you stop the retrieve will often cause a fish to fade. With Mag Raps, I cut the plastic bill off where it says "Rapala" to prevent the lure from doing this. Also, a lure that sinks tail down rather than level or head down is more likely to cause a fish to fade.

5. When a predator fades off a live bait it's usually because the hook is too big or the bait is not healthy. I've seen farm-raised bait ignored when it did not react defensively to the presence of a predator. I believe it's not one-tenth as effective as bait procured from the water you are fishing.

Larry—From Tyke To Tiger(fish)

Seed already planted, circa: late 1950s.

I was born in 1949. As I can clearly recall, and to which everyone who knew me then would attest, in about 1954 my obsessive, compulsive nature was directed toward fishing. By age 11, I was working full-time guiding smallmouth bass fly anglers on the upper St. Croix River in Wisconsin. Twenty-three years later, in the mid '80s, I was producing freshwater TV shows for *The In-Fisherman*. I started my current endeavor, *The Hunt for Big Fish*, now on ESPN2, in 1992. In the last nine years, I've traveled more than 250,000 miles per year (note: Larry's travel agent says 350,000 miles) trying to catch not just exotic fish, but the largest possible fish using the current world record as a barometer. My hope is to learn all I can about every kind of fish and every possible environment. I'm still trying to find out everything I can about all the different places big fish occupy. I want to peer through every keyhole that might reveal a fish large enough to be a problem once hooked.

Tigerfish—Zambezi River, Africa, circa: late 1990s.

lure on the surface at speeds up to 12 knots and keeping track with a GPS on a grid of the drop-off has proven successful.

If heavy cover or shallow water presents a problem, I like to bomb out super-long casts with lures that run on or near the surface while moving at trolling speed, or vertically fish soft plastics or live bait in the pockets on weedless hooks.

Buy the best electronics you can afford and pay close attention to them. I use a Lowrance LMS 350. I even carry it with me as a portable.

As you cover water, you're doing more detailed recon. In water less than 20 feet, I am thinking mostly about what my lure is doing horizontally as long as it's ticking bottom or being sexy on or near the surface. Focus on edges, tips of the points, inside corners and along the base of where any dense weedline roots or emerges in a canopy.

Moving deeper, you have to pay attention vertically. Instead of breaking an area into a 2D grid, you have to look at it like a 3D cube. Keep your eyes peeled for suspended stuff. You may have to modify your tactics to something slower or even vertical. You have to get your lure close enough to the fish that it is at least aware of it.

Sometimes you have to be within a few inches. Sometimes you have to keep it in his space, in his "zone of awareness," for a period of time before he will react. That's what bobbers are for.

Live bait is, of course, another great searching option. It is the ultimate reality check, and there are a million tactical variations. Most cover water more slowly than approaches with artificials.

Why Fish Bite

From the moment they begin feeding after they first hatch, fish are compulsive samplers. They will take a taste of something they have never before sampled if it exhibits the right cues. Early in life, almost every cue is the right one. As a fish gains experience

and receives negative feedback from certain choices, its sampling becomes more refined. I believe latent memories of organisms successfully sampled in the past remain even after a fish works its way up the food chain.

In essence, there are two distinctions:
1. Fish that eat insects.
2. Fish that eat other fish.

Insect Eaters

Early in life, almost all fish get their sustenance from the bottom of the food chain. They eat insects, zooplankton and other small, highly abundant organisms. Most of these organisms have a handful of common characteristics:
1. They are quite tiny and squirmy.
2. They swim, crawl or drift.
3. They are approximately the same color as their environment.
4. Most are highly vulnerable when "dead" drifting, and spend a good deal of time doing it.
5. Some struggle to swim a few inches per minute or can only crawl.
6. Some go only where the wind or current takes them.
7. Others are jet-propelled.
8. Many are in a complex process of grand metamorphosis on their way to becoming adults, and exhibit different behaviors as they transition from one stage to the next.

There is an interesting spatial element to insect feeders. It's about the cube of space in front of the fish's nose that is equivalent to the volume of water that passes through his gills when he takes a gulp.

If a fish is oriented in current and you cast a dark-colored, articulated (jointed) fly or jig just the right distance upstream for the fly to dead-drift into that cube of space in front of the fish's nose, 99 times out of 100 the fish will inhale it. It's like God tapped him on the shoulder and said, "Pal, this is a free meal, take a deep breath or you'll starve to death."

The problem is, when the fish takes the fly presented in this manner you feel nothing. You'll see a white flare of the gill but feel nothing because you are executing a drag-free drift. If the hook catches flesh and stops, current will put tension on the line and you'll feel "a bite." The fish's latent memory of eating tens of thousands of organisms such as this is so strong that the reaction is automatic. Unfortunately, fishing with this presentation is only effective for small areas or for fish you can actually see because it is so slow and tedious. I've found a dark-colored jointed jig or fly that is much larger than the actual insect is more visible to the fish and, if it exhibits the right visual cues, is often more effective than a smaller one.

Fish Eaters

As fish grow, many reach a size where they switch over from a diet of primarily insects to foraging on other fish. The predator/prey reactions when a larger predator fish chooses to eat one of its kin also have many common traits between species. Curiously, they are almost the opposite of what works for insect eaters.

Often predators in both fresh- and saltwater seemingly come out of nowhere rushing up to your lure or bait. Sometimes they take it, other times they fade at the last minute as if something isn't right. If they weren't going to eat it, why waste the energy? In the natural world this kind of behavior could lead to starvation. Introduce man, and this type of behavior is the only thing that keeps fish out of the frying pan. For sure something attracted their attention, but for some reason, some cue, or lack thereof, turned them off.

I've found the most common reason fish fade off lures is that, when the angler sees the fish, he or she puckers the poo poo and slows down the retrieve. At other times, the angler just keeps doing what he's been doing and doesn't react to the presence of the predator by changing lure speed or direction. Result? You get a looker instead of a biter. I've seen marlin, muskies, pike, tigerfish, peacock bass, Nile perch, tarpon, bass, payara and big trout exhibit this frustrating behavior.

Again, the key presentation trigger for a fish that eats other fish is just the opposite of what pushes the button of insect eaters. Rather than dead-drifting a bait like an insect, it's usually best for the prey (your lure) to appear as though it is reacting to the presence of the predator. No wonder trout fishermen often have trouble switching to bass or saltwater, and vice versa.

I mentioned the idea of sampling. Predators have an interesting quality in this regard. Most of the time, anglers think about trying to imitate a specific food fish are feeding on. Sometimes this works, sometimes not. Another approach is to appeal to predators' built-in "natural selection" program.

Natural selection is when a predator fulfills its role in nature by eliminating things that are weak, struggling, clearly out of place and vulnerable. Consider, for example, albinos. How many mature albino fish have you seen? The answer is not many. Most get gobbled up because they stick out like sore thumbs. One of my main go-to lures is an orange Rapala Magnum in sizes from 7 to 18. It may not outproduce a more "natural" color 10:1, but often it's 2:1. It's also a great bait for taking a couple more fish from a school after they've quit biting "normal" stuff.

Live Bait

Sometimes, when predators are lethargic, live-bait rigs have to be modified to make the bait hotter and more active. At other times, you want to set it up so you can cover water quickly. When fish are reluctant to leave cover or chase, sometimes you need to suspend live fish with a float and "anchor" it with a sinker above the hook so the bait can only swim in a circle the radius of the distance of the sinker to the hook.

At other times skipping live bait (head in the water, tail barely out, and swimming like crazy) from a kite will solve all problems. I like to bridle my bait with floss whenever possible because it stays alive and strong much longer than one impaled on a hook. Still, at other times, the most effective presentation is a hunk of dead bait on the bottom. Admittedly, this is no way to cover water, but it is a technique that can never be ignored.

Conclusion

Above all other things, the accuracy and scope of our observations on the water determines our angling success. As revelations about how these observations fit together filters through our consciousness, we are drawn into a great and mysterious labyrinth of possibilities that connect us more closely to the natural world. Each time a fish rises to our fly or takes our offered lure, it somehow proves more than that both we and the fish simply exist. Being able to predict these encounters with a degree of certainty somehow brings existential relief, even joy.

Fish a new lake. Fish a new place. Fish a new species. Try a new tactic. Peer through another keyhole. Allow yourself to explore. My last word of advice: guard carefully the secrets you discover if you want them to remain secret.

Detail Game

Strategy finds fish, but details catch fish.

You can find all the fish in the world, and have them more or less in the mood to hit. But if you don't take care of all the details correctly, you'll go home empty-handed (or, as one of the following stories covers, with a broken rod).

You simply cannot overlook the details of fishing if you expect to find consistent success.

Fortunately, in the course of a year, *North American Fisherman* covers many facets of fishing's detail game. Here are the stories.

LIVE
Dahlberg Holds

by Larry Dahlberg

s a former fly fishing guide of 20-plus years, professional fly tyer and television personality who's sponsored by Rapala, the world's largest manufacturer of artificial lures, the next statement may come as a surprise to you.

If it is presented properly, live bait is ALWAYS the most effective way to make a fish BITE.

Yes, I said ALWAYS. And I DIDN'T say hook or catch, I said BITE.

This story is about what I believe to be some of the most important observations I've made in a lifetime of angling. The few close friends with whom I fish begged me not to reveal some of this information. Yet, I promised Steve Pennaz I'd write a live-bait piece for *North American Fisherman*. I was tempted to leave a few things out, but I've decided to keep my promise to Steve. However, that promise must be accompanied by a promise from you.

This may sound melodramatic, but I have to ask anyone who reads this to promise me up front, on a proverbial stack of Bibles and his great grandmother's grave, that you will not employ any of these big-fish tactics unless you are using a non-offset circle hook. I really mean it. If you don't use a circle hook, there is a high likelihood the most spectacular creature you've ever hooked will die as a result of its encounter with you.

Early Encounters

My first live bait versus artificial revelation came early in life. My father, who started me ice fishing at age 4 and flailing a fly rod for bluegills not long afterward, was strictly an artificial lure man. What he liked best, and still does, is chucking a topwater lure against the bank with deadly accuracy and finessing it along heavy cover.

BAIT
NOTHING Back.

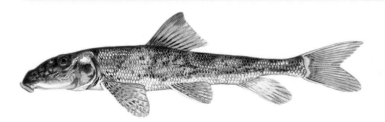

Grampa Louie, on my mother's side, had nearly a dozen kids to feed and was strictly a live-bait man. We'd anchor just upstream from where he figured the fish were and hammer them with huge, fat nightcrawlers he picked on the golf course and raised in a bathtub buried in the earth just outside his doorstep. The only words he ever spoke to me while fishing were "drop the anchor" or "pull up the anchor."

We'd catch more fish in one hole with worms than my dad and I would catch in 10 miles of river throwing artificials. To this day I truly believe the only reason he took me along was so he could legally keep twice as many fish. He was regionally famous for all the big sturgeon he caught. In fact, he almost single-handedly cleaned out what was left of the really big ones in Wisconsin's upper St. Croix during the '50s and '60s.

When he was targeting a big boy, Grampa Louie used 35-pound line and a size 2 ringed-eye O'Shaughnessy commercial setline hook loaded with two big 'crawlers. He'd fish it around major log piles adjacent to deep holes. He always used two lines. When he'd get hung up in a log, he'd just leave it there on a tight line and wait for a fish to find it. In fact, with one line he'd often get hung up on purpose, knowing sooner or later a sturgeon would swim by to suck insect larvae off the log and most likely find his double nightcrawler gob. When he wanted his hook back, he'd just pull and straighten it out. Good trick. Still works.

Frogs For Hawgs

When I was about 11, rumor got to me about some huge largemouths living under a cow bridge. When I looked into the clear water behind the log structure of the bridge, my eyes almost popped out. There rested half a dozen bass from 4 to over 6 pounds!

I threw spoons, my best yellow River Runt, two different colors of Bass-O-Renos. Fast, slow, downstream, sideways, upstream. Deep, shallow and in-between. Nothing worked. Nothing. (Rapalas hadn't been marketed yet, and plastic worms weren't available either.) I finally got one of the smallest ones to hit a Paul Bunyan 66 spinner burned at 15 mph across the pool.

Finally I resorted to my old standby. I quit fishing for a couple of minutes and caught a live green leopard frog. I put a hook through his nose, clamped a dog-eared sinker a foot and a half above it and lowered it into the water so it fell right in front of their noses. The moment I let go of him, the frog used both hands and feet, contorted in front of his nose, in an effort to gain leverage in the futile effort to pry himself off the hook. He was paying absolutely no attention to the bass. Their universal reaction to Mr. Frog's Houdini impression was to move off to the side and let him go by.

I flicked him in the noggin' with one finger to put him to sleep so he'd lay on the hook better. Then, I jigged my frog and diddled with the fish until I was convinced they weren't going to bite. In disgust I took the frog off the hook and tossed it into the river. It lay stunned for a second or two, then began swimming strongly for the shore. On its fifth kick the biggest bass in the school came roaring up off the bottom and engulfed it.

I learned a universal truth that day, and it colored the way I looked at fish, and fishing, forever. Live bait is best rigged in such way that it is not so impeded by the hook(s) or line that it fails to react to the presence of a predator.

Getting back to frogs, they are definitely great bait. It's too bad they're getting so scarce. I used to use them regularly to catch walleyes, catfish, largemouth bass and pike.

They are especially effective early in the year, at the end of winter hibernation, when fish pick them out of the mud. This usually happens in shallow, dark-bottom bays when the water first warms into the high '40s and low '50s. They are also deadly later in the year, fished like a pork rind on back of a jig. I've also had great success fishing them just off the bottom on live-bait rigs for big bass that wouldn't bite anything else.

You've probably heard the old-timers talk about fishing the "frog run" in late summer. It can be amazing. Big, hungry fish in very shallow water. It can actually happen twice. Once, after the frogs have hatched and matured and need to spread out to new territory; and again later when they move out of the ponds and grassy fields, back into the bays where they spend the winter.

Maybe the craziest "killer" frog tactic was something I discovered by accident as a kid. I had a frog that for some reason had become bloated in my pocket. He was frisky and perfectly fine except he looked like a marshmallow with eyes, arms and legs, and looked to be pushing 50 psi. I quickly snapped on a weedless hook, put it through the end of his nose and tossed him under a heavy canopy of vegetation at the confluence of a coldwater creek.

The frog struggled to get underwater but couldn't because he was full of air. Poor Kermit was going crazy on the surface trying to submerge when a 10-pound pike ate him. It was the most beautiful pike bite I had ever seen. The fish's eyes looked like Cat's Eye shooter marbles and it had an expression like a T-Rex.

I found I could replicate this amazingly effective tactic if I used a fine, hollow stem of dry grass to inflate the frog from the port side (there will not be a diagram or photo illustrating this). With the decline

Wild bait rules. The farm-raised sucker (right) is but a pale reflection of its wild-caught cousin (left).

Go Fly A Kite: Extreme Tactics, Extreme Results

Outriggers and planer boards are always good choices for increasing your spread and reducing problems caused by boat spooking, but the ultimate spread, in my opinion, comes from using a fishing kite. Think of it as an "uprigger." First developed for tuna in California in 1918 by a guy named Capt. Farnsworth, the kite is flown on its own short, stout rod rigged with 100-pound or stronger no-stretch line.

Thirty feet or so from the kite is the first of possibly several release clips, just like you'd see on a downrigger. On your main fishing line is a free-sliding swivel that you fasten to the kite's line clip.

When your partner lets out the kite, you let out your line and the kite carries the bait out with it. Since your line slides freely in the swivel, which is hooked to the release clip, you can govern how deep your bait runs. If you let out line, it can go as deep as it wants. If you crank in line, you can hoist the bait out of the water and all way up to the release clip.

At least two dozen boats were fishing a half-mile stretch on the north shore of Minnesota's Lake Mille Lacs and only a couple fish had been seen and none caught. Dahlberg and muskie guide Dave Bentley pulled into the area at 3 p.m. and before 4:30, experimenting with kites, had 18 muskies bite. This method is amazingly effective.

My favorite is to fly the kite out so it delivers the bait right to the doorstep. I then keep the bait right on the surface so its head and gills are in the water, but it kicks up a splash when it wiggles its tail and tries to swim.

I also troll along edges, flying the kite into the shallows or out over open water, alternately letting out and taking in line, which skips the bait along behind the kite. The reasons this works so well: 1. the bait is very visible to the fish; 2. you can take the bait away from a sniffer, causing neutral fish to get more excited; and 3. there is almost no terminal gear in the water—no line, no glare, no line drag on the bait. Deadly.

Editor's Note: AFTCO manufactures saltwater bait kites suitable for freshwater. Bass Pro Shops sells AFTCO's kite kits in its Offshore Angler catalog. For information, contact Bass Pro Shops: (800) BASS-PRO; www.basspro.com.

in frogs I suggest you use them only where they are plentiful, and if you can get them legally. If you decide to inflate one, take a lesson from Bill Clinton and don't inhale.

Unleash The 'Dogs

Waterdogs are one of the most potent of all live baits. You want the smaller, soft, greasy, little immature ones. Not the big, hard growlies just about ready to mature. You can fish them in all the same ways as you fish a frog. My favorite way to fish them is on the back of a jig like a giant piece of pork. They're effective on big bass after they've set up on deep weedlines and humps, especially in late summer and early fall. Every year I lived in Minnesota, I caught at least one largemouth over 7 pounds on a jig and waterdog. For big fish I focused on three different types of scenarios:

1. Outside bends and wood fishing in the lower two-thirds of small reservoirs.

2. Deep cabbage on major structures on super-clear lakes.

3. Lakes and pits designated and managed for trout, but where gamefish like pike and bass have snuck back in.

'Dogs are easy to keep alive and fun to fish with. I used to order them by the thousands and keep them in a big cattle watering tank with a cover on it, outdoors in the shade. With minimal care, even with dragging them back and forth from the lake, they'll last until the fish eat them.

Little Lobsters

Sometimes I seine-netted the spillways below small power dams and caught buckets of crawfish. Using them in the river with only marginal success, I finally climbed a tree so I could watch the fish as I tossed crawfish in the water to see how they reacted. I was amazed. If the crawfish assumed the kung fu fighting position, the bass would often just back up, or move over, and let it pass. But if the crawfish kicked his tail and tried to take off, it was curtains every time. Needless to say, a crawfish that was doubled up and twirling on a hook with a sinker dragging behind it was most often ignored. That is until the fish ate a few escaping crawfish and got "turned on." Then it didn't seem to matter. They'd bite almost anything that came by.

After they'd had their fill, the fish would start ignoring things again, but sometimes the last few crawfish that tried to escape would get eaten. I remember thinking to myself: "This is remarkable. The stimulus that triggers a bass to eat a crawfish isn't that the bait looks exactly like a crawfish; what matters is how the crawfish swims away and reacts to the presence of the bass." This is similar to the lesson I'd learned earlier with the frog.

I discovered that freelining crawfish with a tiny hook in the carapace worked a lot better than anchoring them to the bottom. Taking off the pinchers helped too, otherwise they walked around like a mountain climber with both hands on the rope.

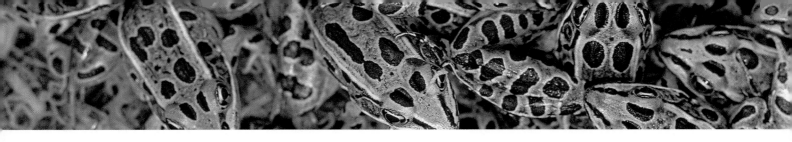

Born Free

One of the most startling observations I've made with live bait is noting the difference between wild bait versus farm-raised. You might think I'm crazy, but I've tested this on dozens of different occasions and in my mind there is no doubt that when the fishing is tough and you are for sure on fish, it makes a big difference.

What happens is, oftentimes, the farm-raised bait doesn't react as vigorously to the presence of a predator. Sometimes it doesn't react at all. I've seen huge pike and muskies swim up to a big farm-raised sucker and bump it with their noses when it didn't try to get away.

A farm-raised bait hasn't learned that predators are bad. It's been raised in an environment devoid of them. The wild sucker is still alive only because it has thus far been quick enough to escape the many predators it encountered every day.

To really test the difference, I bought a few dozen farm-raised suckers 4 to 5 inches long. They were packed in air, tempered to the water they were to be transferred to and fished in, then submerged in a constant flow of fresh water. I also seined a couple dozen wild suckers the same size from a shallow gravel channel behind an island. They were less slippery and much firmer feeling than their domestic brethren and were also leaner, with bigger heads for their length.

The water was dead low and crystal clear. It was almost a month after the opener. Nobody had caught walleyes for two weeks. All the community holes seemed devoid of fish. I slipped my flat-bottom river scow into position quietly with the oars and dropped the anchor.

I lip-hooked a farmie with a size 6 Kahle-style hook, added a couple medium shot and pitched it just up-current from where I knew the deepest slot in the swift, rocky run happened to be. Each cast I got braver, letting it sink deeper and go where it wanted, or where the current took it. A dozen casts produced nothing.

I replaced it with a wild sucker of the same size, and using the same hook and hooking it in the same manner, pitched it to the same spot. As the sucker was

sinking I felt soft thumps as it became startled and began to swim frantically, then a firm thud as a walleye inhaled it. Beautiful 4 pounder. Three casts in a row, I landed nice walleyes. In every major hole for the next eight miles of river the scenario repeated itself.

I told a few fishing friends. They neither believed there could be such a difference, nor that I was hammering walleyes. One shot his mouth off and bet me he could catch as many on plain jigs as I could with live bait. He lost. I caught his limit and mine. Twelve keeper fish, two limits, to zero. I invited a couple of my other buddies to come along and see for themselves. It happened the same way again and again. If you've got good live bait and know how to fish it, you don't need voodoo.

Since then, I've observed a similar phenomenon in saltwater as well. Whether you are fishing with live fish, frogs, crabs, crawfish or shrimp, live and healthy is better than sluggish, and wild is better than domestic. It's worth the effort to keep your bait totally healthy. If it gets stressed once, you can keep it alive, but it's hard to make it really healthy and frisky again.

> *"One of the most startling observations I've made with live bait is noting the difference between wild bait versus farm-raised."*

Just as important, two good baits are better than 20 bad baits. Don't try to put too many baits in a tank. Being alive, and being really hot and frisky are two different things. Oxygen bubbles are no substitute for a steady flow and exchange of fresh water. A quick difference of only 3 degrees Fahrenheit will bean out most fish. Treat your minnows well and they will go to the end of the line and die trying get you a big one.

Remember, too, states have different laws regarding the transport of wild-captured bait. Respect the laws and never release live bait back into the water.

Rigs You'll Dig

What point is there in going all out to keep your bait healthy if you do a "Vlad the Impaler" routine when you put it on the hook? The most common mistake when fishing live bait is to mortally injure the bait with the hook, or to place the hook in such a way that makes it hard for the minnow to breathe. The best way I've seen to solve this problem is a method I first learned in Panama while fishing for black marlin with live bonitos. It's called "floss rigging."

This is very common in saltwater, yet I've never seen anyone try it in freshwater. It's easy on minnows 4 inches and longer. It can be done on smaller bait but it takes a little surgical skill, small needles and finer floss. To properly floss rig a sucker, or other baitfish, see the sidebar "Floss Rigging."

A floss-rigged bait is extremely versatile. For instance:

1. You can freeline it and let it go where it wants.

2. You can add shot ahead of the bait to make it go deeper, or slow it down so it's is easier for a sluggish predator to catch.

3. If you want to fish it on the bottom, use a slip sinker rig.

4. To keep it a fixed distance from the surface or out of rocks, weeds or timber, use a bobber or a balloon.

I particularly like balloons because you can inflate them to any buoyancy, even large enough so they act as a sail and carry the bait out from shore or away from the boat. You can tie them slip or fixed. They're highly visible and can double as markers, yet they're lightweight and take up negligible space.

If you want your bait to swim away or down, it's sometimes best to place the hook in the back on either side of the dorsal fin, or affix it between the tail fin and the vent on the underside. Also, you can try to hook the fish under the skin or use an upholstery or mortician's needle to sew floss to the skin, but it's sometimes hard to get it to hold firm.

A good trick I learned from South African surf expert Rick Jacobs is to poke a small hole just through the skin of the bait where you want the hook to be. Now carve a sharp, ¼- to 1-inch sliver (depending on bait size) from a toothpick and insert it in the hole, horizontally just under the skin and parallel to the body. Push the sliver forward until its entire length is under the skin, then gently slip it backwards under the skin so it's centered under the hole.

You can place your hook directly under the sliver or use floss. It holds like you wouldn't believe and has almost no ill effect on the bait. If you use floss, I suggest hitching the floss loop to the sliver before you

How To Tie A Floss Rig

1 To create a floss rig, gather: a snelled non-offset circle hook; dental floss (or tape); and 12 inches of .018-inch stainless wire, doubled, and pinched sharply to a point. Open it slightly behind the point to allow room to insert floss. If fishing toothy critters, snell the hook with coated wire.

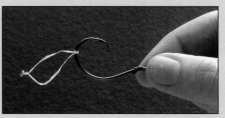

2 Create a loop in a strip of dental floss with a three-times-through loop, or triple-overhand knot. The loop should be 1 to 2 inches in diameter. For larger baitfish, increase loop size and use thicker floss. Then, hitch the loop on the bend of the hook by running the loop through itself.

3 Push the threader all the way through the nostrils of the bait. It helps to hold the bait with a wet towel. Place ¼ inch of the floss loop through the "eye" of the threader, then pull the floss back through the nostril. Note: You can also rig the floss through the eye sockets, ahead of the eyeballs.

4 To secure the hook, put the point of the hook through the loop in the floss, then give the hook a few spins. Pass the point under the twists, between the floss and the skin of the bait, to lock it in place.

insert it under the skin to minimize handling trauma. This is a good way to rig if you're fishing stationary, or current is not a factor.

I'm not quite out of tricks, but I am out of space. Steve, I did the best I could in the space allowed.

Remember!!

Am I suggesting that everyone get rid of their lures and become live baiters? Not for a second! But I am suggesting that the application of good live-bait techniques in areas where fish have become educated will produce big fish. It will also provide you with a no-voodoo reality check and, through observation, may lead you to more successful tactics and strategies to employ when using flies and artificial lures.

One last thing: The best way to clean worm grime out from under your fingernails is to rake your nails across a soft bar of soap then scrub them with a soft brush. The spine of a small catfish works to clean out the cracks and corners and doubles as a toothpick in a pinch...Oh, and I meant it about using circle hooks!

Fight to Win

DAHLBERG'S TIPS FOR DEFEATING GIANT FISH.

by Larry Dahlberg

Perhaps the most common cliche in all of angling is, "The Big One ALWAYS gets away." What a depressing thought. If that were true, those of us who seek big fish could just as well stay home and mow the lawn. In my lifetime of fishing I can count on both hands the number of truly big fish I've lost. But still, those few will forever haunt me, and I will never know how huge they really were.

The emptiest feeling in the world is when a big fish gets off, especially if you don't get a good look at it. The whole point of this article is to help prevent that from happening.

I still remember clearly the first time it happened to me. It was the spring of 1956; I was 6 years old. My Dad, brother and I were fishing sunfish on Big Wood Lake. We anchored our small wooden boat along some reeds in the bay of a little island. I was fly fishing with a small fly rod, light tippet and a black gnat.

Something grabbed my fly so I yanked back and I felt a powerful living-throbbing-going-the-other-way type tug. I leaned back, wrapped the line around my left hand and hung on. The tip of the rod got pointed directly at the fish, and the line, of course, broke. My dad said it was probably a big bass. I knew that I'd screwed up. Worse still: I didn't even get to see the fish.

Why Fish Get Off

A certain percentage of fish both large and small sometimes just "get off." It's one of the realities of angling. I have thought long and hard about how to minimize that reality. When a fish gets unintentionally disconnected it's usually related to one of three factors: the hook, the line or a connection. All other reasons fish get off are subsets of these three things. For example:

1. Hook
a. Gets torn from flesh
b. Straightens out
c. Wasn't stuck good in the first place
d. Falls out due to slack line
e. Angler pulls too hard

A high percentage of fish that get off for hook-related reasons come off when they jump. More about that later.

2. Line
a. Cut (boat, teeth, gillplate, rock)
b. Fray
c. Bad knot
d. Angler pulls too hard
e. Line buries in spool
f. Drag stuck or set too tight
g. Bad line guide

A high percentage of fish that get off for "line" reasons do so when they are close to the boat either during the fight or in the landing process. Obviously the presence of cover compounds the potential for line separation.

Using a premium-grade line is the best way to avoid most problems. And don't be afraid to spool up new line often. It's a small investment when you're talking about the fish of a lifetime.

3. Connection
a. Bad knot
b. Bad swivel or snap
c. Line cut by sharp edge of lure or hook. (combination of 2 and 3, but it happens enough that it's worth mentioning.)

Tips for fighting big fish need to be split into two totally different tackle categories—heavy and light. And when I say heavy, I mean heavy. The low end in my book is 80-pound line. Top end is whatever you want it to be, but I rarely go over 130. You can pull really, really hard on 130.

The International Game Fish Association recognizes records on lines ranging from 2-pound to 130. Classifications and rules for leaders vary between different categories. You can get all the details on their Web site, www.igfa.org, or by calling (954) 927-2628.

Applying Pressure

How hard should you pull? The answer is obvious—as hard as possible without breaking the line or pulling the hook. But most anglers have no idea how

much pressure they actually apply. In most cases, it's far less than they think.

Several years ago I built a simple device to measure the number of pounds I applied versus the number I actually delivered through the rod. The results shocked me. The device consisted of a place to anchor the butt, a scale at the fore grip to measure pounds applied, and another attached to the end of the line to measure pounds delivered.

I found that with a heavy freshwater-class rod oriented so the pull was 90 degrees from the angle of the butt, I could apply 30 pounds of pressure, yet only deliver 3 or 4 pounds! I learned that by lowering the angle (dropping the tip), I could dramatically increase the ratio in my favor. By pointing the rod at the scale and pulling straight away, my ratio was 1:1. Pull 20 pounds, you get 20 pounds on the scale.

As the angle increases to 90 degrees the ratio falls, then begins to favor the angler again as the tip passes 90 degrees. But three problems arise.

First, is stability. Second, is that the leverage of the line against the guides causes them to want to roll to the underside, which exerts a twisting force on the rodtip. The taller the guides, the more the

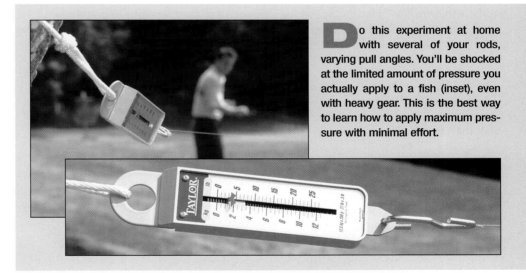

Do this experiment at home with several of your rods, varying pull angles. You'll be shocked at the limited amount of pressure you actually apply to a fish (inset), even with heavy gear. This is the best way to learn how to apply maximum pressure with minimal effort.

twisting effect, which increases the tendency for the rod to break.

But the biggest concern was that the 90-degree angle compresses all of the rod's flex into the upper third (the weakest point). It's called high sticking, and it will break a rod faster than a rogue screen door on a windy day.

Likewise, fighting a fish with the rodtip pointed directly at it would negate the rod's ability to act as a shock absorber that protects the line from sudden stress. You've got to find an angle in between—a sweet spot where you gain the greatest amount of line with every lift—for each fish you fight.

Try this. Tie a 10-pound weight to your line and place it on the floor a couple of feet in front of you.

Find The Right Angle

Many anglers make the mistake of "high-sticking," holding the rodtip high while fighting the fish (A). Dahlberg says the high-stick puts the least pressure on the fish. A straight pull (C) creates the most pressure, but takes the rod out of play as a shock absorber. A rod position in between (B) is most desirable as it allows you to pressure the fish while still using the rod to dampen sudden surges.

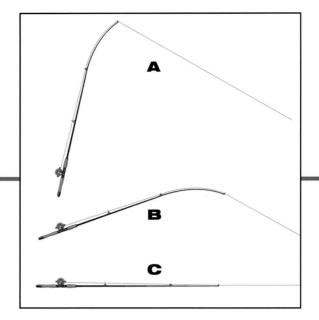

With three feet of line out try lifting the weight by raising the rodtip. Unless you have an old, crummy rod you don't care about, don't lift too hard. You'll find it very, very difficult to lift the weight, or to control it if you do get it off the ground.

Now stand on a chair and crank the tip to within a couple inches of the weight. Rather than levering it by raising the tip and lowering the butt, lift the whole rod straight up, without changing the butt angle. The weight comes off the ground and you can actually control it.

To experiment, I suggest you line up all your rods, and with the help of a friend, tie the line to a scale and pull like you would on a fish. Try different angles and distances, and have your partner read off the numbers on the scale. You will be surprised at the results, and there's a good chance that, in 10 minutes, you'll get more information about fighting fish than you have gained in a lifetime.

As you try different rods from stiff to soft it will become apparent that length and action also have a great deal to do with how pressure is applied. A rod with a super fast tip and powerful butt loads (quits bending) quickly. It will continue to gain in actual delivered pressure until you, or the rod, reaches the limit of physical strength.

It's a case of simple leverage. The longer and stiffer the butt section the quicker it will load, but your actual mechanical advantage will be less.

If you have a rod that bends right down into the handle, you might have to stand on a ladder or walk halfway across the room to load it.

Lift Instead Of Lever

Anglers typically use the rod as a lever, with the fulcrum point somewhere near the reel seat area, to lift heavy fish (A). This method requires the angler to exert substantial force, yet provides little control. A better way is to reel the rodtip close to the water's surface and lift the entire rod as much as possible (B).

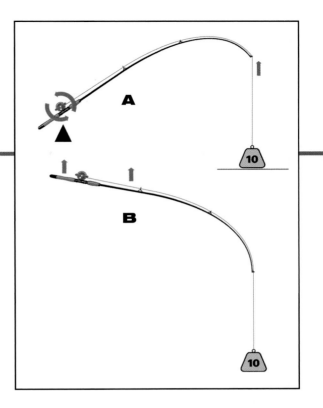

But once it is bent over at the handle, your mechanical advantage is tremendous.

The problem here is that when such a rod is loaded with a great deal of pressure, the shape of its cross section changes from round to oval. If it gets too out of round it collapses.

This exercise is about two factors—how hard you are actually pulling, and how to deliver maximum pressure with the least effort. If you're using super-heavy tackle, it's 99 percent of the game. Fighting a big fish on light tackle requires more than applying maximum pressure. You have to keep it within certain parameters. Absorbing the shock of a headshake or quick movement is critical to prevent break-offs.

Back to the question of how hard you have to pull. A 100-pound fish weighs 100 pounds when it's out of the water. But in the water, the same fish would make the scale read approximately 5 pounds. The ratio of fish flesh in the air versus fish flesh in the water is in the neighborhood of 20:1. It gives you a guide as to the amount of pressure needed to lift a fish.

A 10-pound bass that isn't fighting back can be lifted with as little as eight ounces of pressure. It's going to take 50 pounds to lift a 1,000-pound marlin even if it's asleep.

Avoid Mistakes

My theory is that you want to apply the maximum pressure your tackle will allow so you can land the fish quickly and reduce the chance of post-release mortality. Plus, the quicker you land a fish the fewer possibilities there are that something else will go wrong.

When you first hook a fish it usually goes a little crazy. After that, it settles down and the remainder of the fight takes place. I like to keep enough initial heat on so the fish has to work to gain line, and to keep it from building up a head of steam, especially if cover is a factor. When the fish stops after its initial run, I get as close to it as I can by moving the boat or running down the shoreline, then resume heavy pressure.

The idea is to force the fish to feel the same way you would after you've sprinted 100 yards, stopped to catch your breath, and then realize the bear is still chasing you. There is both an aerobic factor and a muscle fatigue factor. If you never let the fish rest, (this means you can't rest either) it's amazing how quickly it can be landed.

The two common mistakes anglers make are: 1) making too long a lifting stroke; and 2) trying to crank the fish in using the reel.

"Short stroking" is the most efficient way to gain line back and put consistent pressure on a fish to keep it coming your way. It involves finding the sweet spot and gaining line back with short, rapid pumps. The moment you've lifted the rodtip and gained a couple feet (inches, in some cases) of line, lower it and crank in what you've gained, then pump again. The tip should never be up more that a fraction of a second. Pump, crank, pump, crank.

Most anglers lift, then just hold the tip up and lean back. Mistake! The moment the tip is up, it's time to lower it and crank the handle.

With heavy line I like to pull until I hear the line start to ping or feel all the stretch come out. Once it's

> ## "The quicker you land a fish the fewer possibilities there are that something will go wrong."

Dahlberg's Big Fish Rig

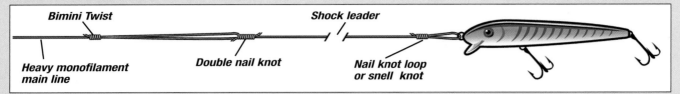

Bimini Twist

Shock leader

Heavy monofilament main line

Double nail knot

Nail knot loop or snell knot

Dahlberg's typical big-fish rig starts with a Bimini Twist, followed by a shock leader from 6 to 18 inches long when casting; 6 or more feet in length when fishing live bait. He connects the hard mono leader to the Bimini with a double nail knot and uses a nail knot loop or snell to tie on the lure or hook.

quit stretching, you better be careful because it's at the breaking point and the margin of error has been reduced to near zero. The drag or your arms must absorb any shock at this point because the rod is fully loaded and its ability to absorb significant shock has been lost.

Reel World

And, of course, you should never use the reel as a winch. Cranking a spinning reel against the drag gets you nowhere and just twists the line. With a level-wind, you run the risk of burying the line in itself on the spool. Use the reel to take in line that you've gained by lifting the fish with the rod.

The reel does its work when the fish runs. A high-quality drag is essential when fighting huge fish on heavy tackle. The reason is heat. It can build up so much most drags become undependable. In fact, it can get so hot the reel will sizzle when you spit on it.

Shimano's Tiagra, my favorite for really big fish, actually has a heat-compensating piston that senses the temperature increase and compensates for this problem.

The lightest I usually set the drag for tuna or marlin is at about one-third the breaking strength of the line. I set it with a direct pull straight off the reel with the rodtip pointing at the scale. Once the fish has settled down I often increase the drag, but usually by applying thumb pressure to the spool or pinching the line between the fore grip and my left thumb.

On slower-moving fish like sharks, sturgeon, halibut and catfish I often set the drag at two-thirds (or more) of the line's break strength. But you have to be ready to back off on it when the pinging begins.

"When I'm near heavy cover and anticipate hooking a big fish, I think about position before I even make a cast."

When using 130-pound line I often set the drag so tight that it will register 5 pounds when the reel is in freespool. In this case, I make sure I'm tied to something solid in the boat.

Because their drag surfaces are smaller, light-tackle and freshwater reels are not as dependable under heavy pressure as larger, saltwater reels. Plus, the frame and other parts of smaller reels can twist or warp, causing binding and chatter.

Another factor that comes into play with a small reel is that, as the amount of line on the spool is reduced, it takes an increasing amount of pressure to slip the drag. In other words, as the fish gets farther and farther away from you the drag actually increases. For this reason, even if I'm using 20- or 30-pound line, I usually run a drag setting of less than 5 pounds and rely on my thumb to act as the drag when I'm pumping or trying to turn a fish. I apply only a minimum amount of pressure when the fish is actually making a run. The most dependable light-tackle reel I've found is the Shimano Calcutta; it has a good drag and resists torque.

Stay In Position

In addition to knowing how much pressure you can apply to a big fish, you also have to maintain the right position. The boat needs to be in the right place for maximum effect, and you need to be in the right place in the boat so you don't get "pinched" in a position where the fish can break off on the propeller or anchor rope.

I like to stay as close as is reasonable to the fish. That way I'm not fighting line stretch. I also try to maneuver the boat so I pull the fish in the direction he actually wants to go, rather than pulling dead against the direction the fish is facing. This tactic usually keeps the fish active, close to the surface and off balance; all of which accelerate the anaerobic/lactic shock that fatigues it.

When I'm near heavy cover and anticipate hooking a big fish, I think about position before I even make a cast. If one strikes, what will I do?

If I'm fishing flowing water, I ask myself what effect the current will have. I make sure the boat is facing the right way, and that I'm ready to hit the high-bypass switch on the trolling motor. If someone else is running the boat, they must understand the game plan, too.

When I hook a large fish on light tackle, I often apply almost zero pressure during its initial run, and instead focus on reducing the distance between us. At the same time I get into a position where I can use the fish's momentum and direction to lead it away from cover. Very often when you reduce pressure the fish will settle down.

Often with large fish like sturgeon, I wait until I'm directly overtop before lifting. I short-stroke them to the surface with as much pressure as the line will stand, then reduce it to a minimum when the fish blasts off after coming to the top. This is especially effective on sturgeon because their mouths are located so far behind the actual tip of the nose. If you have difficulty lifting a fish off bottom, try circling it quickly with the boat and applying pressure from different angles. Sometimes, by getting ahead of the fish you can plane it to the surface. I've found this especially effective on tuna and hammerhead sharks.

It's always a hard call as to how much heat to apply in an attempt to keep the fish from gaining cover. If a fish does beat you to the bushes it's usually best to reduce pressure to almost zero, then go in and try to free the line before resuming efforts to land the critter.

When fishing heavy cover it's usually a good rule to keep your casting length to a minimum and to put good heat on the fish

The Bimini Twist

The Bimini Twist is a favorite tool among anglers who target big fish because of its incredible strength and dependability. But learning to tie this knot can be intimidating. Here are eight simple steps that will lead you through the process.

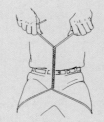

Step 1

Measure a little more than twice the length you want for the double-line loop. Bring the tag end back to the standing line and twist the loop 18 to 23 times.

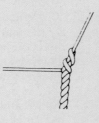

Step 2

Slowly spread the loop in order to slide the twists together about 10 inches below the tag end. Spread the lines evenly, keeping the same angle on each side, so they do not wrap on top of one another. Step both feet through the loop and bring it up around your knees so pressure can be placed on the twist column by spreading your knees.

Step 3

With the twists snugged, hold the standing line in one hand with tension just slightly off vertical. With other hand, pull the tag at a right angle to the twists. Keeping tension on the loop with your knees, gradually ease tension of tag end so it will roll over the column of twists, beginning just below the top twist. As the loop continues to spread, the tag end will wrap back down over the twists.

Step 4

Spread legs apart slowly to maintain pressure on loop. Steer tag end into a tight spiral coil as it continues to roll over the twisted line. Make sure the twists lie side-by-side and don't roll over each other.

Step 5

When the tag end has coiled over the column of twists, continue knee pressure on the loop and pinch the end of knot to keep it from unraveling. Place a finger in the crotch of line to prevent the last turn from slipping, and make a simple half-hitch with tag end around nearest leg of loop and pull up tight.

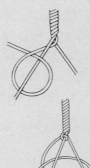

Step 6

With the half-hitch holding the knot, release knee pressure but keep the loop stretched. Use the tag to make a half-hitch around both legs of loop, but do not pull tight.

Step 7

Make two or three more turns with the tag end around both legs of the loop, winding inside the bend of line formed by the loose half-hitch and toward the knot. Pull tag end slowly, forcing the loops to form a spiral.

Step 8

Moisten spirals and pull loops tight against main knot. Leave about ¼-inch of a tag end when trimming. Tying a Bimini Twist takes practice, but it's worth the effort.

Danger Zone

Always be aware of the danger zone, the area that's equal in radius to the length of line between you and the fish, before you make a cast. Any obstacle within this circle could be a hazard to your boating a trophy. In this situation, Dahlberg says he would first cast to the outside tree limbs, hoping to draw the fish into the open. If that fails to elicit a strike, he'll make a straight-on approach to the spot he thinks holds the fish, then turn the trolling motor 180 degrees. The moment the strike occurs, he'd hit the high-bypass button on the motor, backing the boat and pulling the fish away from cover.

immediately upon the strike. That way you can use the fish's momentum to help carry it as far from the obstructions as possible early in the battle.

When fighting from a boat I always position myself in the corner closest to the fish. When a fish gets close, you want to be prepared to move quickly from one end to the other to maintain control.

With a really huge fish, especially in a small boat, I'll often start the motor to keep the boat away from the fish. Otherwise, with a lightweight boat, you pull yourself to the fish rather than the other way around and end up with a green fish at boatside, with 6 feet of line out. Then, the best thing is to keep it moving. Swim it in circles, swim it around the bow or stern. Don't let it lie there with its mouth open shaking its head.

Another no-no (especially with light line) is to seesaw the same length of line over the rodtip as you lift and crank. If I get in a standoff with a fish, I like to move off a few feet so I don't have the exact same spot on the line wearing against the guides. Also during the fight, I pay close visual attention to the line to see if any nicks or frays have developed. If I should see a questionable spot on the line I reduce pressure, loosen the drag and play the fish very lightly.

I've seen anglers do epic battles with large fish in heavy current. The fish makes a downstream run, then the angler struggles to drag it back against the flow. I never do that. Rather, I'll reposition so I'm even with, or preferably downstream, from the fish. If it runs downstream I'll run with it, and use the current to help me slide the fish up onto the bank.

This technique can turn a battle with a large salmon or sea-run trout into a quick three- or four-

minute encounter instead of a 30-minute ordeal that ends with a pulled hook.

There are many ideas as to what an angler should do if a fish jumps. With tarpon, popular theory is to "Bow to the King." In other words, slack off pressure when the fish goes airborne. If you don't bow, a tarpon will often land on the tight line and snap it. At other times the lure will go flying. This is especially true if the fish is a long way from the boat.

When a jumping tarpon is close to me I usually try to maintain a tight line and tip the fish in the direction it is heading, with pressure applied at a downward angle. If I feel pressure decreasing, I continue to crank the reel.

At the same time I'll anticipate where the fish is headed and may find myself in a quick shuffle to reposition in the boat to avoid getting "pinched."

With other species that jump when hooked, there's less risk the fish will land on the line and break it. In this case, I try to keep the pressure on.

"The idea is to force the fish to feel the same way you would after you've sprinted 100 yards, stopped to catch your breath, and then realized the bear is still chasing you."

Slack line increases the chance the fish will throw the lure or hook as it shakes its head.

Landing Big Fish

Most large fish are lost at the boat while attempting to land them. My earlier suggestion of keeping the fish moving holds true here. From a boat you have a choice of netting, gaffing or hand-landing. From shore you beach the fish. With a really huge fish, if you can find a clean sand or gravel beach, there is no easier way to land it than to take it to shore.

If you are a net guy, make sure the bag is as deep as your fish is long. Also don't stab at the fish. Just hold the net in one hand, support the bag in the other and swim the fish head first into the hoop. Don't hurry and make sure the angler lets up pressure as soon as the fish gets pointed into the net.

Once the fish is in the net bag you can point the end of the handle straight at the sky and the net will close on the fish. Don't try to lift it like you are throwing hay with a pitchfork. That's a good way to break the yoke of the net or bend the handle. Just lift it straight up with the handle in a vertical position.

Hoop diameter is not as important as bag depth. If the hooks of your lure get entangled in the leading edge of the net, you want it to be deep enough that the fish can't flip its tail and vault out.

Lip gaffs are trickier to use than nets and can tear a fish up if you're not careful, but they often work better on fish that are too big for the net. Just be sure to avoid the fish's gills. Your best shot is usually behind the lower jaw, either inserted from above or below. If the gaff is tied to your wrist, be careful so the fish doesn't start flopping and tear your arm off.

Sometimes, after I've secured the fish on the gaff, I'll pin the fish to the side of the boat by sticking the gaff in the wooden gunwale and pulling back hard.

Hand landing is one of my favorite ways to land big fish of less than 50 pounds. The use of a glove is recommended. Often if you are wearing a glove, you can grab the fish at the base of the tail and with the other hand on the leader or under the fish's belly just lift them into the boat.

Another method is to slip four fingers behind the gillplate (NOT in the gills), leading with your index finger. Keep your fingers together and tuck in your thumb. Be very careful to observe where the hooks are lodged. If they are too close to where you're going to do business, don't stick your hand in there.

Good terminal connections are critical to consistently landing big fish. When hunting for big ones I always tie a bimini twist in my main line before my terminal knot. Usually I use a length of shock leader either in the form of nylon coated wire, Monel wire or Stren Hi-Impact mono leader material, either in flourocarbon or regular, depending on the teeth of the fish I'm chasing.

Most of the wear and tear takes place in the last foot or two of line, so it's always a good idea to reinforce it with the double line from the bimini twist, a shock leader, or both.

The big one that got away? I don't want to hear about it. I'd rather you send me a picture of the big one you caught after an epic, line-pinging, drag-screeching battle that ended in a live release. The picture will be quicker than a depressing long-winded story, plus you'll sleep better. 🐟

Below: Dahlberg subdued this Nicaragua tarpon in 35 minutes on a flippin' stick, a Calcutta 400 reel, 20-pound MagnaThin and a 150-pound Hi-Impact shock leader.

Rigs that Saved the Day

SPENCE'S SOLUTIONS FOR TOUGH FISHING CONDITIONS.

by Field Editor Spence Petros

It was easy back in the '60s. Find a few "hidden" spots that most everyone else missed, such as small offshore humps or sharp inside turns along a deep weed edge, and you were almost certain to catch fish. Lots of 'em. But a few hundred knowledgeable structure fishermen quickly became a few thousand, and now legions of anglers have learned to uncover the sunken treasures that were once honeyholes to a select few.

At the same time, tackle has gotten better, and savvy anglers have jumped on advances like deep-diving, snag-resistant crankbaits, soft plastics that look and move better than the real thing, sinkers that rarely hang, low-stretch superlines, holographic lure finishes and scalpel-sharp premium hooks.

Which is why—perhaps now more than ever—the best piece of fishing equipment is still a quick mind. If you can adjust to weather and water conditions, the mood of the fish, and other factors like fishing pressure or boat traffic, you'll outfish those who can't, 10 to 1.

New Tricks

Last summer I spent a lot of time on a handful of waters I've fished for over 40 years. Going into the season, I thought, "I'm just going to go out and catch fish, what more could I possibly learn on these lakes?" Yet even then, a few on-the-water adjustments made a big difference.

In one case, slab crappies held tight to large pier foundations in gin-clear, four- to six-foot depths. Problem was, in prime low-light conditions, it was tough to see the exact outline of the cover

well enough to retrieve a small jig parallel to and inches from the edge. Sure, it was easy when it was calm and bright, but then most of the crappies would only follow.

My solution? Fish during bright, calm conditions to locate crappies that would briefly shadow the jig, then quickly pitch a lively minnow below a small slip float back at them. It worked like a charm.

On another clear lake, spawning and post-spawn bass were hugging a moss-covered bottom in eight to 10 feet. The clingy moss stopped any bottom-bumping presentations, and for about 10 days the larger bass wouldn't react to fast-moving baits fished off bottom. Soft plastic jerk worms tempted some fish, but it was an extremely early or late bite.

After trying different options, I found the win-

ning presentation was a 6-inch Berkley Tournament Strength Power Nightcrawler, nose-hooked on a size 4 Tru-Turn hook, about two feet behind a pegged, ⅛-ounce bullet sinker. I counted the rig down and cranked it steadily, just above the moss.

Extra-long casts were critical in the clear water, so I used a light, 7-foot spinning rod and 4-pound test mono. When a bass took the worm, my wispy rod doubled, signaling the strike. I drove the thin-wire hook home with a long, sweeping set and seven or eight fast turns of the reel handle.

The rig worked well. I boated 17 to 25 bass during four consecutive afternoon trips on this heavily pressured, tough-bite lake. Now the technique is in my bag of tricks for use again under similar situations.

These are just two examples of how old-fashioned ingenuity can save the day. Many times,

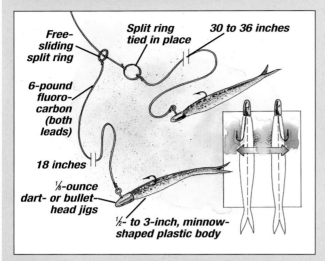

Two Shot Jump Rig

Free-sliding split ring

Split ring tied in place

30 to 36 inches

6-pound fluoro-carbon (both leads)

18 inches

⅛-ounce dart- or bullet-head jigs

½- to 3-inch, minnow-shaped plastic body

Cast the double-jig rig to bass-busting baitfish on the surface, or the edges of otherwise calm schools of bait. When rigging, hook the plastic at 5- to 10-degree opposing angles so the jigs dart in opposite directions (inset).

I've invented new rigs or modified standard presentations to deal with challenging fishing conditions. The following are a few more favorites that have bailed me out on numerous occasions.

Jump Jig Rig

If you fish clear water, you've no doubt seen marauding bass attack massive schools of shiners or shad. The surface boils, baitfish fly out of the water, then poof—the mayhem's over as quickly as it began.

If you're fast enough to toss a small, minnow-bodied crank or grub into the melee, you might get bit. But it's hard being in the right place at the right time, then following up with that perfect cast.

This kind of surface action is common from late spring through early summer, whenever baitfish schools cruise weed tops, inside weed edges and shallow water. To be prepared, I keep a rod rigged with a special double-jig rig (if legal) within quick reach.

I call it the Two-Shot Jump Rig, and I cast it both to surfacing bass as well as the edges of otherwise calm schools of bait—if I suspect bass are around. The rig stands out, yet appears natural, seems easy for opportunistic bass to catch, casts well and hooks most fish.

The setup features two ⅛-ounce jigs dressed with ½- to 3-inch minnow-shaped plastic bodies. Rig the plastics at 5- to 10-degree opposing angles so the baits jump in opposite directions.

I first separated my leadheads with a small three-way swivel, until double-headers strained and popped my light line. Now, one jig trails 30 to 36 inches behind a split ring tied in-line, while the other rides 18 inches below a free-sliding split ring rigged ahead of it. I fish the rig with a 6½- to 7-foot spinning rod and long-casting reel spooled with 6-pound fluoro.

Cast the rig to breaking bass or the edges of baitfish schools. Count the jigs down three to six seconds, with your rod parallel to the water. Snap the rodtip up to a 1:30 position, pause a second, then snap the tip to 12 o'clock. Let the jigs fall back to their starting depth, while turning the reel handle slowly about one full crank to eliminate slack. A strike usually registers as a "tick" while the lure sinks. Hooked bass often attract other fish, so don't bring 'em in too fast.

I also fish the rig along inside weed edges, over subsurface beds, along rocky shorelines and just about anywhere I spot schools of shiners or shad, including deep, open water. Expect to catch nearly anything that feeds on minnows.

Big Game Leader

Superlines work great for trolling up muskies and pike. The only drawback is, they're not as abrasion-resistant as mono—especially when scraped across rocks while pulling a big crankbait.

My solution? I use a 3- to 4-foot wire leader when trolling on or near bottom. The length prevents rocks from cutting my line, and is a lifesaver

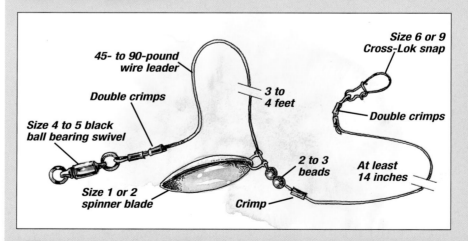

Lethal Leader

45- to 90-pound wire leader

Double crimps

Size 4 to 5 black ball bearing swivel

Size 1 or 2 spinner blade

3 to 4 feet

Size 6 or 9 Cross-Lok snap

Double crimps

2 to 3 beads

Crimp

At least 14 inches

An extra-long leader prevents rocks and debris from fraying low-stretch superline, and helps when a trophy 'ski or pike starts rolling. The small spinner adds flash and vibration; experiment with blade design and color to match water clarity and light conditions. Keep the spinner 14 inches or more ahead of the lure to avoid ruining the bait's action.

when a feisty muskie or pike starts rolling. I use 45- to 90-pound test seven-strand wire, double-crimping each end for extra strength. I don't want anything coming unraveled.

I often add a size 1 spinner and a couple of beads 14 inches or so above the snap (any closer and you risk altering the bait's action). The blade helps in low-light conditions, dingy water and on pressured lakes, where something a little different is often a big plus. Use a crimp to hold it in place—split shot will slide.

Wood Crappies

Many crappie anglers concentrate their efforts on spring, when the fish are shallow and easy to catch, but savvy speck fans also focus on summer and fall—a time when slabs often congregate around woody cover related to underwater structure like drop-offs or creek channels. Still, knowing the fish are holding in and around wood is one thing; pulling them out with a minimal amount of fish-spooking snags is another.

Many top fishermen hover over deep brush or timber and gingerly lower a dropper-type live bait rig until it makes contact, then lift the rig up a few inches to keep their minnows just above the snag. In theory, it's great—but rigs snag, especially when the water is choppy, or when they're fished by anyone with less than an expert sense of feel.

A few modifications can make this old rig even more effective. For starters, tie 'em with fluoro-carbon line. Its near-invisibility and great abrasion resistance make it ideal for wood-hugging crappies. Second, while many anglers opt for heavy lines and thin-wire hooks—which, when hung, straighten under steady pressure—I prefer weedless steel, especially in clear water.

One of the best is Lindy-Little Joe's No-Snagg hook, which features a sharp, short-shank hook protected by an easy-to-set, seven-strand weed guard that can be adjusted for more or less tension. I've fished the design for 15 years, with line as light as 6-pound test (note: with light lines, use a long, slow, sweeping hookset).

Although most fishermen tie a bell sinker to the bottom of the line, there are better options. One is using one or two extra-large split shot, which usu-

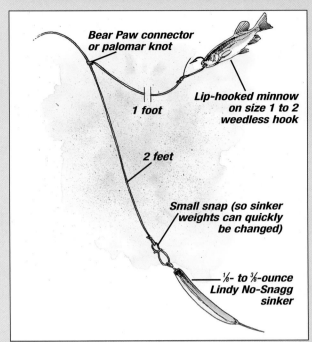

Deep-Water Crappie Rig

Bear Paw connector or palomar knot

1 foot

Lip-hooked minnow on size 1 to 2 weedless hook

2 feet

Small snap (so sinker weights can quickly be changed)

⅛- to ⅜-ounce Lindy No-Snagg sinker

The sinker and weedless hook of Spence's modified dropper rig all but eliminate snags in brush, without sacrificing hooking power. You can use a palomar knot to attach the dropper, but Spence favors a Bear Paw line connector for two reasons. It helps keep the hook away from the main line, and may be attached without tying knots on the main line. To fish twin droppers, use a stiffer line to the hook—it's less apt to wrap around the main line.

ally slide off when the weight gets hung. Lindy's No-Snagg sinkers are another.

If you're fishing monofilament or fluoro, use a 5-foot, 9-inch to 6-foot rod with a little backbone. With low-stretch superline, soften up the rod action and increase the length. You need a little give somewhere.

Trolling Meat

When the top lake trout guide in camp said he was going to show us a hot technique for big lakers, I got excited. But when I found out he liked to sit on shore, waiting for a trout to pluck his chunk of sucker meat off the bottom, my enthusiasm waned.

Out of courtesy, I sat calmly for an hour, waiting for a strike, before taking a boat out to the nearest drop-off and trolling a crankbait. That, too, was a slow

"Knowing the fish are holding in and around wood is one thing; pulling them out with a minimal amount of fish-spooking snags is another."

Trout Meat Rig

A 6-inch-long, scaled sucker fillet is deadly for lakers and big browns, especially in water temperatures below 55 degrees. Leave the skin on—it helps keep the meat on the hook. Keep the meat slim, too; ¼ to ⅜ of an inch produces the most action, creates less drag, and gives you the highest hooking percentage. The crankbait is mainly for depth control, but may pick up occasional strikes. Tip: to minimize tangles, the trailing line (to the meat) should be about 2 feet longer than the dropper. Also, let the rig out slowly, under tension, as the boat is moving.

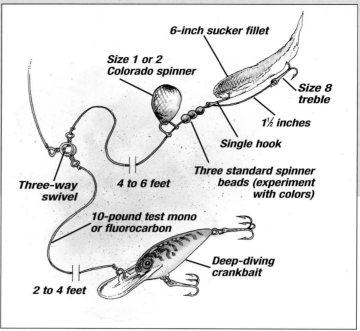

6-inch sucker fillet
Size 1 or 2 Colorado spinner
Size 8 treble
1½ inches
Single hook
Three standard spinner beads (experiment with colors)
Three-way swivel
4 to 6 feet
10-pound test mono or fluorocarbon
Deep-diving crankbait
2 to 4 feet

proposition. During the next hour, two trout butted my lure, but I failed to hook either one.

Undaunted, I kept trolling, glancing now and then at the fillet of sucker meat lying on the floor of the boat, and thinking how nice it would be to fish it at a decent rate of speed.

As the trolling bite languished, it dawned on me to put a size 6 treble on a 3- to 4-inch trailer behind the single hook of a walleye spinner, add about a 6-inch strip of sucker meat and let a ½-ounce egg sinker take it down to the strike zone.

The rig worked pretty well. I caught six trout to the four landed by my three shore-bound companions. Still, the rig needed work. Running depth was highly speed-dependent and I couldn't be sure how deep it went.

So I snapped a crankbait to the dropper line of a three-way rig and let the spinner-and-meat combo ride on the trailing line. It worked great, and I showed our sedentary guide a thing or two about Yankee ingenuity.

I've since had excellent success with the meat rig on other trips, badly outfishing just about anything else for trout scattered within 35 feet of the surface—especially in water cooler than 55 degrees.

But one day, several years and hundreds of trout later, it was my turn for a reminder that even the best rigs occasionally need tweaking. The fishing was slow; problem was, the lakers were too deep for my wonder rig. A few hours into the day I pulled up next to the boat of my friend and fellow NAFC member Jim Saric, bemoaning the fact that I only had a few fish.

Saric laughed. He was doing just fine with "my" rig. The difference? He'd made a slight modification; a heavy bead-chain sinker above the three-way swivel gave him an extra five to 10 feet of depth.

I'd been outfoxed.

Since that day I've experimented with extra weights to pull the rig's crankbait deeper. And, with the help of a thin-diameter, 10- to 14-pound superline, I now have no problem fishing it down to 50 feet.

The rig works well on other trout, particularly big browns. I can see savvy anglers across the country using it on cold-water trout. If suckers aren't part of the native forage base, use a strip of smelt, alewife or herring. Where bait isn't allowed, a long, skinny pork rind will do. In states where it's illegal to fish lines with multiple hooks, take the hooks off the crankbait and use it as a tool to control depth and speed.

Running depth is easy to gauge. Keep the spinner fairly small—a size 1 or 2 Colorado—the meat slim, say ¼-to ⅜-inch thick (scaled, with the skin left on), and you'll sacrifice little of the lure's original depth.

> *"If you can adjust to weather and water conditions, the mood of the fish, and other factors like fishing pressure or boat traffic, you'll outfish those who can't, 10 to 1."*

Popping Whites

It was getting frustrating. Very frustrating. Here a friend and I were on a beautiful, early July morning, fishing the swirling waters below a big dam on the Mississippi, in a spot I sensed held hundreds, maybe thousands of white bass—and getting shut down, cold.

To make matters worse, jumbo whites were erupting on schools of terrified baitfish all around us. They'd break the surface and inhale a few minnows—pop, pop, pop—but before we could react, their brief feeding frenzies would end. I tried waiting, rod cocked for a quick cast to breaking fish, but the action was sporadic, spread out, and it was almost impossible to get a jig into the fracas during the few fleeting seconds it lasted.

Random casts with a variety of subsurface presentations also drew blanks. All feeding activity appeared centered around baitfish driven to the surface.

Suddenly it dawned on me that the "pop-pop" noises made by the feeding whites sounded a lot like a cupped-face, topwater bass lure. I quickly rummaged through my tackle box and found an old Hula Popper. A quick cast showed me the bait could talk the talk, but since it didn't really resemble the actual forage, I doubted it would walk the walk.

I tried adding a short, mono leader with a white streamer fly, but it wrapped around the popper's rear treble hook on almost every cast. After more trial and error, I removed the offending treble and linked a small jig to the bait with a stiff, 18-inch section of 10-pound test mono. Bingo! The rig was a home run. Cast after cast produced white bass; we stopped counting after releasing 175 fish.

Spence modifies classic rigs and invents new ones to beat challenging fishing conditions.

Popper Rig

Commotion from the topwater draws white bass to the surface, where they zero in on the trailing jig. Make several sharp pops to mimic feeding whites, followed by a short pause. Repeat. On the cast, slow or stop the rig just before it hits the water to avoid tangles.

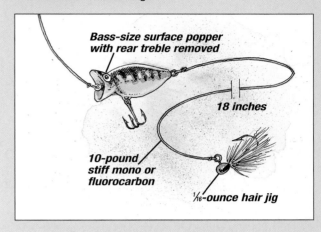

Bass-size surface popper with rear treble removed

18 inches

10-pound stiff mono or fluorocarbon

1/16-ounce hair jig

The key was casting into the general area of surface activity, popping the lure sharply three or four times, then pausing a few seconds between pops to let the "injured" jig sink. The white bass never got wise to the presentation. We caught 'em as long as they were feeding on or near the surface, and I've enjoyed similar successes for like-minded bass many times since.

Through the years, my system has evolved. I now use a longer spinning rod, about 6½ to 7 feet, spooled with 10-pound Berkley FireLine, and similar-weight fluorocarbon for leader material. I prefer durable hair jigs weighing about ¹⁄₁₆ ounce. Leadheads dressed with plastic are okay, too, provided you glue 'em to the jighead.

The loud pops made by a Hula Popper or Rebel Pop-R generally work best, especially in heavy current, over deep water, or under choppy conditions. But sometimes the subdued pop of a Storm Chug Bug or Bill Lewis SpitFire, which create less surface disturbance, is better. You can also vary the intensity of the pops and splashes by raising or lowering your rodtip. If the action is spotty, experiment with the sharpness and length of your pulls, along with rod positioning.

If you're fishing with a buddy, try casting your poppers a few feet apart and ripping up the surface. Or, if you're adventurous, tie two jigs behind the popper. This rig is more difficult to cast, but it sure can double your fun. Just remember to slow down the lure just before it hits the water so the jigs don't foul the main line.

There's an old saying that if you build a better mousetrap, the world will be yours. Likewise, when you learn to create better fishin' rigs, success will naturally follow.

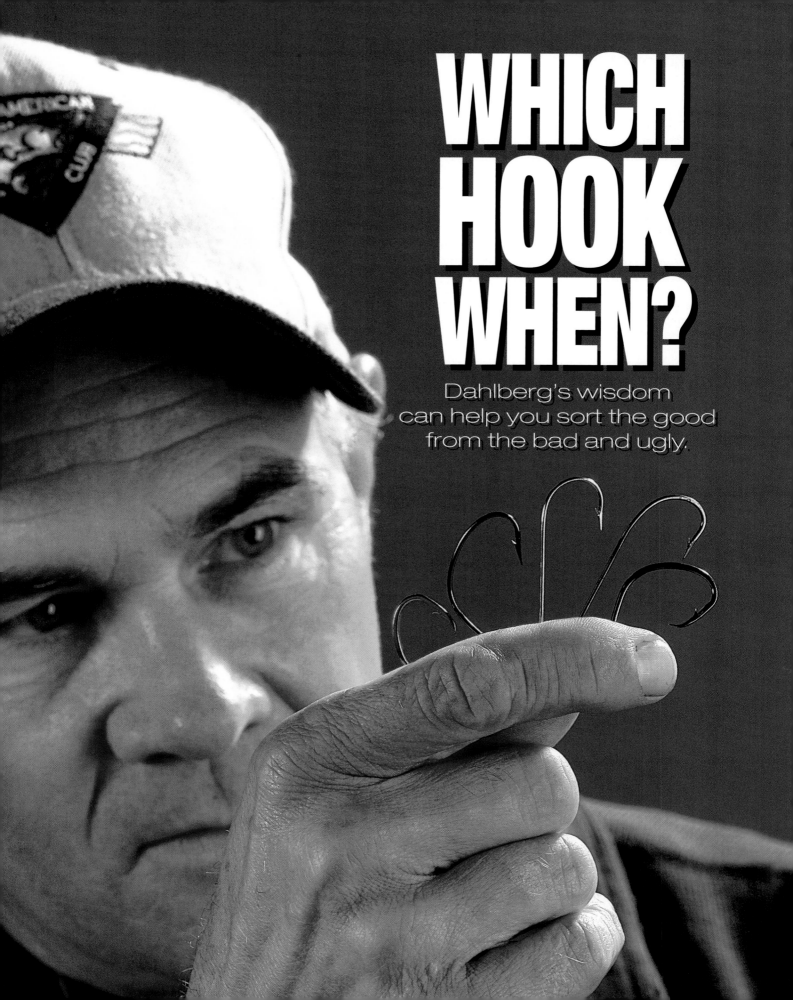

WHICH HOOK WHEN?

Dahlberg's wisdom
can help you sort the good
from the bad and ugly.

by Larry Dahlberg

The first real consideration I can remember giving to fishhooks was at Burnett Larsen's Hardware store in Grantsburg, Wisconsin. I was about 15 years old and planning to make a streamer out of Mylar for a lady named Mrs. Daniels who'd almost killed us both while trying to cast a Prescott Spinner on an earlier outing.

The only hook available in the size I needed was a black, kirbed model with a large ringed eye. I know now that it was a size 2/0 trotline hook for catfish.

The shank was so heavy I knew Mrs. Daniels would be hung up constantly in the shallow rocks I was planning to fish. I decided I could add a pencil cork along the shank to make it more buoyant. I gave the fly a red marabou tail, and added a shock of gold Mylar at the head. It was my Mepps spinner imitation.

The next time Mrs. Daniels showed up, I had her drop the new fly in the water while I rowed across the topside of the riffles. The fish bit it like crazy, but her 6-weight fly rod wasn't stiff enough or her wrist strong enough to sink that big, dull hook into a fish.

I finally had her point the rod straight at the fly with about 30 feet of line out while I rowed cross-current in the tailout. She caught the first smallmouth of her 10-year fishing career. In fact, she caught so many she tore the heads off matches to keep track.

Rather than solving the hook-up problem by using the momentum of the boat, another solution might have been to sharpen the hook in a triangular fashion, and reduce the size of the barb by 50 percent or more. Hook files had been invented, but apparently I had not yet been introduced to them.

The years passed and after searching the Herter's catalog and the combined inventories of everyone I knew that had any hooks, I discovered the Herter's 933R (actually a Mustad 3366, which is still one of my favorites for deer hair flies). It was inexpensive, lightweight and had a fairly stiff shank, small barb and sharp point. Using flies tied with it, Mrs. Daniels could hook her own smallmouths fair and square, if she was paying attention.

During the last dozen or so seasons guiding fly fishermen to smallmouths, I devoted my "off time" to investigating other aspects of angling. I spent several seasons experimenting with live bait of all kinds, mostly targeting walleyes in the river, but catching lots of smallmouths in the process. When not on the river I spent my time harassing largemouth bass with everything from frogs to mudpuppies. Other than using great bait, which is a huge part of it, I found success was also dependent upon hook selection.

Rather than simply trying to tell you what hook to use for a specific purpose, let me share my observations and look at some of the options available today in the world of fishhooks.

Hook Science

As I've hinted in my story about Mrs. Daniels, in hook selection, there are three major considerations: 1. Hooking power, 2. Holding power, and 3. How the weight or shape of the hook affects the bait or lure to which it is connected. Point and barb design, metal quality (stiffness), shank length and diameter are all factors that can affect any of these three criteria.

When most of us think about hook penetration we focus on making sure the point is sharp. In fact, there's been an argument for as long as I can remember as to the best way to manufacture a sharp hook point. One school says to triangulate it to create a cutting edge on the inside of the barb. The other claims it's better to have a tapered, conical point. I've also seen sharpeners that put an edge on the outside of the barb.

One of the most interesting is the spade-type point offered on many hooks from Owner Corp. In cross-section, their "Cutting Point" actually has a "+" shape.

Which hook point offers the best penetration? It's fairly easy to test. In fact, I once saw a device designed to measure the pressure it took to push the point of a clamped hook through a latex membrane that simulated a fish's flesh.

This type of test quickly reveals three things: 1. Given identical barb size and wire diameter, all properly sharpened hooks, whether they're conical or triangulated on either side, penetrate effectively, 2. Small barbs penetrate more easily than large barbs, and 3. Points that taper slowly penetrate better than those with a steep taper.

> **"Given identical barb size and wire diameter, all properly sharpened hooks, whether they're conical or triangulated on either side, penetrate effectively."**

Angle Of Penetration

Both the long-shank hook on the left and the short-shank hook on the right have a straight point. Notice how the short-shank hook tips downward so the point's angle of penetration is nearly 45 degrees from the direction of pull; very inefficient. We used a clinch knot on this hook, the same as on the long-shank hook. By snelling a short-shank hook, you improve the angle, but only slightly. Note that the long-shank hook doesn't tip as much, so the angle of penetration is somewhat flatter and will pierce tissue more easily. Still, it's far from parallel to the direction of pull, and thus is nearly as inefficient as the short-shank hook.

In my own workshop I took things a step further by testing penetration on more bone-like materials. More importantly, I attached the hook to a monofilament line so it could twist and turn like it does in a real fishing situation. As a result, I made some very interesting discoveries that have helped me boat hundreds of fish that I otherwise would not have caught.

Put To The Test

The "angle of penetration" experiment illustrates what I believe to be the most important hook fundamentals: Tie a short-shank hook with a straight point (like you'd use to fish a yarn fly for steelhead, or a leech for walleyes) onto a piece of monofilament fishing line. On the other end tie a straight-point, long-shank Aberdeen hook.

Place one hook point on the tip of each thumb and pull the line tight. Both hooks will tip when their points catch. Note how the short-shank hook tips to nearly a 45-degree angle while the long-shank hook

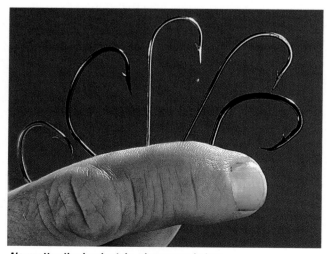

No matter the hook style, sharpness is key.

only tips a few degrees. You'll see that while the penetration angle of the long-shank hook is better (flatter) than the short-shank hook, neither hooks' point is on the same vector as the line.

Now try the test on something less soft and tender than your thumb, like stiff cardboard. As you increase pressure, the soft, thin, Aberdeen hook begins to open, reducing it's penetration angle to less than that of the short-shank hook. In fact, the hook's flexibility will allow it to open up another 20 or 30 degrees.

Now try the same experiment with a long-shank hook featuring a curved point. While the straight point might catch flesh more quickly than a curved point, it's obvious that when the hook tips under pressure, the curved point penetrates instantly, almost parallel with the line. And because it digs in and slides forward, the point of pressure on the hook moves into the bend, reducing the force acting to open the hook.

One could argue that a curved point is less likely to catch soft flesh, especially if you're using light mono, have a great deal of line out and are dealing with substantial stretch. This problem can be overcome by offsetting the point slightly to the side with a pair of pliers. Hooks that are designed this way are called "kirbed," and do indeed yield better hooking percentages.

How do you get a hook with a straight point to pull more parallel to the line? Change its shape. Tie on a wide-gap hook, or what is popularly known as the Kahle-style, and perform the same test. You'll see the point penetrates parallel to the line. Now perform the test using cardboard, pitting one hook against the other.

You'll notice that, though the wide-gap hook may penetrate best initially, it may stop halfway into the cardboard if the barb is too large or dull. A hook with a less efficient shape may pass through the cardboard more easily if it has a smaller, sharper or more gradually tapering barb.

Now try both long- and short-shank hooks with curved points. The curved point compensates when you tighten the line and allows the point to penetrate at a much more efficient angle. Follow up by trying a piece of plywood instead of cardboard; something hard like the jawbone of a fish. The first thing you'll notice when you pull fairly hard is that the long-shank hook begins to flex.

A thin-wire hook will open up and eventually let go. A wide-gap style with the same shank stiffness will stick deeper on the initial pull, but will also flex and want to open. A forged wide-gap hook, or one made of super high-grade steel, will retain its shape and penetrate much more efficiently than any of the more flexible hooks.

Flexible Benefits

So, why aren't all hooks made with curved points and stiff shafts? Because in fishing, you always have some kind of compromise. Say you're fishing crappies in wood. Crappies have very soft mouths, so hook penetration is not an issue. Breaking off when you get hung up in the wood is an issue.

A soft, thin Aberdeen hook easily straightens when you apply pressure, even with light line, and can be pulled free from the snag. Plus, once retrieved, the hook can be reshaped without risk of breaking it.

A hook made of stiff, high-grade steel that hangs up would most likely stay in the brush. And, if you did manage to straighten it, the stiff hook might snap like a twig when you tried to reshape it.

Fortunately, anglers don't usually have to make sure the hook point has to penetrate bone, cartilage or tough gristle. But, I've found in the circumstances where this is the case (big catfish, pike, muskies, tarpon, sailfish, tigerfish, payara and freshwater dorado), penetration becomes a critical issue. Light, stretchy line and a fairly large bait and hook compound the problem.

Finer Points

In my experience, the curved, flattened, tapering point of the Owner SSW hook offers the best penetration. As I mentioned earlier, the cross-section of the point is a "+" shape rather than being round. This fiendishly clever design decreases the surface area of the cross section while providing support to combat flexing. Also, the diameter of the shaft is extremely thin, but very stiff.

The trade-off is that achieving stiffness with the thin shaft can make the hook brittle if it's not perfectly tempered. Sometimes they break under pressure, and are nearly impossible to resharpen.

Hooks with cone-shape points and small, gradually tapering barbs made of super high-quality steel are also able to penetrate more efficiently than the hooks available a dozen or so years ago. Partly because of their out-of-the-box sharpness, partly

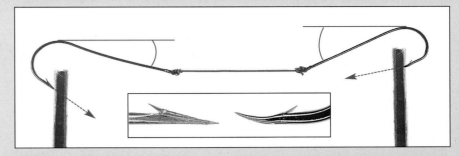

Straight Point Vs. Curved Point

Here, two long-shank hooks are compared. The hook on the left has a straight point; the hook on the right, a curved point (see inset). Stiff cardboard represents bony tissue. You'll note the hook on the left is starting to open, while the curved point hook on the right retains its shape. The reason? Penetration! The downward angle of the straight point resists penetration, often to the point of hook failure. The hook with the curved point, however, digs in instantly and slides forward, moving the point of pressure into the bend, thereby reducing the force acting to open the hook.

because of the reduced barb size and partly because they better resist flexing and bending under pressure.

Interestingly, the sharper the point and/or the more efficient the shape, the less of a problem flexing becomes. Once the point catches and begins to sink in, the odds of the hook opening up are reduced because the point of pressure moves toward and into the bend of the hook.

Most of the time when hooks open up, they have not penetrated to the point where they are holding in the corner of the bend. They open up when the point has hit bone, putting a great deal of pressure on the tip.

Shape not being a consideration, all premium hook points in both triangulated and cone versions

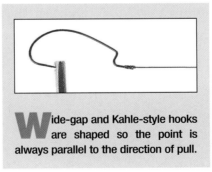

Wide-gap and Kahle-style hooks are shaped so the point is always parallel to the direction of pull.

have phenomenal penetration. Some anglers argue that the cutting edge of the triangulated hook creates a bigger hole, enabling the fish to shake the hook more easily. Although this seems a possibility to me, I have never found it to be the case. Even using a strong pair of pliers, the large, sharply triangulated barbs on the trebles most of us use on our striper or muskie lures are difficult to remove from a fish's elastic flesh.

You can test hookpoint strength on a small hook by pulling it sideways across your thumbnail. Back in the early 1970s I had an entire box of 50 hooks where the points snapped off during the thumbnail test. In addition, there were hooks of the same model in other boxes that came in the same master carton, where every point curled over.

Nowadays most premium hook points will neither snap nor bend, and will make a deep crease in your thumbnail. The only way to ruin them is to remove too much material, or weaken the point with too much heat when sharpening.

On hooks that tip when the point digs in, I sharpen the inside of the barbs in a very sharp triangle. If you look at the angle of penetration, it's obvious a sharp leading edge will help the point sink in. Tests through a membrane will bear out the obvious. In most cases, and on all hooks larger than 8/0, I also reduce the height of the barb considerably—as much as 50 to 75 percent.

Conversely, a hook sharpened so the edge is on the outside of the barb (as is accomplished with the double files I've seen used), is virtually ineffectual. It's like sharpening the wrong side of a knife. You'd do better using this file to sharpen your teeth or toenails. It might save time spent digging for the line clipper.

Hooks For Special Occasions

Manufacturers have come up with dozens of specialty hooks. Some are designed to fit a specific type of artificial lure. Others are meant to improve hook-up rates, while still more simply to add appeal to a live-bait offering. Here are a couple of examples that deserve consideration:

Fluorescent, phosphorescent and lacquered hooks,

Just about every hook company offers colored hooks these days. Whether they're laquered (left) or painted (right), the extra splash of color can turn a tough bite around.

what a brilliant idea! By adding color to the hook, manufactures have given fishermen yet another great option for presenting live bait. The bright color attracts the fish's curiosity better than bait alone would, plus it's not so overpowering that it's likely to turn off neutral fish.

Hooks like Shaw Grigsby's HP Hook and David Fritts' Carolina Special are hybrids that take advantage of features from several different hook shapes, and are designed to increase the effectiveness of soft plastic lures. In my view, they are a great improvement.

If not for the use of today's high-quality steel and high-tech manufacturing processes, the lightweight shank, coupled with the wide gap, found on these hooks would open up like they were made of rubber if you had to put serious heat on a fish.

Holding Power

Holding power comes into play after the hook has penetrated. It is a function of hook stiffness and shape. Obviously, the stiffer and stronger the shank, the less likely it will open under heavy pressure.

Shape is important because it affects where and how leverage is applied against the bend of the hook. While wide-gap hooks penetrate best, they also tend to open more easily because the actual point of pressure against the bend is farther from the shank

(almost to the barb), allowing more leverage to open it. That's why, when using this style hook, it's critical to have the best steel money can buy.

In my experience, the treble hooks used on large lures seem to have the most problems with opening up. Usually, the longer the lure, the higher the likelihood the hooks will open. In most cases, the problem occurs with the front or middle treble when the fish is hooked in the corner of the mouth with a hook stuck in both the upper and lower jawbone. The reason is that the length of the lure provides leverage against the hooks. The fish spins and something has to give.

Adding a split ring often helps. Another solution is to go to a much heavier, thicker hook shank (see "The X System," page 157). But the very best solution is to add a split ring and go to a treble made

Selecting the right hook can mean the difference between success and failure. Dahlberg, with his wife, Marilyn, found a hook that penetrated even the toothy maw of this tigerfish.

of super high-grade steel that is both strong and stiff. (On a side note, I'd also like to say that someone needs to start making a high-grade split ring, one that's strong but has a thin diameter so it fits through hook eyes. In fact, I think they owe it to us.)

The way to test a hook for strength and quality is to try to open it up with a pair of pliers. If it's hard to bend and springs back when you ease off, it's going to perform better than one that's hard to bend, but doesn't spring back.

When using live bait, the weight and size of the hook can be the deciding factor in getting bites. I don't think it's so much a matter of the fish seeing the hook, as much as how the hook affects the bait's ability to swim strongly and stay alive. The smallest, thinnest hook you can get away with yields the best results.

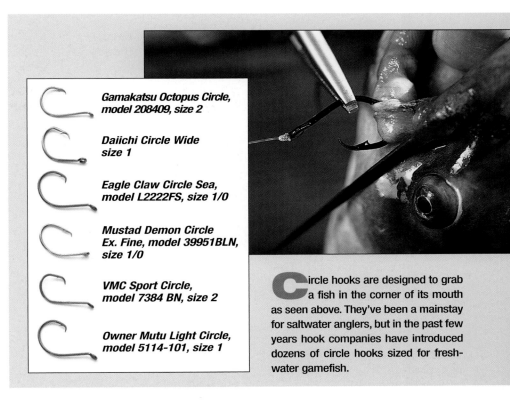

Gamakatsu Octopus Circle, model 208409, size 2

Daiichi Circle Wide size 1

Eagle Claw Circle Sea, model L2222FS, size 1/0

Mustad Demon Circle Ex. Fine, model 39951BLN, size 1/0

VMC Sport Circle, model 7384 BN, size 2

Owner Mutu Light Circle, model 5114-101, size 1

Circle hooks are designed to grab a fish in the corner of its mouth as seen above. They've been a mainstay for saltwater anglers, but in the past few years hook companies have introduced dozens of circle hooks sized for freshwater gamefish.

Perfect Circle

Unlike conventional hooks, penetration of a circle hook has nothing to do with achieving a parallel vector between the line and point. Instead, penetration occurs when the shank acts as a lever, rotating the point into tissue.

Although they resist getting hung up better than conventional hooks, and are easier for beginners to hook fish with, the main reason to use circle hooks is to reduce post-release mortality. It's my belief the use of circle hooks should be mandated in all fisheries where special regulations such as catch-and-release or slot sizing are in place.

One warning, however: many manufacturers offer offset (kirbed) circle hooks. In my experience, offset circle hooks have a high percentage of gut,

throat and gill hookups, which defeats their purpose. Don't buy them. If you have had trouble hooking fish on circle hooks, here are a few helpful tips:

1. Snell the hook so the line comes out of the eye toward the barb. I learned this from a commercial fisherman on the Indian Ocean, and it makes a difference.

2. Don't jerk. Tighten the line and let the fish set the hook.

3. Make sure you are are at an angle to the fish when you tighten the line. You can be behind it, directly over it or to the side, but unless the line passes out of the fish's mouth at an angle, you won't hook it. The best scenario is for the fish to be running away when you apply pressure.

Great Hooks

There have been enormous strides in the quality of fishhooks, especially in the quality of the steel and manufacturing technology. The result is better out-of-the-box sharpness, higher strength and better performance.

Many new shapes have evolved as well, but the majority of marketing emphasis is usually centered on penetrating power and the hook point. As you can see when performing the simple experiments we've illustrated, there's a whole lot more involved. The key to applying this to your own fishing is understanding the trade-offs and compromises in each design.

The X System

Hook size is designated by numbers. They are available in even-numbered sizes ranging from a tiny size 28 (about the size of this letter j) to a size 2. Although odd-number sizes are found in Europe, a size 1 in the U.S. is one size (or you could say a half-size) larger than size 2. After size 1, the nomenclature changes to 1/0 (pronounced "one-ought," or "one-oh") and continues with 2/0, 3/0, 4/0 etc. as size increases.

Manufacturers also use a system to designate relative shank length and diameter. Manufacturers may designate something like this on the box; Size 6, 4X Long, 2X Strong. That means the gap is a standard size 6, the length is that of a hook four sizes up (in this case 1/0) and the shank is the diameter of a hook 2 sizes larger (in this case a size 2).

Index